Barclay's
Guide to the
New Testament

Barclay's
Guide to the
New Testament

William Barclay

WESTMINSTER
JOHN KNOX PRESS
LOUISVILLE · KENTUCKY

Cover design by Eric Walljasper, Minneapolis, MN

First edition
Published by Westminster John Knox Press
Louisville, Kentucky

This book is printed on acid-free paper that meets the American National Standards Institute Z39.48 standard. ♾

PRINTED IN THE UNITED STATES OF AMERICA

08 09 10 11 12 13 14 15 16 17—10 9 8 7 6 5 4 3 2 1

Library of Congress Cataloging-in-Publication Data

Barclay, William, 1907–1978.
  Barclay's guide to the New Testament / William Barclay.—1st ed.
     p. cm.
  Includes indexes.
  ISBN 978-0-664-23256-6 (alk. paper)
  1. Bible. N.T.—Introductions. I. Title. II. Title: Guide to the New Testament.
  BS2330.3.B33   2008
  225.6'1—dc22   2007046593

Contents

1.	Matthew: The Royal Gospel	1
2.	Mark: The Essential Gospel	12
3.	Luke: The Universal Gospel	22
4.	John: The Precious Gospel	29
5.	Acts: From Jerusalem to Rome	57
6.	The Letters of Paul	64
7.	Romans: The Essence of Paul's Thought	69
8.	1 & 2 Corinthians: Wisdom and Reconciliation	81
9.	Galatians: Law and Grace	91
10.	Ephesians: The Supreme Letter	96
11.	Philippians: The Letter of Joy	108
12.	Colossians: Resisting a Great Heresy	115
13.	1 & 2 Thessalonians: Advice and Reproof	128
14.	1 & 2 Timothy and Titus: Hearing the Voice of Paul	134
15.	Philemon: More than a Slave	149
16.	Hebrews: Access to God	158
17.	James: An Early Christian Sermon	169
18.	1 Peter: The Lovely Letter	205

CONTENTS

19.	2 Peter: Against Immoral Teachers	237
20.	1 John: A Defence of the Faith	245
21.	2 & 3 John: Love and Truth	265
22.	Jude: Affirming the One True God	277
23.	Revelation: Visions of God's Power	297
	Scripture Index	321
	Subject Index	331

1

Matthew

The Royal Gospel

The Synoptic Gospels

Matthew, Mark and Luke are usually known as the *synoptic gospels*. *Synoptic* comes from two Greek words which mean *to see together*, and literally means *able to be seen together*. The reason for that name is this. These three gospels each give an account of the same events in Jesus' life. There are in each of them additions and omissions; but broadly speaking their material is the same and their arrangement is the same. It is therefore possible to set them down in parallel columns, and so to compare the one with the other.

When that is done, it is quite clear that there is the closest possible relationship between them. If, for instance, we compare the story of the feeding of the 5,000 (Matthew 14:12–21; Mark 6:30–44; Luke 9:10–17), we find exactly the same story told in almost exactly the same words.

Another instance is the story of the healing of the man who was sick with the palsy (Matthew 9:1–8; Mark 2:1–12; Luke 5:17–26). These three accounts are so similar that even a small explanatory remark – 'he then said to the paralytic' – occurs in all three as an explanation in exactly the same place. The correspondence between the three gospels is so close that we are bound to come to the conclusion either that all three are drawing their material from a common source, or that two of them must be based on the third.

The Earliest Gospel

When we examine the matter more closely, we see that there is every reason for believing that Mark must have been the first of the gospels to be written, and that the other two, Matthew and Luke, are using Mark as a basis.

Mark can be divided into 105 sections. Of these sections, 93 occur in Matthew and 81 in Luke. Of Mark's 105 sections, there are only four which do not occur either in Matthew or in Luke.

Mark has 661 verses; Matthew has 1,068 verses; Luke has 1,149 verses. Matthew reproduces no fewer than 606 of Mark's verses, and Luke reproduces 320. Of the 55 verses of Mark which Matthew does not reproduce, Luke reproduces 31; so there are only 24 verses in the whole of Mark which are not reproduced somewhere in Matthew or Luke.

It is not only the substance of the verses which is reproduced; the very words are reproduced. Matthew uses 51 per cent of Mark's words; and Luke uses 53 per cent.

Both Matthew and Luke as a general rule follow Mark's order of events. Occasionally either Matthew or Luke differs from Mark; but they never *both* differ against him; always at least one of them follows Mark's order.

Improvements on Mark

Since Matthew and Luke are both much longer than Mark, it might just possibly be suggested that Mark is a summary of Matthew and Luke; but there is one other set of facts which shows that Mark is earlier. It is the custom of Matthew and Luke to improve and to polish Mark, if we may put it in such a way. Let us take some instances.

Sometimes Mark seems to limit the power of Jesus; at least, an ill-disposed critic might try to prove that he was doing so. Here are three accounts of the same incident:

> Mark 1:34: And he cured *many* who were sick with various diseases, and cast out *many* demons;
>
> Matthew 8:16: And he cast out the spirits with a word, and cured *all* who were sick;
>
> Luke 4:40: And he laid his hands on *each* of them and cured them.

Let us take three other similar examples:

> Mark 3:10: For he had cured *many*;
>
> Matthew 12:15: And he cured *all* of them;
>
> Luke 6:19: And healed *all* of them.

Matthew and Luke both change Mark's *many* into *all* so that there may be no suggestion of any limitation of the power of Jesus Christ.

There is a very similar change in the account of the events of Jesus' visit to Nazareth. Let us compare the account of Mark and of Matthew.

> Mark 6:5–6: And *he could do* no deed of power there . . . and he was amazed at their unbelief;
>
> Matthew 13:58: And *he did not do* many deeds of power there, because of their unbelief.

Matthew shrinks from saying that Jesus *could not* do any deeds of power, and changes the form of the expression accordingly.

Sometimes Matthew and Luke leave out little touches in Mark in case they could be taken to belittle Jesus. Matthew and Luke omit three statements in Mark:

Mark 3:5: He looked around at them with anger, he
was grieved at their hardness of heart;

Mark 3:21: And when his family heard it, they went
out to restrain him for people were saying, '*He
has gone out of his mind*';

Mark 10:14: He was indignant.

Matthew and Luke hesitate to attribute human emotions
of anger and grief to Jesus, and shudder to think that anyone
should even have suggested that Jesus was mad.

Sometimes Matthew and Luke slightly alter things in Mark
to get rid of statements which might seem to show the apostles
in a bad light. We take but one instance, from the occasion on
which James and John sought to ensure themselves of the
highest places in the coming kingdom. Let us compare the
introduction to that story in Mark and in Matthew:

Mark 10:35: *James and John*, the sons of Zebedee, came
forward to him, and said to him . . .;

Matthew 20:20: Then the mother of the sons of Zebedee
came to him with her sons, and kneeling before
him, she asked a favour of him.

Matthew hesitates to ascribe motives of ambition directly to
the two apostles, and so he ascribes them to their mother.

All this makes it clear that Mark is the earliest of the
gospels. Mark gives a simple, vivid, direct narrative; but
Matthew and Luke have already begun to be affected by
doctrinal and theological considerations which make them
much more careful of what they say.

The Teaching of Jesus

We have seen that Matthew has 1,068 verses; and that Luke
has 1,149 verses; and that between them they reproduce 582

Mark's gospel - what Jesus did
Matthew Luke - drew from that + what
MATTHEW *Jesus SAID*

of Mark's 661 verses. That means that in Matthew and Luke there is much more material than Mark supplies. When we examine that material, we find that more than 200 verses of it are almost identical. For instance, such passages as Luke 6:41–2 and Matthew 7:3, 5; Luke 10:21–2 and Matthew 11:25–7; Luke 3:7–9 and Matthew 3:7–10 are almost exactly the same.

But here we notice a difference. The material which Matthew and Luke drew from Mark was almost entirely material dealing with the events of Jesus' life; but these 200 additional verses common to Matthew and Luke tell us not what Jesus *did*, but what Jesus *said*. Clearly in these verses Matthew and Luke are drawing from *a common source book of the sayings of Jesus*.

That book does not now exist; but to it scholars have given the letter Q which stands for *Quelle*, which is the German word for *source*. In its day it must have been an extraordinarily important book, for it was the first handbook of the teaching of Jesus.

Matthew's Place in the Gospel Tradition

It is here that we come to Matthew the apostle. Scholars are agreed that the first gospel as it stands does not come directly from the hand of Matthew. One who had himself been an eyewitness of the life of Christ would not have needed to use Mark as a source book for the life of Jesus in the way Matthew does. But one of the earliest Church historians, a man called Papias, gives us this intensely important piece of information: 'Matthew collected the sayings of Jesus in the Hebrew tongue.'

So, we can believe that it was none other than Matthew who wrote that book which was the source from which everyone who wished to know what Jesus taught must draw. And

5

it was because so much of that source book is incorporated in the first gospel that Matthew's name was attached to it. We must be forever grateful to Matthew, when we remember that it is to him that we owe the Sermon on the Mount and nearly all we know about the teaching of Jesus. Broadly speaking, to Mark we owe our knowledge of the *events* of Jesus' life; to Matthew we owe our knowledge of the substance of Jesus' *teaching*.

Matthew the Tax-gatherer

About Matthew himself we know very little. We read of his call in Matthew 9:9. We know that he was a tax-gatherer and that he must therefore have been a bitterly hated man, for the Jews hated the members of their own race who had entered the civil service of their conquerors. Matthew would be regarded as nothing better than a collaborator.

But there was one gift which Matthew would possess. Most of the disciples were fishermen. They would have little skill and little practice in putting words together and writing them down; but Matthew would be an expert in that. When Jesus called Matthew, as he sat in the office where he collected the customs duty, Matthew rose up and followed him and left everything behind him except one thing – his pen. And Matthew nobly used his literary skill to become the first man ever to compile an account of the teaching of Jesus.

The Gospel of the Jews

Let us now look at the chief characteristics of Matthew's gospel so that we may watch for them as we read it.

First and foremost, Matthew *is the gospel which was written for the Jews*. It was written by a Jew in order to convince Jews.

One of the great objects of Matthew is to demonstrate that all the prophecies of the Old Testament are fulfilled in Jesus, and that, therefore, he must be the Messiah. It has one phrase which runs through it like an ever-recurring theme: 'This was to fulfil what the Lord had spoken by the prophet.' That phrase occurs in the gospel as often as sixteen times. Jesus' birth and Jesus' name are the fulfilment of prophecy (1:21–3); so are the flight to Egypt (2:14–15); the slaughter of the children (2:16–18); Joseph's settlement in Nazareth and Jesus' upbringing there (2:23); Jesus' use of parables (3:34–5); the triumphal entry (21:3–5); the betrayal for thirty pieces of silver (27:9); and the casting of lots for Jesus' garments as he hung on the cross (27:35). It is Matthew's primary and deliberate purpose to show how the Old Testament prophecies received their fulfilment in Jesus; how every detail of Jesus' life was foreshadowed in the prophets; and thus to compel the Jews to admit that Jesus was the Messiah.

The main interest of Matthew is in the Jews. Their conversion is especially near and dear to the heart of its writer. When the Syro-Phoenician woman seeks his help, Jesus' first answer is: 'I was sent only to the lost sheep of the house of Israel' (15:24). When Jesus sends out the Twelve on the task of evangelization, his instruction is: 'Go nowhere among the Gentiles, and enter no town of the Samaritans, but go rather to the lost sheep of the house of Israel' (10:5–6). Yet it is not to be thought that this gospel by any means excludes the Gentiles. Many are to come from the east and the west to sit down in the kingdom of God (8:11). The gospel is to be preached to the whole world (24:14). And it is Matthew which gives us the marching orders of the Church: 'Go therefore and make disciples of all nations' (28:19). It is clear that Matthew's first interest is in the Jews, but that it foresees the day when all nations will be gathered in.

The Jewishness of Matthew is also seen in its attitude to the law. Jesus came not to destroy, but to fulfil the law. The least part of the law will not pass away. People must not be taught to break the law. The righteousness of the Christian must exceed the righteousness of the scribes and Pharisees (5:17–20). Matthew was written by one who knew and loved the law and who saw that even the law has its place in Christian life.

Once again there is an apparent paradox in the attitude of Matthew to the scribes and Pharisees. They are given a very special authority: 'The scribes and the Pharisees sit on Moses' seat; therefore, do whatever they teach you and follow it' (23:2). But at the same time there is no gospel which so sternly and consistently condemns them.

Right at the beginning, there is John the Baptist's savage denunciation of them as a brood of vipers (3:7–12). They complain that Jesus eats with tax-collectors and sinners (9:11). They ascribe the power of Jesus, not to God, but to the prince of devils (12:24). They plot to destroy him (12:14). The disciples are warned against the leaven, the evil teaching, of the scribes and Pharisees (16:12). They are like evil plants doomed to be rooted up (15:13). They are quite unable to read the signs of the times (16:3). They are the murderers of the prophets (21:41). There is no chapter of condemnation in the whole New Testament like Matthew 23, which is condemnation not of what the scribes and the Pharisees teach, but of what they are. He condemns them for falling so far short of their own teaching, and far below the ideal of what they ought to be.

There are certain other special interests in Matthew. Matthew *is especially interested in the Church*. It is in fact the only one of the synoptic gospels which uses the word Church at all. Only Matthew introduces the passage about the Church after Peter's confession at Caesarea Philippi (Matthew 16:13–23; cf. Mark 8:27–33; Luke 9:18–22). Only Matthew says that disputes are to be settled by the Church (18:17). By the time Matthew came to be written, the Church had become a great organization and institution, and indeed the dominant factor in the life of the Christian.

Matthew *has a specially strong apocalyptic interest.* That is to say, Matthew has a specially strong interest in all that Jesus said about his own second coming, about the end of the world, and about the judgment. Matthew 24 gives us a fuller account of Jesus' apocalyptic discourse than any of the other gospels. Matthew alone has the parables of the talents (25:14–30), the wise and the foolish virgins (25:1–13), and the sheep and the goats (25:31–46). Matthew has a special interest in the last things and in judgment.

But we have not yet come to the greatest of all the characteristics of Matthew. *It is supremely the teaching gospel.*

We have already seen that the apostle Matthew was responsible for the first collection and the first handbook of the teaching of Jesus. Matthew was the great systematizer. It was his habit to gather together in one place all that he knew about the teaching of Jesus on any given subject. The result is that in Matthew we find five great blocks in which the teaching of Jesus is collected and systematized. All these sections have to do with the kingdom of God. They are as follows:

(a) The Sermon on the Mount, or the law of the kingdom (5–7).

(b) The duties of the leaders of the kingdom (10).

(c) The parables of the kingdom (13).

(d) Greatness and forgiveness in the kingdom (18).

(e) The coming of the King (24–5).

9

Matthew does more than collect and systematize. It must be remembered that Matthew was writing in an age when printing had not been invented, when books were few and far between because they had to be handwritten. In an age like that, comparatively few people could possess a book; and, therefore, if they wished to know and to use the teaching and the story of Jesus, they had to carry them in their memories.

Matthew therefore always arranges things in a way that is easy for the reader to memorize. He arranges things in threes and sevens. There are three messages to Joseph; three denials of Peter; three questions of Pilate; seven parables of the kingdom in chapter 13; and seven woes to the scribes and Pharisees in chapter 23.

The genealogy of Jesus with which the gospel begins is a good example of this. The genealogy is to prove that Jesus is the Son of David. In Hebrew there are no figures; when figures are necessary, the letters of the alphabet stand for the figures. In Hebrew there are no written vowels. The Hebrew letters for David are DWD; if these letters are taken as figures and not as letters, they add up to fourteen; and the genealogy consists of three groups of names, and in each group there are fourteen names. Matthew does everything possible to arrange the teaching of Jesus in such a way that people will be able to assimilate and to remember it.

Every teacher owes a debt of gratitude to Matthew, for Matthew wrote what is above all the teacher's gospel.

Matthew has one final characteristic. Matthew's *dominating idea is that of Jesus as King*. He writes to demonstrate the royalty of Jesus.

Right at the beginning, the genealogy is to prove that Jesus is the Son of David (1:1–17). The title, Son of David, is used more often in Matthew than in any other gospel (15:22,

21:9, 21:15). The wise men come looking for him who is King of the Jews (2:2). The triumphal entry is a deliberately dramatized claim to be King (21:1–11). Before Pilate, Jesus deliberately accepts the name of King (27:11). Even on the cross, the title of King is affixed, even if it is in mockery, over his head (27:37). In the Sermon on the Mount, Matthew shows us Jesus quoting the law and five times abrogating it with a regal: 'But I say to you . . .' (5:22, 28, 34, 39, 44). The final claim of Jesus is: 'All authority . . . has been given to me' (28:18).

Matthew's picture of Jesus is of the man born to be King. Jesus walks through his pages as if in the purple and gold of royalty.

2

Mark

The Essential Gospel

The Synoptic Gospels

The first three gospels, Matthew, Mark and Luke, are always known as the synoptic gospels. The word *synoptic* comes from two Greek words which mean *to see together*; and these three are called the synoptic gospels because they can be set down in parallel columns and their common matter looked at together. It would be possible to argue that of them all Mark is the most important. It would indeed be possible to go further and to argue that it is the most important book in the world, because it is agreed by nearly everyone that it is the earliest of all the gospels and therefore the first life of Jesus that has come down to us. Mark may not have been the first person to write the life of Jesus. Doubtless there were earlier simple attempts to set down the story of Jesus' life; but Mark's gospel is certainly the earliest life of Jesus that has survived.

The Pedigree of the Gospels

When we consider how the gospels came to be written, we must try to think ourselves back to a time when there was no such thing as a printed book. The gospels were written long before printing had been invented, and compiled when every book had to be carefully and laboriously written out by hand. It is clear that, as long as that was the case, only a few copies of any book could exist.

MARK

How do we know, or how can we deduce, that Mark was the first of all the gospels? When we read the synoptic gospels even in English we see that there are remarkable similarities between them. They contain the same incidents often told in the same words; and they contain accounts of the teaching of Jesus which are often almost identical. If we compare the story of the feeding of the 5,000 in the three gospels (Mark 6:30–44; Matthew 14:12–21; Luke 9:10–17), we see that it is told in almost exactly the same words and in exactly the same way. A very clear instance of this is the story of the healing of the man who was sick with the palsy (Mark 2:1–12; Matthew 9:1–8; Luke 5:17–26). The accounts are so similar that even a little parenthesis – 'he said to the paralytic' – occurs in all three in exactly the same place. The correspondences are so close that we are forced to one of two conclusions. Either all three are taking their material from some common source, or two of the three are based on the third.

When we study the matter closely we find that Mark can be divided into 105 sections. Of these, ninety-three occur in Matthew and eighty-one in Luke. Only four are not included either in Matthew or in Luke. Even more compelling is this. Mark has 661 verses; Matthew has 1,068 verses; Luke has 1,149 verses. Of Mark's 661 verses, Matthew reproduces no fewer than 606. Sometimes he alters the wording slightly but he even reproduces 51 per cent of Mark's actual words. Of Mark's 661 verses, Luke reproduces 320, and he actually uses 53 per cent of Mark's actual words. Of the fifty-five verses of Mark which Matthew does not reproduce, thirty-one are found in Luke. So the result is that there are only twenty-four verses in Mark which do not occur somewhere in Matthew and Luke. This makes it look very much as if Matthew and Luke were using Mark as the basis of their gospels.

What makes the matter still more certain is this. Both Matthew and Luke very largely follow Mark's order of events. Sometimes Matthew alters Mark's order and sometimes Luke does. But when there is a change in the order Matthew and Luke never agree together against Mark. Always one of them retains Mark's order of events.

A close examination of the three gospels makes it clear that Matthew and Luke had Mark before them as they wrote; and they used his gospel as the basis into which they fitted the extra material which they wished to include.

It is thrilling to remember that when we read Mark's gospel we are reading the first life of Jesus, on which all succeeding lives have necessarily been based.

Mark, the Writer of the Gospel

Who then was this Mark who wrote the gospel? The New Testament tells us a good deal about him. He was the son of a well-to-do lady of Jerusalem whose name was Mary, and whose house was a rallying point and meeting place of the early Church (Acts 12:12). From the very beginning Mark was brought up in the very centre of the Christian fellowship.

Mark was also the nephew of Barnabas, and when Paul and Barnabas set out on their first missionary journey they took Mark with them to be their secretary and attendant (Acts 12:25). This journey was a most unfortunate one for Mark. When they reached Perga, Paul proposed to strike inland up to the central plateau; and for some reason Mark left the expedition and went home (Acts 13:13).

He may have gone home because he was scared to face the dangers of what was notoriously one of the most difficult and dangerous roads in the world, a road hard to travel and haunted by bandits. He may have gone home because it was increasingly clear that the leadership of the expedition was being assumed by Paul, and Mark may have felt with disapproval that his uncle was being pushed into the background. He may have gone home because he did not approve of the work which Paul was doing. Writing in the fourth century, John Chrysostom – perhaps with a flash of imaginative insight – says that Mark went home because he wanted his mother!

Paul and Barnabas completed their first missionary journey and then proposed to set out upon their second. Barnabas was anxious to take Mark with them again. But Paul refused to have anything to do with the man 'who had deserted them in Pamphylia' (Acts 15:37–40). So serious was the difference between them that Paul and Barnabas split company, and, as far as we know, never worked together again.

For some years, Mark vanishes from history. Tradition has it that he went down to Egypt and founded the church of Alexandria there. Whether or not that is true we do not know, but we do know that when Mark re-emerges it is in the most surprising way. We learn to our surprise that when Paul writes the letter to the Colossians from prison in Rome Mark is there with him (Colossians 4:10). In another prison letter, to Philemon, Paul numbers Mark among his fellow workers (verse 24). And, when Paul is waiting for death and very near the end, he writes to Timothy, his right-hand man, and says, 'Get Mark and bring him with you, for he is useful in my ministry' (2 Timothy 4:11). It is a far cry from the time when Paul contemptuously dismissed Mark as a quitter. Whatever had happened, Mark had redeemed himself. He was the one man Paul wanted at the end.

Mark's Sources of Information

The value of any story will depend on the writer's sources of information. Where, then, did Mark get his information about the life and work of Jesus? We have seen that his home was from the beginning a Christian centre in Jerusalem. Often he must have heard people tell of their personal memories of Jesus. But it is most likely that he had a source of information without a superior.

Towards the end of the second century there was a man called Papias who liked to obtain and transmit such information as he could glean about the early days of the Church. He tells us that Mark's gospel is nothing other than a record of the preaching material of Peter, the greatest of the apostles. Certainly Mark stood so close to Peter, and so near to his heart, that Peter could call him 'my son Mark' (1 Peter 5:13). Here is what Papias says:

> Mark, who was Peter's interpreter, wrote down accurately, though not in order, all that he recollected of what Christ had said or done. For he was not a hearer of the Lord or a follower of his. He followed Peter, as I have said, at a later date, and Peter adapted his instruction to practical needs, without any attempt to give the Lord's words systematically. So that Mark was not wrong in writing down some things in this way from memory, for his one concern was neither to omit nor to falsify anything that he had heard.

We may then take it that in his gospel we have what Mark remembered of the preaching material of Peter himself.

So, then, we have two great reasons why Mark is a book of supreme importance. First, it is the earliest of all the gospels; if it was written just shortly after Peter died, its date will be about AD 65. Second, it embodies the record of what Peter preached and taught about Jesus. We may put it this way: Mark is the nearest approach we will ever possess to an eyewitness account of the life of Jesus.

The Lost Ending

There is a very interesting point about Mark's gospel. In its original form it stops at Mark 16:8. We know this for two reasons. First, the verses which follow (Mark 16:9–20) are not in any of the great early manuscripts; only later and inferior manuscripts contain them. Second, the style of the Greek is so different that these verses and the rest of the gospel cannot have been written by the same person.

But the gospel cannot have been *meant* to stop at Mark 16:8. What then happened? It may be that Mark died, perhaps even suffered martyrdom, before he could complete his gospel. More likely, it may be that at one time only one copy of the gospel remained, and that a copy in which the last part of the roll on which it was written had got torn off. There was a time when the Church did not much use Mark, preferring Matthew and Luke. It may well be that Mark's gospel was so neglected that all copies except for a mutilated one were lost. If that is so, we were within an ace of losing the gospel which in many ways is the most important of all.

The Characteristics of Mark's Gospel

Let us look at the characteristics of Mark's gospel so that we may watch for them as we read and study it.

(1) It is the nearest thing we will ever get to a report of Jesus' life. Mark's aim was to give a picture of Jesus as he was. The scholar B. F. Westcott called it 'a transcript from life'. A. B. Bruce of Glasgow's Free Church College said that it was written 'from the viewpoint of loving, vivid recollection', and that its great characteristic was *realism*.

If we are ever to get anything approaching a biography of Jesus, it must be based on Mark, for it is his delight to tell the facts of Jesus' life in the simplest and most dramatic way.

(2) Mark never forgot the divine side of Jesus. He begins his gospel with the declaration of faith, 'The beginning of the gospel (good news) of Jesus Christ, the Son of God.' He leaves us in no doubt what he believed Jesus to be. Again and again he speaks of the impact Jesus made on the minds and hearts of those who heard him. The awe and astonishment which he evoked are always in the forefront of Mark's mind. 'They were astounded at his teaching' (1:22). 'They were all amazed' (1:27). Such phrases occur again and again. Not only was this astonishment in the minds of the crowds who listened to Jesus; it was still more in the minds of the inner circle of the disciples. 'And they were filled with great awe, and said to one another, "Who then is this, that even the wind and the sea obey him?"' (4:41). 'And they were utterly astounded' (6:51). 'They were greatly astounded' (10:26).

To Mark, Jesus was not simply one of us; he was God among us, constantly moving people to a wondering amazement with his words and deeds.

(3) At the same time, no gospel gives such a human picture of Jesus. Sometimes its picture is so human that the later writers alter it a little because they are almost afraid to say what Mark said. To Mark, Jesus is simply 'the carpenter' (6:3). Later Matthew alters that to 'the carpenter's son' (Matthew 13:55), as if to call Jesus a village tradesman is too daring. When Mark is telling of the temptations of Jesus, he writes, 'The Spirit immediately *drove* him out into the wilderness' (1:12). Matthew and Luke do not like this word *drove* used of Jesus, so they soften it down and say, 'Jesus was *led up* by the Spirit into the wilderness' (Matthew 4:1; cf. Luke 4:1). No one tells us so much about the emotions of Jesus as Mark does. Jesus sighed deeply in his spirit (8:12; cf. 7:34). He was moved with compassion (6:34). He was amazed at their unbelief (6:6). He was moved with righteous anger (3:5, 8:33,

10:14). Only Mark tells us that when Jesus looked at the rich young ruler he loved him (10:21). Jesus could feel the pangs of hunger (11:12). He could be tired and want to rest (6:31).

It is in Mark's gospel, above all, that we get a picture of a Jesus who shared emotions and passions with us. The sheer humanity of Jesus in Mark's picture brings him very near to us.

(4) One of the great characteristics of Mark is that over and over again he inserts the little vivid details into the narrative which are the hallmark of an eyewitness. Both Matthew and Mark tell of Jesus taking the little child and setting him in the midst. Matthew (18:2) says, 'He called a child, whom he put among them.' Mark adds something which lights up the whole picture (9:36). In the words of the Revised Standard Version, 'And he took a child and put him in the midst of them; and *taking him in his arms*, he said to them . . .' In the lovely picture of Jesus and the children, when Jesus rebuked the disciples for keeping the children from him, only Mark finishes, '*and he took them up in his arms, laid his hands on them, and blessed them*' (10:13–16; cf. Matthew 19:13–15; Luke 18:15–17). All the tenderness of Jesus is in these little vivid additions. When Mark is telling of the feeding of the 5,000, he alone tells how they sat down *in hundreds and in fifties*, looking like vegetable beds in a garden (6:40); and immediately the whole scene rises before us. When Jesus and his disciples were on the last journey to Jerusalem, only Mark tells us, '*and Jesus was walking ahead of them*' (10:32; cf. Matthew 20:17; Luke 18:31); and in that one vivid little phrase all the loneliness of Jesus stands out. When Mark is telling the story of the stilling of the storm, he has one little sentence that none of the other gospel writers have. 'He was in the stern, *asleep on the cushion*' (4:38). And that one touch makes the picture vivid before our eyes.

There can be little doubt that all these details are due to the fact that Peter was an eyewitness and was seeing these things again with the eye of memory.

(5) Mark's realism and his simplicity come out in his Greek style.

(a) His style is not carefully developed and polished. He tells the story as a child might tell it. He adds statement to statement connecting them simply with the word 'and'. In the third chapter of the gospel, in the Greek, there are thirty-four clauses or sentences one after another introduced by 'and' after one principal verb. It is the way in which an eager child would tell the story.

(b) He is very fond of the words 'and straightaway', 'and immediately'. They occur in the gospel almost thirty times. It is sometimes said of a story that 'it marches'. But Mark's story does not so much march; he rushes on in a kind of breathless attempt to make the story as vivid to others as it is to himself.

(c) He is very fond of the historic present. That is to say, in the Greek he talks of events in the present tense instead of in the past. 'And when Jesus heard it, he *says* to them, "Those who are strong do not need a doctor, but those who are ill"' (2:17). 'And when they *come* near to Jerusalem, to Bethphage and to Bethany, to the Mount of Olives, he *sends* two of his disciples, and *says* to them, "Go into the village opposite you . . ."' (11:1–2). 'And immediately, while he was still speaking, Judas, one of The Twelve, *comes*' (14:43).

Generally speaking we do not keep these historic presents in translation, because in English they do not sound well; but they show how vivid and real the thing was to Mark's mind, as if it was happening before his very eyes.

(d) He quite often gives us the very Aramaic words which Jesus used. To Jairus' daughter, Jesus said, '*Talitha cumi*'

(5:41). To the deaf man with the impediment in his speech, he said, '*Ephphatha*' (7:34). The dedicated gift is '*Corban*' (7:11). In the garden, he says, '*Abba*, Father' (14:36). On the cross, he cries, '*Eloi, Eloi, lema sabachthani?*' (15:34).

There were times when Peter could hear again the very sound of Jesus' voice and could not help passing it on to Mark in the very words that Jesus spoke.

The Essential Gospel

It would not be unfair to call Mark *the essential gospel*. We will do well to study with loving care the earliest gospel we possess, the gospel where we hear again the preaching of Peter himself.

3

Luke

The Universal Gospel

A Lovely Book and its Author

The Gospel according to St Luke has been called the loveliest book in the world. When once an American asked him if he could recommend a good life of Christ, the theologian James Denney answered, 'Have you tried the one that Luke wrote?' There is a legend that Luke was a skilled painter; there is even a painting of Mary in a Spanish cathedral to this day which purports to be by him. Certainly he had an eye for vivid things. It would not be far wrong to say that the third gospel is the best life of Christ ever written. Tradition has always believed that Luke was the author and we need have no qualms in accepting that tradition. In the ancient world it was the regular thing to attach books to famous names; no one thought it wrong. But Luke was never one of the famous figures of the early Church. If he had not written the gospel no one would have attached it to his name.

Luke was a Gentile; and he has the unique distinction of being the only New Testament writer who was not a Jew. He was a medical man, a doctor by profession (Colossians 4:14), and maybe that very fact gave him the wide sympathy he possessed. It has been said that a minister sees men and women at their best; a lawyer sees them at their worst; and a doctor sees them as they are. Luke saw men and women and loved them all.

LUKE

The book was written to a man called Theophilus. He is called *most excellent Theophilus* and the title given him is the normal title for a high official in the Roman government. No doubt Luke wrote it to tell an earnest inquirer more about Jesus; and he succeeded in giving Theophilus a picture which must have bound his heart closer to the Jesus of whom he had heard.

The Symbols of the Gospels

Every one of the four gospels was written from a certain point of view. Very often on stained-glass windows the writers of the gospels are pictured; and usually to each there is attached a symbol. The symbols vary but one of the commonest allocations is this.

The emblem of *Mark* is a *man*. Mark is the simplest and most straightforward of the gospels. It has been well said that its characteristic is *realism*. It is the nearest to being a report of Jesus' life.

The emblem of *Matthew* is a *lion*. Matthew was a Jew writing for Jews and he saw in Jesus the Messiah, the lion of the tribe of Judah, the one whom all the prophets had predicted.

The emblem of *John* is the *eagle*. The eagle can fly higher than any other bird. It is said that of all creatures only the eagle can look straight into the sun. John is the theological gospel; its flights of thought are higher than those of any of the others. It is the gospel where the philosopher can find themes to think about for a lifetime and to solve only in eternity.

The symbol of *Luke* is the *calf*. The calf is the animal for sacrifice; and Luke saw in Jesus the sacrifice for all the world. In Luke above all, the barriers are broken down and Jesus is for Jew and Gentile, saint and sinner alike. He is the Saviour of the world. Keeping that in mind, let us now set down the characteristics of this gospel.

23

A Historian's Care

First and foremost, Luke's gospel is an exceedingly careful bit of work. His Greek is notably good. The first four verses are well-nigh the best Greek in the New Testament. In them he claims that his work is the product of the most careful research. His opportunities were ample and his sources must have been good. As the trusted companion of Paul he must have known all the great figures of the Church, and we may be sure that he had them tell their stories to him. For two years he was Paul's companion in imprisonment in Caesarea. In those long days he had every opportunity for study and research and he must have used them well.

An example of Luke's care is the way in which he dates the emergence of John the Baptist. He does so by no fewer than six contemporary datings. 'In the fifteenth year of the reign of Tiberius Caesar [1], Pontius Pilate being governor of Judaea [2], Herod being tetrarch of Galilee [3], and his brother Philip being tetrarch of the region of Ituraea and Trachonitis [4], and Lysanias tetrarch of Abilene [5] in the high priesthood of Annas and Caiaphas [6], the word of God came to John' (Luke 3:1–2, Revised Standard Version). Here is a man who is writing with care and who will be as accurate as it is possible for him to be.

The Gospel for the Gentiles

It is clear that Luke wrote mainly for Gentiles. Theophilus was a Gentile, as was Luke himself, and there is nothing in the gospel that a Gentile could not grasp and understand. (1) As we have seen, Luke begins his dating from the reigning *Roman* emperor and the current *Roman* governor. The *Roman* date comes first. (2) Unlike Matthew, he is not greatly interested in the life of Jesus as the fulfilment of Jewish prophecy. (3)

He very seldom quotes the Old Testament at all. (4) He has a habit of giving Hebrew words in their Greek equivalent so that a Greek would understand. Simon the *Cananaean* becomes Simon the *Zealot* (cf. Luke 6:15; Matthew 10:4). *Calvary* is called not by its Hebrew name, *Golgotha*, but by its Greek name, *Kranion*. Both mean *the place of a skull.* He never uses the Jewish term *Rabbi* of Jesus but always a Greek word meaning *Master.* When he is tracing the descent of Jesus, he traces it not to Abraham, the founder of the Jewish race, as Matthew does, but to Adam, the founder of the human race (cf. Matthew 1:2; Luke 3:38).

Because of this Luke is the easiest of all the gospels to read. He was writing, not for Jews, but for people very like ourselves.

The Gospel of Prayer

Luke's gospel is specially the gospel of prayer. At all the great moments of his life, Luke shows us Jesus at prayer. He prayed at his baptism (3:21); before his first collision with the Pharisees (5:16); before he chose the Twelve (6:12); before he questioned his disciples as to who they thought he was; before his first prediction of his own death (9:18); at the transfiguration (9:29); and upon the cross (23:46). Only Luke tells us that Jesus prayed for Peter in his hour of testing (22:32). Only he tells us the prayer parables of the friend at midnight (11:5–13) and the unjust judge (18:1–8). To Luke the unclosed door of prayer was one of the most precious in all the world.

The Gospel of Women

In Palestine the place of women was low. In the Jewish morning prayer a man thanks God that he has not made him 'a Gentile, a slave or a woman'. But Luke gives a very special place to women. The birth narrative is told from Mary's point of view. It is in Luke that we read of Elizabeth, of Anna, of the widow at Nain, of the woman who anointed Jesus' feet in the house of Simon the Pharisee. It is Luke who makes vivid the pictures of Martha and Mary and of Mary Magdalene. It is very likely that Luke was a native of Macedonia where women held a more emancipated position than anywhere else; and that may have something to do with it.

The Gospel of Praise

In Luke the phrase *praising God* occurs oftener than in all the rest of the New Testament put together. This praise reaches its peak in the three great hymns that the Church has sung throughout all her generations – the *Magnificat* (1:46–55), the *Benedictus* (1:68–79) and the *Nunc Dimittis* (2:29–32). There is a radiance in Luke's gospel which is a lovely thing, as if the sheen of heaven had touched the things of earth.

The Universal Gospel

But the outstanding characteristic of Luke is that it is the universal gospel. All the barriers are down; Jesus Christ is for all people without distinction.

(a) The kingdom of heaven is not shut to the Samaritans (9:51–6). Luke alone tells the parable of the Good Samaritan (10:30–7). The one grateful leper is a Samaritan (17:11–19). John can record a saying that the Jews have no dealings with the Samaritans (John 4:9). But Luke refuses to shut the door on anyone.

(b) Luke shows Jesus speaking with approval of Gentiles whom an orthodox Jew would have considered unclean. He shows us Jesus citing the widow of Zarephath and Naaman the Syrian as shining examples (4:25–7). The Roman centurion is praised for the greatness of his faith (7:9). Luke tells us of that great word of Jesus, 'People will come from east and west, from north and south, and will eat in the kingdom of God' (13:29).

(c) Luke is supremely interested in the poor. When Mary brings the offering for her purification it is the offering of the poor (2:24). When Jesus is, as it were, setting out his credentials to the emissaries of John, the climax is, 'The poor have good news brought to them' (7:22). He alone tells the parable of the rich man and the poor man (16:19–31). In Luke's account of the beatitudes the saying of Jesus runs, not, as in Matthew (5:3), 'Blessed are the poor in spirit', but simply, 'Blessed are you who are poor' (Luke 6:20). Luke's gospel has been called 'the gospel of the underdog'. His heart runs out to everyone for whom life is an unequal struggle.

(d) Above all Luke shows Jesus as the friend of outcasts and sinners. He alone tells of the woman who anointed Jesus' feet and bathed them with her tears and wiped them with her hair in the house of Simon the Pharisee (7:36–50); of Zachaeus, the despised tax-gatherer (19:1–10); of the penitent thief (23:43); and he alone has the immortal story of the prodigal son and the loving father (15:11–32). When Matthew tells how Jesus sent his disciples out to preach, he says that Jesus told them not to go to the Samaritans or the Gentiles (Matthew 10:5); but Luke omits that altogether. All four gospel writers quote from Isaiah 40 when they give the message of John the Baptist, 'Prepare the way of the Lord; make straight in the desert a highway for our God'; but only Luke continues the quotation to its trium-phant conclusion, 'And all flesh shall see the salvation of God' (Isaiah 40:3–5; Matthew 3:3; Mark 1:3; John 1:23; Luke 3:4, 6). Luke of all the gospel writers sees no limits to the love of God.

The Book Beautiful

As we study this book we must look for these characteristics. Somehow of all the gospel writers one would have liked to meet Luke best of all, for this Gentile doctor with the tremendous vision of the infinite sweep of the love of God must have been a lovely individual. F. W. Faber wrote the lines:

> There's a wideness in God's mercy,
>   Like the wideness of the sea;
> There's a kindness in his justice,
>   Which is more than liberty.
>
> For the love of God is broader
>   Than the measures of man's mind;
> And the heart of the Eternal
>   Is most wonderfully kind.

Luke's gospel is the demonstration that this is true.

4
John
The Precious Gospel

The Gospel of the Eagle's Eye

For many Christian people, the Gospel according to St John is the most precious book in the New Testament. It is the book on which above all they feed their minds and nourish their hearts, and in which they rest their souls. Very often on stained-glass windows and the like, the gospel writers are represented in symbol by the figures of the four animals that the writer of the Revelation saw around the throne (Revelation 4:7). The emblems are variously distributed among the gospel writers, but a common allocation is that the *man* stands for Mark, which is the plainest, the most straightforward and the most human of the gospels; the *lion* stands for Matthew, for he specially saw Jesus as the Messiah and the Lion of the tribe of Judah; the *ox* stands for Luke, because it is the animal of service and sacrifice, and Luke saw Jesus as the great servant of men and women and the universal sacrifice for all people; and the *eagle* stands for John, because it alone of all living creatures can look straight into the sun and not be dazzled, and, of all the New Testament writers, John has the most penetrating gaze into the eternal mysteries and the eternal truths and the very mind of God. Many people find themselves closer to God and to Jesus Christ in John than in any other book in the world.

The Gospel that is Different

But we have only to read the Fourth Gospel in the most cursory way to see that it is quite different from the other three. It omits so many things that they include. The Fourth Gospel has no account of the birth of Jesus, of his baptism, of his temptations; it tells us nothing of the Last Supper, nothing of Gethsemane and nothing of the ascension. It has no word of the healing of any people possessed by devils and evil spirits. And, perhaps most surprising of all, it has none of the parable stories Jesus told which are such a priceless part of the other three gospels. In these other three gospels, Jesus speaks either in these wonderful stories or in short, epigrammatic, vivid sentences which stick in the memory. But in the Fourth Gospel, the speeches of Jesus are often a whole chapter long and are often involved, argumentative pronouncements quite unlike the pithy, unforgettable sayings of the other three.

Even more surprising, the account in the Fourth Gospel of the facts of the life and ministry of Jesus is often different from that in the other three.

(1) John has a different account of the *beginning* of the ministry of Jesus. In the other three gospels, it is quite definitely stated that Jesus did not emerge as a preacher until after John the Baptist had been imprisoned. 'Now after John was arrested, Jesus came to Galilee, proclaiming the good news of God' (Mark 1:14; cf. Luke 3:18, 20; Matthew 4:12). But in John there is a quite considerable period during which the ministry of Jesus overlapped with the activity of John the Baptist (John 3:22–30, 4:1–2).

(2) John has a different account of the *scene* of Jesus' ministry. In the other three gospels, the main scene of the ministry is Galilee, and Jesus does not reach Jerusalem until

the last week of his life. In John, the main scene of the
ministry is Jerusalem and Judaea, with only occasional with-
drawals to Galilee (2:1–13, 4:35–5:1, 6:1–7:14). In John,
Jesus is in Jerusalem for a Passover which occurred at the
same time as the cleansing of the Temple, as John tells the
story (2:13); he is in Jerusalem at the time of an unnamed
feast (5:1); he is there for the Feast of Tabernacles (7:2, 10);
he is there at the Feast of Dedication in the wintertime
(10:22). In fact, according to the Fourth Gospel, Jesus never
left Jerusalem after that feast; after chapter 10 he is in
Jerusalem all the time, which would mean a stay of months,
from the wintertime of the Feast of the Dedication to the
springtime of the Passover at which he was crucified.

In point of fact, in this particular matter John is surely right.
The other gospels show us Jesus mourning over Jerusalem as
the last week came on. 'Jerusalem, Jerusalem, the city that
kills the prophets and stones those who are sent to it! How
often have I desired to gather your children together as a hen
gathers her brood under her wings, and you were not willing!'
(Matthew 23:37 = Luke 13:34). It is clear that Jesus could not
have said that unless he had paid repeated visits to Jerusalem
and made repeated appeals to it. It was impossible for him to
say that on a first visit. In this, John is unquestionably right.

It was in fact this difference of scene which provided the
great Church historian Eusebius with one of the earliest
explanations of the difference between the Fourth Gospel and
the other three. He said that in his day (about AD 300) many
people who were scholars held the following view. Matthew
at first preached to the Hebrew people. The day came when
he had to leave them and go to other nations. Before he went,
he set down his story of the life of Jesus in Hebrew, 'and thus
compensated those whom he was obliged to leave for the
loss of his presence'. After Mark and Luke had published

their gospels, John was still preaching the story of Jesus orally. 'Finally he proceeded to write for the following reason. The three gospels already mentioned having come into the hands of all and into his hands too, they say that he fully accepted them and bore witness to their truthfulness; *but there was lacking in them an account of the deeds done by Christ at the beginning of his ministry* . . . They therefore say that John, being asked to do it for this reason, gave in his gospel an account of the period which had been omitted by the earlier evangelists, and of the deeds done by the Saviour during that period; that is, of the deeds done before the imprisonment of John the Baptist . . . John therefore records the deeds of Christ which were performed *before* the Baptist was cast into prison, but the other three evangelists mention the events which happened *after* that time . . . The *Gospel according to John* contains the *first* acts of Christ, while the others give an account of the *latter* part of his life' (Eusebius, *The Ecclesiastical History*, 5:24).

So then according to Eusebius there is no contradiction at all between the Fourth Gospel and the other three; the difference is due to the fact that the Fourth Gospel is describing a ministry in Jerusalem, at least in its earlier chapters, which preceded the ministry in Galilee, and which took place while John the Baptist was still at liberty. It may well be that this explanation of Eusebius is at least in part correct.

(3) John has a different account of the *duration* of Jesus' ministry. The other three gospels, on the face of it, imply that it lasted only one year. Within the ministry, there is only one Passover Feast. In John, there are *three* Passovers: one at the cleansing of the Temple (2:13), one near the feeding of the 5,000 (6:4), and the final Passover at which Jesus went to the cross. According to John, the ministry of Jesus would take a

minimum of two years, and probably a period nearer three years, to cover its events. Again, John is unquestionably right. If we read the other three gospels closely and carefully, we can see that he is right. When the disciples plucked the ears of corn (Mark 2:23), it must have been springtime. When the 5,000 were fed, they sat down on the *green grass* (Mark 6:39); therefore it was springtime again, and there must have been a year between the two events. There follows the tour through Tyre and Sidon, and the transfiguration. At the transfiguration, Peter wished to build three booths and to stay there. It is most natural to think that it was the time of the Feast of Tabernacles or Booths and that that is why Peter made the suggestion (Mark 9:5). That would make the date early in October. There follows the space between that and the last Passover in April. Therefore, behind the narrative of the other three gospels lies the fact that Jesus' ministry actually did last for at least three years, as John represents it.

(4) It sometimes even happens that John differs in matters of fact from the other three. There are two outstanding examples. First, John puts the cleansing of the Temple at the *beginning* of Jesus' ministry (2:13–22); the others put it at the *end* (Mark 11:15–17; Matthew 21:12–13; Luke 19:45–6). Second, when we come to study the narratives in detail, we will see that John dates the crucifixion of Jesus on the day before the Passover, while the other gospels date it on the day of the Passover.

We can never shut our eyes to the obvious differences between John and the other gospels.

John's Special Knowledge

One thing is certain – if John differs from the other three gospels, it is not because of ignorance and lack of information.

The plain fact is that, if he omits much that they tell us, he also tells us much that they do not mention. John alone tells of the marriage feast at Cana of Galilee (2:1–11); of the coming of Nicodemus to Jesus (3:1–15); of the woman of Samaria (4); of the raising of Lazarus (11); of the way in which Jesus washed his disciples' feet (13:1–17); of Jesus' wonderful teaching about the Holy Spirit, the Comforter, which is scattered through chapters 14–17. It is only in John that some of the disciples really come alive. It is in John alone that Thomas speaks (11:16, 14:5, 20:24–9); that Andrew becomes a real personality (1:40–1, 6:8–9, 12:22); that we get a glimpse of the character of Philip (6:5–7, 14:8–9); that we hear the carping protest of Judas at the anointing at Bethany (12:4–5). And the strange thing is that these little extra touches are intensely revealing. John's pictures of Thomas and Andrew and Philip are like little cameos or vignettes in which the character of each man is etched in a way we cannot forget.

Further, again and again John has little extra details which read like the memories of one who was there. The loaves which the young boy brought to Jesus were *barley* loaves (6:9); when Jesus came to the disciples as they crossed the lake in the storm, they had rowed between three and four miles (6:19); there were six stone water pots at Cana of Galilee (2:6); it is only John who tells of the four soldiers gambling for the seamless robe as Jesus dies (19:23); he knows the exact weight of the myrrh and aloes which were used to anoint the dead body of Jesus (19:39); and he remembers how the perfume of the ointment filled the house at the anointing at Bethany (12:3). Many of these things are such apparently unimportant details that they are inexplicable unless they are the memories of someone who was there.

However much John may differ from the other three gospels, that difference is to be explained not by ignorance but rather by the fact that he had more knowledge or better sources or a more vivid memory than the others.

Further evidence of the specialized information of the writer of the Fourth Gospel is his *detailed knowledge of Palestine and of Jerusalem*. He knows how long it took to build the Temple (2:20); that the Jews and the Samaritans had a permanent quarrel (4:9); the low Jewish view of women (4:9); and how the Jews regard the Sabbath (5:10, 7:21–3, 9:14). His knowledge of the geography of Palestine is intimate. He knows of two Bethanys, one of which is beyond Jordan (1:28, 12:1); he knows that Bethsaida was the home of some of the disciples (1:44, 12:21); that Cana is in Galilee (2:1, 4:46, 21:2); and that Sychar is near Shechem (4:5). He has what one might call a street-by-street knowledge of Jerusalem. He knows the sheepgate and the pool near it (5:2); the pool of Siloam (9:7); Solomon's Porch (10:23); the brook Kidron (18:1); the pavement which is called Gabbatha (19:13); and Golgotha, which is like a skull (19:17). It must be remembered that Jerusalem was destroyed in AD 70 and that John did not write until around AD 100; and yet from his memory he knows Jerusalem like the back of his hand.

The Circumstances in which John Wrote

We have seen that there are very real differences between the Fourth Gospel and the other three gospels; and we have seen that, whatever the reason, it was not lack of knowledge on John's part. We must now go on to ask, what was the aim with which John wrote? If we can discover this, we will discover why he selected and treated his facts as he did.

The Fourth Gospel was written in Ephesus around AD 100. By that time, two special features had emerged in the situation of the Christian Church. First, *Christianity had gone out into the Gentile world*. By that time, the Christian Church was no longer predominantly Jewish; it was in fact overwhelmingly Gentile. The vast majority of its members now came not from a Jewish but a Greek background. That being so, *Christianity had to be restated.* It was not that the truth of Christianity had changed; but the terms and the categories in which it found expression had to be changed.

Take but one instance. A Greek might take up the Gospel according to St Matthew and immediately on opening it would be confronted with a long genealogy. Genealogies were familiar enough to Jews, but quite unintelligible to Greeks. Moving on, the reader would be confronted with a Jesus who was the Son of David, a king of whom the Greeks had never heard, and the symbol of a racial and nationalist ambition which had no significance for the Greeks. The picture presented was of Jesus as the Messiah, a term of which Greeks had never heard. Must Greeks who wished to become Christians be compelled to reorganize their entire thinking into Jewish categories? Must they learn a good deal about Jewish history and Jewish apocalyptic literature (which told about the coming of the Messiah) before they could become Christians? As the biblical scholar E. J. Goodspeed phrased it: 'Was there no way in which [they] might be introduced directly to the values of Christian salvation without being for ever routed, we might even say, detoured, through Judaism?' Greeks were among the world's greatest thinkers. Was it necessary for them to abandon all their own great intellectual heritage in order to think entirely in Jewish terms and categories of thought?

John faced that problem fairly and squarely. And he found one of the greatest solutions which ever entered the human mind. Later on, in the commentary, we shall deal much more fully with John's great solution. At the moment, we touch on it briefly. The Greeks had two great conceptions.

(a) They had the conception of the *Logos*. In Greek, *logos* means two things – it means *word* and it means *reason*. Jews were entirely familiar with the all-powerful word of God. 'God said, "Let there be light"; and there was light' (Genesis 1:3). Greeks were entirely familiar with the thought of reason. They looked at this world; they saw a magnificent and dependable order. Night and day came with unfailing regularity; the year kept its seasons in unvarying course; the stars and the planets moved in their unaltering path; nature had her unvarying laws. What produced this order? Greeks answered unhesitatingly: the *Logos*, the mind of God, is responsible for the majestic order of the world. They went on: what is it that gives human beings power to think, to reason and to know? Again they answered unhesitatingly: the *Logos*, the mind of God, dwelling within an individual makes that person a thinking rational being.

John seized on this. It was in this way that he thought of Jesus. He said to the Greeks: 'All your lives you have been fascinated by this great, guiding, controlling mind of God. The mind of God has come to earth in the man Jesus. Look at him and you see what the mind and thought of God are like.' John had discovered a new category in which Greeks might think of Jesus, a category in which Jesus was presented as nothing less than God acting in human form.

(b) They had the conception of two worlds. The Greeks always conceived of two worlds. The one was the world in which we live. It was a wonderful world in its way but a world of shadows and copies and unrealities. The other was the real world, in which the great realities, of which our earthly things are only poor, pale copies, stand for ever. To the Greeks, the unseen world was the real one; the seen world was only shadowy unreality.

Plato systematized this way of thinking in his doctrine of forms or ideas. He held that in the unseen world there was the perfect pattern of everything, and the things of this world were shadowy copies of these eternal patterns. To put it simply, Plato held that somewhere there was a perfect pattern of a table of which all earthly tables are inadequate copies; somewhere there was the perfect pattern of the good and the beautiful of which all earthly goodness and earthly beauty are imperfect copies. And the great reality, the supreme idea, the pattern of all patterns and the form of all forms was God. The great problem was how to get into this world of reality, how to get out of our shadows into the eternal truths.

John declares that that is what Jesus enables us to do. He *is* reality come to earth. The Greek word for *real* in this sense is *alēthinos*; it is very closely connected with the word *alēthēs*, which means *true*, and *alētheia*, which means *the truth*. The Authorized and Revised Standard Versions translate *alēthinos* as *true*; they would be far better to translate it as *real*. Jesus is the *real* light (1:9); Jesus is the *real* bread (6:32); Jesus is the *real* vine (15:1); to Jesus belongs the *real* judgment (8:16). Jesus alone has reality in our world of shadows and imperfections.

Something follows from that. Every action that Jesus did was, therefore, not only an act in time but a window which allows us to see into reality. That is what John means when he talks of Jesus' miracles as *signs* (*sēmeia*). The wonderful works of Jesus were not simply wonderful; they were windows opening on to the reality which is God. This explains why John tells the miracle stories in a quite different way from the other three gospel writers. There are two differences.

(a) In the Fourth Gospel, we miss the note of compassion which is in the miracle stories of the others. In the others, Jesus is moved with compassion for the leper (Mark 1:41); his sympathy goes out to Jairus (Mark 5:22); he is sorry for the father of the epileptic boy (Mark 9:14); when he raises to life the son of the widow of Nain, Luke says with an infinite tenderness: 'He gave him to his mother' (Luke 7:15). But in John the miracles are not so much deeds of compassion as deeds which demonstrate the glory of Christ. After the miracle at Cana of Galilee, John comments: 'Jesus did this, the first of his signs, in Cana of Galilee, *and revealed his glory*' (2:11). The raising of Lazarus happens '*for God's glory*' (11:4). The blind man's blindness existed to allow a demonstration of the glory of the works of God (John 9:3). To John, it was not that there was no love and compassion in the miracles; but in every one of them he saw the glory of the reality of God breaking into time and into human affairs.

(b) Often the miracles of Jesus in the Fourth Gospel are accompanied by a long discourse. The feeding of the 5,000 is followed by the long discourse on the bread of life (chapter 6); the healing of the blind man springs from the saying that Jesus is the light of the world (chapter 9); and the raising of Lazarus leads up to the saying that Jesus is the resurrection and the life (chapter 11). To John, the miracles were not simply single events in time; they were insights into what God is always doing and what Jesus always is; they were windows into the reality of God. Jesus did not merely once feed 5,000 people; that was an illustration that he is forever the real bread of life. Jesus did not merely once open the eyes of a blind man; he is forever the light of the world. Jesus did not merely once raise Lazarus from the dead; he is forever and for everyone the resurrection and the life. To John, a miracle was never an isolated act; it was always a window into the reality of what Jesus always was and always is and always did and always does.

It was with this in mind that the great scholar Clement of Alexandria (about AD 230) arrived at one of the most famous and true of all verdicts about the origin and aim of the Fourth Gospel. It was his view that the gospels containing the genealogies had been written first – that is, Luke and Matthew; that then Mark, at the request of many who had heard Peter preach, composed his gospel, which embodied the preaching material of Peter; and that then 'last of all, John, perceiving that what had reference to the bodily things of Jesus' ministry had been sufficiently related, and encouraged by his friends, and inspired by the Holy Spirit, wrote *a spiritual gospel*' (quoted in Eusebius, *The Ecclesiastical History*, 6:14). What Clement meant was that John was interested not so much in the mere facts as in the meaning of the facts, that it was not facts he was after but truth. John did not see the events of Jesus' life simply as events in time; he saw them as windows looking into eternity, and he pressed towards the spiritual meaning of the events and the words of Jesus' life in a way that the other three gospels did not attempt.

That is still one of the truest verdicts on the Fourth Gospel ever reached. John did write, not a historical, but a spiritual gospel.

So, first of all, John presented Jesus as the mind of God in a person come to earth, and as the one person who possesses reality instead of shadows and is able to lead men and women out of the shadows into the real world of which Plato and the great Greeks had dreamed. The Christianity which had once been clothed in Jewish categories had taken to itself the greatness of the thought of the Greeks.

The Rise of the Heresies

The second of the great facts confronting the Church when the Fourth Gospel was written was *the rise of heresy*. It was now about seventy years since Jesus had been crucified. By this time, the Church was an organization and an institution. Theologies and creeds were being thought out and stated; and inevitably the thoughts of some people went down mistaken ways, and heresies resulted. A heresy is seldom a complete untruth; it usually results when one facet of the truth is unduly emphasized. We can see at least two of the heresies which the writer of the Fourth Gospel sought to combat.

(a) There were certain Christians, especially Jewish Christians, who gave too high a place to John the Baptist. There was something about him which had an inevitable appeal to the Jews. He walked in the prophetic succession and talked with the prophetic voice. We know that in later times there was an accepted sect of John the Baptist within the orthodox Jewish faith. In Acts 19:1–7, we come upon a little group of twelve on the fringe of the Christian Church who had never got beyond the baptism of John.

Over and over again, the Fourth Gospel quietly, but definitely, relegates John to his proper place. Over and over again, John himself denies that he has ever claimed or possessed the highest place, and without qualification yields that place to Jesus. We have already seen that in the other gospels the ministry of Jesus did not begin until John the Baptist had been put into prison, but that in the Fourth Gospel their ministries overlap. The writer of the Fourth Gospel may well have used that arrangement to show John and Jesus in actual meeting and to show that John used these meetings to admit, and to urge others to admit, the supremacy of Jesus. It is carefully pointed out that John is not 'that light' (1:8). He is shown as quite definitely disclaiming all messianic aspirations (1:20ff., 3:28, 4:1, 10:41). It is not even permissible to think of him as the highest witness (5:36). There is no criticism at all of John the Baptist in the Fourth Gospel; but there is a rebuke to those who would give him a place which ought to belong to Jesus and to Jesus alone.

(b) A certain type of heresy which was very widely spread in the days when the Fourth Gospel was written is called by the general name of Gnosticism. Without some understanding of it, much of John's greatness and much of his aim will be missed. The basic doctrine of Gnosticism was that matter is essentially evil and spirit is essentially good. The Gnostics went on to argue that on that basis God himself cannot touch matter and therefore did not create the world. What he did was to put out a series of emanations. Each of these emanations was further from him, until at last there was one so distant from him that it could touch matter. That emanation was the creator of the world.

By itself that idea is bad enough, but it was made worse by an addition. The Gnostics held that each emanation knew less and less about God, until there was a stage when the emanations were not only ignorant of God but actually hostile to him. So they finally came to the conclusion that the creator god was not only different from the real God, but was also quite ignorant of and actively hostile to him. Cerinthus, one of the leaders of the Gnostics, said that 'the world was created, not by God, but by a certain power far separate from him, and far distant from that Power who is over the universe, and ignorant of the God who is over all'.

The Gnostics believed that God had nothing to do with the creating of the world. That is why John begins his gospel with the ringing statement: 'All things came into being through him, and without him not one thing came into being' (1:3). That is why John insists that 'God so loved the *world*' (3:16). In face of the Gnostics who so mistakenly spiritualized God into a being who could not possibly have anything to do with the world, John presented the Christian doctrine of the God who made the world and whose presence fills the world that he has made.

The beliefs of the Gnostics impinged on their ideas of Jesus.

(a) Some of the Gnostics held that Jesus was one of the emanations which had proceeded from God. They held that he was not in any real sense divine; that he was only a kind of demi-god who was more or less distant from the real God; that he was simply one of a chain of lesser beings between God and the world.

(b) Some of the Gnostics held that Jesus had no real body. A body is matter and God could not touch matter; therefore Jesus was a kind of phantom without real flesh and blood. They held, for instance, that when he stepped on the ground he left no footprint, for his body had neither weight nor substance. They could never have said: 'The Word became *flesh*' (John 1:14). St Augustine tells how he had read much in the work of the philosophers of his day; he had found much that was very like what was in the New Testament, but, he said: '"The Word was made flesh and dwelt among us" I did not read there.' That is why John in his First Letter insists that Jesus came *in the flesh*, and declares that anyone who denies that fact is moved by the spirit of the antichrist (1 John 4:3). This particular heresy is known as *Docetism*. Docetism comes from the Greek word *dokein* which means *to seem*; and the heresy is so called because it held that Jesus only *seemed* to be a man.

(c) Some Gnostics held a variation of that heresy. They held that Jesus was a man into whom the Spirit of God came at his baptism; that the Spirit remained with him throughout his life until the end; but since the Spirit of God could never suffer and die, it left him before he was crucified. They gave Jesus' cry on the cross as: 'My power, my power, why have you forsaken me?' And in their books they told of people talking on the Mount of Olives to a form which looked exactly like Jesus while the man Jesus died on the cross.

So then the Gnostic heresies were expressed in two possible alternative beliefs. They believed either that Jesus was not really divine but simply one of a series of emanations from God, or that he was not in any sense human but a kind of phantom in the shape of a man. The Gnostic beliefs at one and the same time destroyed the real godhead and the real humanity of Jesus.

The Humanity of Jesus

The fact that John is out to correct both these Gnostic tendencies explains a curious paradoxical double emphasis in his gospel. On the one hand, there is no gospel which so uncompromisingly stresses the real humanity of Jesus. Jesus was angry with those who bought and sold in the Temple courts (2:15); he was physically tired as he sat by the well which was near Sychar in Samaria (4:6); his disciples offered him food in the way in which they would offer it to any hungry man (4:31); he had sympathy with those who were hungry and with those who were afraid (6:5, 20); he knew grief and he wept tears as any mourner might do (11:33, 35, 38); in the agony of the cross the cry of his parched lips was: 'I am thirsty' (19:28). The Fourth Gospel shows us a Jesus who was no shadowy, docetic figure; it shows us one who knew the weariness of an exhausted body and the wounds of a distressed mind and heart. It is the truly human Jesus whom the Fourth Gospel sets before us.

The Deity of Jesus

On the other hand, there is no gospel which sets before us such a view of the deity of Jesus.

(a) John stresses the *pre-existence* of Jesus. 'Before Abraham was,' said Jesus, 'I am' (8:58). He talks of the glory which he had with the Father before the world was made (17:5). Again and again he speaks of his coming down from heaven (6:33–8). John saw in Jesus one who had always been, even before the world began.

(b) The Fourth Gospel stresses more than any of the others the *omniscience* of Jesus. It is John's view that apparently miraculously Jesus knew the past record of the woman of Samaria (4:16–17); apparently without anyone telling him, he knew how long the man beside the healing pool had been ill (5:6); before he asked it, he knew the answer to the question he put to Philip (6:6); he knew that Judas would betray him (6:61–4); and he knew of the death of Lazarus before anyone told him of it (11:14). John saw in Jesus one who had a special and miraculous knowledge independent of anything which he might be told. He needed to ask no questions because he knew the answers.

(c) The Fourth Gospel stresses the fact, as John saw it, that Jesus always acted entirely on his own initiative and was not influenced by anyone else. It was not his mother's request which moved him to the miracle at Cana in Galilee; it was his own personal decision (2:4); the urging of his brothers had nothing to do with the visit which he paid to Jerusalem at the Feast of Tabernacles (7:10); no one took his life from him – no one could; he laid it down purely voluntarily (10:18, 19:11). As John saw it, Jesus had a divine independence from all human influence. He was self-determined.

To counter the Gnostics and their strange beliefs, John presents us with a Jesus who was undeniably human and who yet was undeniably divine.

The Author of the Fourth Gospel

We have seen that the aim of the writer of the Fourth Gospel was to present the Christian faith in such a way that it would commend itself to the Greek world to which Christianity had gone out, and also to combat the heresies and mistaken ideas which had arisen within the Church. We go on to ask: 'Who is that writer?' Tradition answers unanimously that the author was John the apostle. We shall see that beyond doubt the authority of John lies behind the gospel, although it may well be that its actual form and style of writing did not come from his hand. Let us, then, collect what we know about him.

He was the younger son of Zebedee, who possessed a fishing boat on the Sea of Galilee and was sufficiently well off to be able to employ hired servants to help him with his work (Mark 1:19–20). His mother was Salome, and it seems likely that she was the sister of Mary, the mother of Jesus (Matthew 27:56; Mark 16:1). With his brother James, he obeyed the call of Jesus (Mark 1:20). It would seem that James and John were in partnership with Peter in the fishing trade (Luke 5:7–10). He was one of the inner circle of the disciples, for the lists of the disciples always begin with the names of Peter, James and John, and there were certain great occasions when Jesus took these three specially with him (Mark 3:17, 5:37, 9:2, 14:33).

In character he was clearly a turbulent and ambitious man. Jesus gave to him and to his brother the name *Boanerges*, which the gospel writers take to mean *Sons of Thunder*. John and his brother James were completely exclusive and intolerant (Mark 9:38; Luke 9:49). So violent was their temper that they were prepared to blast a Samaritan village out of existence because it would not give them hospitality when they were on their journey to Jerusalem (Luke 9:54). Either they or their mother Salome had the ambition that when Jesus came into his kingdom, they might be his principal ministers of state (Mark 10:35; Matthew 20:20). In the other three gospels, John appears as a leader of the apostolic band, one of the inner circle, and yet a turbulent, ambitious and intolerant character.

In the Book of Acts, John always appears as the companion of Peter, and he himself never speaks at all. His name is still one of the three names at the head of the apostolic list (Acts 1:13). He is with Peter when the lame man is healed at the Beautiful Gate of the Temple (Acts 3:1ff.). With Peter, he is brought before the Sanhedrin and faces the Jewish leaders with a courage and a boldness that astonishes them (Acts 4:1–13). With Peter, he goes from Jerusalem to Samaria to survey the work done by Philip (Acts 8:14).

In Paul's letters, he appears only once. In Galatians 2:9, he is named as one of the pillars of the Church along with Peter and James, and with them is depicted as giving his approval to the work of Paul.

John was a strange mixture. He was one of the leaders of the Twelve; he was one of the inner circle of Jesus' closest friends; at the same time he was a man of temper and ambition and intolerance, and yet of courage.

We may follow John into the stories told of him in the early Church. Eusebius tells us that he was banished to Patmos in the reign of Domitian (Eusebius, *The Ecclesiastical History*, 3:23). In the same passage, Eusebius tells a characteristic story about John, a story which he received from Clement of Alexandria. John became a kind of bishop of Asia Minor and was visiting one of his churches near Ephesus. In the congregation, he saw a tall and exceptionally fine-looking young man. He turned to the elder in charge of the congregation and said to him: 'I commit that young man into your charge and into your care, and I call this congregation to witness that I do so.' The elder took the young man into his own house and cared for him and instructed him, and the day came when he was baptized and received into the Church. But very soon afterwards, he fell in with evil friends and embarked on such a career of crime that he ended up by becoming the leader of a band of murdering and pillaging brigands. Some time afterwards, John returned to the congregation. He said to the elder: 'Restore to me the trust which I and the Lord committed to you and to the church of which you are in charge.' At first the elder did not understand of what John was speaking. 'I mean', said John, 'that I am asking you for the soul of the young man whom I entrusted to you.' 'Alas!' said the elder, 'he is dead.' 'Dead?' said John. 'He is dead to God,' said the elder. 'He fell from grace; he was forced to flee from the city for his crimes and now he is a bandit in the mountains.' Immediately John went to the mountains. Deliberately he allowed himself to be captured by the robber band. They brought him before the young man, who was now the chief of the band; and, in his shame, the young man tried to run away from him. John, though an old man, pursued him. 'My son,' he cried, 'are you running away from your father? I am feeble and far advanced in age; have pity on me, my son; fear not; there is yet hope of salvation for you. I will stand for you before the Lord Christ. If need be, I will gladly die for you as he died for me. Stop, stay, believe! It is Christ who has sent me to you.' The appeal broke the heart of the young man. He stopped, threw away his weapons, and wept. Together he and John came down the mountainside and he was brought back into the Church and into the Christian way. There we see the love and the courage of John still in operation.

Eusebius (3:28) tells another story of John which he got from the works of the second-century theologian, Irenaeus. We have seen that one of the leaders of the Gnostic heresy was a man called Cerinthus. 'The apostle John once entered a bath to bathe; but, when he learned that Cerinthus was within, he sprang from his place and rushed out of the door, for he could not bear to remain under the same roof with him. He advised those who were with him to do the same. "Let us flee," he said, "lest the bath fall, for Cerinthus, the enemy of the truth, is within."' There we have another glimpse of the temper of John. Boanerges was not quite dead.

Writing in the fifth century, John Cassian tells another famous story about John. One day he was found playing with a tame partridge. A narrower and more rigid brother rebuked him for thus wasting his time, and John answered: 'The bow that is always bent will soon cease to shoot straight.'

It is the great biblical scholar Jerome who tells the story of the last words of John. When he was dying, his disciples asked him if he had any last message to leave them. 'Little children,' he said, 'love one another.' Again and again he repeated it; and they asked him if that was all he had to say. 'It is enough,' he said, 'for it is the Lord's command.'

Such then is our information about John; and he emerges as a figure of fiery temper, of wide ambition, of undoubted courage and, in the end, of gentle love.

The Beloved Disciple

If we have been following our references closely, we will have noticed one thing. All our information about John comes from the first three gospels. It is the astonishing fact that the Fourth Gospel never mentions the apostle John from beginning to end. But it does mention two other people.

First, it speaks of *the disciple whom Jesus loved*. There are four mentions of him. He was leaning on Jesus' breast at the Last Supper (John 13:23–5); it is into his care that Jesus committed Mary as he died upon his cross (19:25–7); it was Peter and he whom Mary Magdalene met on her return from the empty tomb on the first Easter morning (20:2); and he was present at the last resurrection appearance of Jesus by the lakeside (21:20).

Second, the Fourth Gospel has a kind of character whom we might call the *witness*. As the Fourth Gospel tells of the spear thrust into the side of Jesus and the issue of the water and the blood, there comes the comment: 'He who saw this has testified so that you also may believe. His testimony is true, and he knows that he tells the truth' (19:35). At the end of the gospel comes the statement that it was the beloved disciple who testified of these things, 'and we know that his testimony is true' (21:24).

Here we are faced with rather a strange thing. In the Fourth Gospel, John is never mentioned; but the beloved disciple is, and in addition there is a witness of some kind to the whole story. It has never really been doubted in tradition that the beloved disciple is John. A few have tried to identify him with Lazarus, for Jesus is said to have loved Lazarus (John 11:3, 5); or with the rich young ruler, of whom it is said that Jesus, looking on him, loved him (Mark 10:21). But although the gospel never says so in so many words, tradition has always identified the beloved disciple with John, and there is no real need to doubt the identification.

But a very real point arises – suppose John himself actually did the writing of the gospel, would he really be likely to speak of himself as the disciple whom Jesus loved? Would he really be likely to pick himself out like this, and, as it were, to say: 'I was his favourite; he loved me best of all'? It is surely very unlikely that John would confer such a title on himself. If it was conferred by others, it is a lovely title; if it was conferred by himself, it comes perilously near to an almost incredible self-conceit.

Is there any way, then, that the gospel can be John's own eyewitness story, and yet at the same time have been actually written down by someone else?

The Production of the Church

In our search for the truth, we begin by noting one of the outstanding and unique features of the Fourth Gospel. The most remarkable thing about it is the long speeches of Jesus. Often they are whole chapters long, and are entirely unlike the way in which Jesus is portrayed as speaking in the other three gospels. The Fourth Gospel, as we have seen, was written about the year AD 100, that is, about seventy years after the crucifixion. Is it possible after these seventy years to look on these speeches as word-for-word reports of what Jesus said? Or can we explain them in some way that is perhaps even greater than that? We must begin by holding in our minds the fact of the speeches and the question which they inevitably raise.

And we have something to add to that. It so happens that in the writings of the early Church we have a whole series of accounts of the way in which the Fourth Gospel came to be written. The earliest is that of Irenaeus, who was bishop of Lyons about AD 177; and Irenaeus was himself a pupil of the Bishop of Smyrna, Polycarp, who in turn had actually been a pupil of John. There is therefore a direct link between Irenaeus and John. Irenaeus writes:

> John, the disciple of the Lord, who also leant upon his
> breast, himself also *published* the gospel in Ephesus,
> when he was living in Asia.

The suggestive thing there is that Irenaeus does not merely
say that John *wrote* the gospel; he says that John *published*
(*exedōke*) it in Ephesus. The word that Irenaeus uses makes
it sound not like the private publication of some personal
memoir but like the public issue of some almost official
document.

The next account is that of Clement, who was head of the
great school of Alexandria about AD 230. He writes:

> Last of all, John perceiving that the bodily facts had
> been made plain in the gospel, *being urged by his
> friends*, composed a spiritual gospel.

The important thing here is the phrase *being urged by his
friends*. It begins to become clear that the Fourth Gospel is
far more than one man's personal production and that there is
a group, a community, a church behind it. On the same lines,
a tenth-century manuscript called the *Codex Toletanus*, which
prefaces the New Testament books with short descriptions,
prefaces the Fourth Gospel thus:

> The apostle John, whom the Lord Jesus loved most,
> last of all wrote this gospel, *at the request of the bishops
> of Asia*, against Cerinthus and other heretics.

Again we have the idea that behind the Fourth Gospel there
is the authority of a group and of a church.

We now turn to a very important document, known as the
Muratorian Canon. It is so called after a scholar Muratori
who discovered it. It is the first list of New Testament books
which the Church ever issued and was compiled in Rome
about AD 170. Not only does it list the New Testament books,

it also gives short accounts of the origin and nature and contents of each of them. Its account of the way in which the Fourth Gospel came to be written is extremely important and illuminating.

> At the request of his fellow-disciples and of his bishops, John, one of the disciples, said: 'Fast with me for three days from this time and whatsoever shall be revealed to each of us, whether it be favourable to my writing or not, let us relate it to one another.' On the same night it was revealed to Andrew that John should relate all things, *aided by the revision of all.*

We cannot accept all that statement, because it is not possible that Andrew, the apostle, was in Ephesus in AD 100; but the point is that it is stated as clearly as possible that, while the authority and the mind and the memory behind the Fourth Gospel are that of John, it is clearly and definitely the product, not of one man, but of a group and a community.

Now we can see something of what happened. About the year AD 100 there was a group living in Ephesus whose leader was John. They revered him as a saint and they loved him as a father. He must have been almost 100 years old. Before he died, they thought most wisely that it would be a great thing if the aged apostle set down his memories of the years when he had been with Jesus. But in the end they did far more than that. We can think of them sitting down and reliving the old days. One would say: 'Do you remember how Jesus said . . . ?' And John would say: 'Yes, and now we know that he meant . . .'

In other words, this group was not only writing down what Jesus *said*; that would have been a mere feat of memory. They were writing down what Jesus *meant*; that was the guidance of the Holy Spirit. John had thought about every word that Jesus had said; and he had thought under the guidance of the Holy Spirit who was so real to him. Professor W. M. Macgregor of Trinity College, Glasgow, had a sermon entitled: 'What Jesus becomes to a man who has known him long.' That is a perfect description of the Jesus of the Fourth Gospel. A. H. N. Green Armytage puts the point perfectly in his book *John Who Saw*. Mark, he says, suits the *missionary* with his clear-cut account of the facts of Jesus' life; Matthew suits the *teacher* with his systematic account of the teaching of Jesus; Luke suits the *parish minister or priest* with his wide sympathy and his picture of Jesus as the friend of all; but John is the gospel of the *contemplative*.

He goes on to speak of the apparent contrast between Mark and John. 'The two gospels are in a sense the same gospel. Only, where Mark saw things plainly, bluntly, literally, John saw them subtly, profoundly, spiritually. We might say that John lit Mark's pages by the lantern of a lifetime's meditation.' In his *Lyrical Ballads*, William Wordsworth defined poetry as 'Emotion recollected in tranquillity'. That is a perfect description of the Fourth Gospel. That is why John is unquestionably the greatest of all the gospels. Its aim is not to give us what Jesus said, like a newspaper report, but to give us what Jesus meant. In it, the risen Christ still speaks. John is not so much The Gospel according to St John; it is rather *The Gospel according to the Holy Spirit*. It was not John of Ephesus who wrote the Fourth Gospel; it was the Holy Spirit who wrote it through John.

The Writer of the Gospel

We have one question still to ask. We can be quite sure that the mind and the memory behind the Fourth Gospel is that of

John the apostle; but we have also seen that behind it is a witness who was the writer, in the sense that he was the one who actually wrote it all down. Can we find out who he was? We know from what the early Church writers tell us that there were actually two Johns in Ephesus at the same time. There was John the apostle; but there was another John, who was known as John the elder.

Papias, who loved to collect all that he could find about the history of the New Testament and the story of Jesus, gives us some very interesting information. He was Bishop of Hierapolis, which is quite near Ephesus, and his dates are from about AD 70 to about AD 145. That is to say, he was actually a contemporary of John. He writes how he tried to find out 'what Andrew said or what Peter said, or what was said by Philip, by Thomas, or by James, or by John, or by Matthew, or by any other of the disciples of the Lord; and what things Aristion and *the elder John*, the disciples of the Lord, say'. In Ephesus there was the *apostle* John and the *elder* John; and the elder John was so well-loved a figure that he was actually known as *The Elder*. He clearly had a unique place in the Church. Both Eusebius and Dionysius the Great tell us that even in their own days in Ephesus there were two famous tombs, the one of John the apostle and the other of John the elder.

Now let us turn to the two little letters, 2 John and 3 John. The *letters* come from the same hand as the gospel, and how do they begin? The *Second* Letter begins: 'The elder to the elect lady and her children' (2 John 1). The *Third* Letter begins: 'The elder to the beloved Gaius' (3 John 1). Here we have our solution. The one who actually penned the letters was John the elder; the mind and memory behind them was the aged John the apostle, the master whom John the elder always described as 'the disciple whom Jesus loved'.

55

The Precious Gospel

The more we know about the Fourth Gospel, the more precious it becomes. For seventy years, John had thought of Jesus. Day by day, the Holy Spirit had opened out to him the meaning of what Jesus said. So when John was near the century of life and his days were numbered, he and his friends sat down to remember. John the elder held the pen to write for his master, John the apostle; and the last of the apostles set down not only what he had heard Jesus say but also what he now knew Jesus had meant. He remembered how Jesus had said: 'I still have many things to say to you, but you cannot bear them now. When the Spirit of truth comes, he will guide you into all the truth' (John 16:12–13). There were many things which seventy years ago he had not understood; there were many things which in these seventy years the Spirit of truth had revealed to him. These things John set down even as the eternal glory was dawning upon him. When we read this gospel, let us remember that we are reading the gospel which of all the gospels is most the work of the Holy Spirit, speaking to us of the things which Jesus meant, speaking through the mind and memory of John the apostle and by the pen of John the elder. Behind this gospel is the whole church at Ephesus, the whole company of the saints, the last of the apostles, the Holy Spirit and the risen Christ himself.

5

Acts

From Jerusalem to Rome

A Precious Book

In one sense, Acts is the most important book in the New Testament. It is the simple truth that, if we did not possess Acts, we would have no information whatever about the early Church apart from what we could deduce from the letters of Paul.

There are two ways of writing history. There is the way which attempts to trace the course of events from week to week and from day to day; and there is the way which, as it were, opens a series of windows and gives us vivid glimpses of the great moments and personalities of any period. The second way is the way of Acts.

We usually speak of the Acts of the Apostles. But the book neither gives nor claims to give an exhaustive account of the acts of the apostles. Apart from Paul, only three apostles are mentioned in it. In Acts 12:2, we are told in one brief sentence that James, the brother of John, was executed by Herod. John appears in the narrative, but never speaks. It is only about Peter that the book gives any real information – and very soon, as a leading player, he passes from the scene. In the Greek, there is no 'The' before Acts; the correct title is Acts of Apostolic Men; and what Acts aims to do is to give us a series of typical exploits of the heroic figures of the early Church.

The Writer of the Book

Although the book never says so, from the earliest times Luke has been held to be its writer. About Luke, we really know very little; there are only three references to him in the New Testament – Colossians 4:14, Philemon 24 and 2 Timothy 4:11. From these, we can say two things with certainty. First, Luke was a doctor; second, he was one of Paul's most valued helpers and most loyal friends, for he was a companion of Paul in his last imprisonment. We can deduce the fact that he was a Gentile. Colossians 4:11 concludes a list of mentions and greetings from those who are 'of the circumcision', that is, from Jews; verse 12 begins a new list, and we naturally conclude that the new list is of Gentiles. So we have the very interesting fact that Luke is the only Gentile author in the New Testament.

We could have guessed that Luke was a doctor because of his instinctive use of medical words. In Luke 4:35, in telling of the man who had the spirit of an unclean devil, he says: 'When the demon had thrown him down' and uses the correct medical word for convulsions. In Luke 9:38, when he draws the picture of the man who asked Jesus: 'I beg you to look at my son', he employs the conventional word for a doctor paying a visit to a patient. The most interesting example is in the saying about the camel and the needle's eye. All three of the writers of what have come to be known as the synoptic gospels give us that saying (Matthew 19:24; Mark 10:25; Luke 18:25). For *needle*, both Mark and Matthew use the Greek *raphis*, the ordinary word for a tailor's or a household needle. Luke alone uses *belonē*, the technical word for a surgeon's needle. Luke was a doctor, and a doctor's words came most naturally to his pen.

ACTS

The Recipient of the Book

Luke wrote both his gospel and Acts to a man called Theophilus (Luke 1:3; Acts 1:1). We can only guess who Theophilus was. Luke 1:3 calls him 'most excellent Theophilus'. The phrase really means 'Your Excellency' and indicates a man high up in the service of the Roman government. There are three possibilities.

(1) Just possibly, Theophilus is not a real name at all. In those days, it might well have been dangerous to be a Christian. *Theophilus* comes from two Greek words – *theos*, which means *God*, and *philein*, which means *to love*. It may be that Luke wrote to someone who loved God, whose real name he did not mention for safety's sake.

(2) If Theophilus was a real person, he must have been a high government official. Perhaps Luke wrote to show him that Christianity was a lovely thing and that Christians were good people. Maybe his writing was an attempt to persuade a government official not to persecute Christians.

(3) There is a more romantic theory than either of these, based on the facts that Luke was a doctor and that doctors in the ancient days were often slaves. It has been suggested that Luke was the doctor of Theophilus, that Theophilus had been gravely ill, that by Luke's skill and devotion he was brought back to health, and that in gratitude he gave Luke his freedom. Then, it may be, Luke wanted to show how grateful he was for this gift; and, since the most precious thing he had was the story of Jesus, he wrote it down and sent it to his benefactor.

Luke's Aim in Writing Acts

Anyone who writes a book does so for a reason, and maybe for more than one reason. Let us now consider why Luke wrote Acts.

(1) One of his reasons was to commend Christianity to the Roman government. Again and again, he goes out of his way to show how courteous Roman magistrates were to Paul. In Acts 13:12, Sergius Paulus, the governor of Cyprus, becomes a Christian. In 18:12ff., Gallio is absolutely fair-minded in Corinth. In 16:35ff., the magistrates at Philippi discover their mistake and apologize publicly to Paul. In 19:31, the Asiarchs in Ephesus are shown to be concerned that no harm should come to Paul. Luke was pointing out that, in the years before he wrote, Roman officials had often been well-disposed and always just and fair to Christianity.

Further, Luke takes pains to show that Christians were good and loyal citizens and had always been regarded as such. In Acts 18:14, Gallio declares that there is no question of crime or villainy. In 19:37, the secretary of Ephesus gives the Christians a good report. In 23:29, Claudius Lysias is careful to say that he has nothing against Paul. In 25:25, Festus declares that Paul has done nothing worthy of death, and in the same chapter Festus and Agrippa agree that Paul might well have been released had he not appealed to Caesar.

Luke was writing in the days when Christians were disliked and persecuted; and he told his story in such a way as to show that the Roman magistrates had always been perfectly fair to Christianity and that they had never regarded the Christians as evil. In fact, the very interesting suggestion has been made that Acts is nothing other than the brief prepared for Paul's defence when he stood trial before the Roman emperor.

(2) One of Luke's aims was to show that Christianity was for all people of every country. This was one of the things the Jews found it hard to grasp. They had the idea that they were God's chosen people and that God had no use for any other nation. Luke sets out to prove otherwise. He shows

Philip preaching to the Samaritans; he shows Stephen making Christianity universal and being killed for it; he shows Peter accepting Cornelius into the Church; he shows the Christians preaching to the Gentiles at Antioch; he shows Paul travelling far and wide winning men and women of every kind for Christ; and in Acts 15 he shows the Church making the great decision to accept the Gentiles on equal terms with the Jews.

(3) But these were merely secondary aims. Luke's chief purpose is set out in the words of the risen Christ in 1:8: 'You will be my witnesses in Jerusalem, in all Judaea and Samaria, and to the ends of the earth.' It was to show the expansion of Christianity – to show how that religion which began in a little corner of Palestine had in not much more than thirty years reached Rome.

The Church historian C. H. Turner has pointed out that Acts falls into six panels, each ending with what might be called a progress report. The six panels are:

(a) 1:1–6:7; this tells of the church at Jerusalem and the preaching of Peter; and it finishes with the summary: 'The word of God continued to spread; the number of the disciples increased greatly in Jerusalem, and a great many of the priests became obedient to the faith.'

(b) 6:8–9:31; this describes the spread of Christianity through Palestine and the martyrdom of Stephen, followed by the preaching in Samaria. It ends with the summary: 'Meanwhile the church throughout Judaea, Galilee and Samaria had peace and was built up. Living in the fear of the Lord and in the comfort of the Holy Spirit, it increased in numbers.'

(c) 9:32–12:24; this includes the conversion of Paul, the extension of the Church to Antioch, and the reception of Cornelius, the Gentile, into the Church by Peter. Its summary is: 'The word of God continued to advance.'

(d) 12:25–16:5; this tells of the extension of the Church through Asia Minor and the preaching tour of Galatia. It ends: 'So the churches were strengthened in the faith and increased in numbers daily.'

(e) 16:6–19:20; this describes the extension of the Church to Europe and the work of Paul in great Gentile cities like Corinth and Ephesus. Its summary runs: 'So the word of the Lord grew mightily and prevailed.'

(f) 19:21–28:31; this tells of the arrival of Paul in Rome and his imprisonment there. It ends with the picture of Paul 'proclaiming the kingdom of God and teaching about the Lord Jesus Christ with all boldness and without hindrance'.

This plan of Acts answers its most puzzling question – why does it finish where it does? It finishes with Paul in prison awaiting judgment. We would so much have liked to know what happened to him; and the end remains a mystery. But Luke stopped there because he had achieved his purpose; he had shown how Christianity began in Jerusalem and swept across the world until it reached Rome. One New Testament scholar has said that the title of Acts might be: 'How they brought the Good News from Jerusalem to Rome.'

Luke's Sources

Luke was a historian, and the sources from which a historian draws information are all important. Where then did Luke get his facts? In this connection, Acts falls into two parts.

(1) There are the first fifteen chapters, describing events of which Luke had no personal knowledge. He most probably had access to two sources.

(a) There were the records of the local churches. They may never have been set down in writing, but the churches had their stories. In this section, we can distinguish three records. There is the record of the *Jerusalem church*, which we find in chapters 1–5 and in chapters 15–16. There is the record of the *church at Caesarea*, which covers 8:26–40 and 9:31–10:48. There is the record of the *church at Antioch*, which includes 11:19–30 and 12:25–14:28.

(b) It is very likely that there were cycles of stories which were the Acts of Peter, the Acts of John, the Acts of Philip and the Acts of Stephen. Beyond a doubt, Luke's friendship with Paul would bring him into touch with all the great figures of all the churches, and all their stories would be at his disposal.

(2) There are chapters 16–28. Luke had personal knowledge of much that is included in this section. When we read Acts carefully, we notice a strange thing. Most of the time, Luke's narrative is in the third-person plural; but in certain passages it changes over to the first-person plural, and 'they' becomes 'we'. The 'we' passages are as follows: Acts 16:10–17, 20:5–16, 21:1–18 and 27:1–28:16. On all these occasions, Luke must have been present. He must have kept a travel diary, and in these passages we have eyewitness accounts. As for the times when he was not present, many were the hours he must have spent in prison with Paul, and many were the stories Paul must have told him, There can have been no great figure Luke did not know, and in every case he must have got his story from someone who was there.

When we read Acts, we may be quite sure that no historian ever had better sources or used those sources more accurately.

6

The Letters of Paul

The Letters of Paul

There is no more interesting body of documents in the New Testament than the letters of Paul. That is because, of all forms of literature, a letter is most personal. Demetrius, one of the ancient Greek literary critics, once wrote: 'Everyone reveals his own soul in his letters. In every other form of composition it is possible to discern the writer's character, but in none so clearly as the epistolary' (Demetrius, *On Style*, 227). It is precisely because he left us so many letters that we feel we know Paul so well. In them, he opened his mind and heart to the people he loved so much; and in them, to this day, we can see that great mind grappling with the problems of the early Church, and feel that great heart throbbing with love for men and women, even when they were misguided and mistaken.

The Difficulty of Letters

At the same time, there is often nothing so difficult to understand as a letter. Demetrius (*On Style*, 223) quotes a saying of Artemon, who edited the letters of Aristotle. Artemon said that a letter ought to be written in the same manner as a dialogue, because it was one of the two sides of a discussion. In other words, reading a letter is like listening to one side of a telephone conversation. So, when we read the letters of

Paul, we often find ourselves in difficulty. We do not possess the letter which he was answering, we do not fully know the circumstances with which he was dealing, and it is only from the letter itself that we can deduce the situation which prompted it. Before we can hope to understand fully any letter Paul wrote, we must try to reconstruct the situation that produced it.

The Ancient Letters

It is a great pity that Paul's letters were ever called *epistles.* They are in the most literal sense *letters.* One of the great lights shed on the interpretation of the New Testament has been the discovery and the publication of the *papyri.* In the ancient world, *papyrus* was the substance on which most documents were written. It was composed of strips of the pith of a certain bulrush that grew on the banks of the Nile. These strips were laid one on top of the other to form a substance very like brown paper. The sands of the Egyptian desert were ideal for preservation; for papyrus, although very brittle, will last forever as long as moisture does not get at it. As a result, from the Egyptian rubbish heaps, archaeologists have rescued hundreds of documents – marriage contracts, legal agreements, government forms and, most interesting of all, private letters. When we read these private letters, we find that there was a pattern to which nearly all conformed, and we find that Paul's letters reproduce exactly that pattern. Here is one of these ancient letters. It is from a soldier, called Apion, to his father Epimachus. He is writing from Misenum to tell his father that he has arrived safely after a stormy passage.

> Apion sends heartiest greetings to his father and lord Epimachus. I pray above all that you are well and fit; and that things are going well with you and my sister

and her daughter and my brother. I thank my Lord Serapis [his god] that he kept me safe when I was in peril on the sea. As soon as I got to Misenum I got my journey money from Caesar – three gold pieces. And things are going fine with me. So I beg you, my dear father, send me a line, first to let me know how you are, and then about my brothers, and thirdly, that I may kiss your hand, because you brought me up well, and because of that I hope, God willing, soon to be promoted. Give Capito my heartiest greetings, and my brothers and Serenilla and my friends. I sent you a little picture of myself painted by Euctemon. My military name is Antonius Maximus. I pray for your good health. Serenus sends good wishes, Agathos Daimon's boy, and Turbo, Gallonius's son. (G. Milligan, *Selections from the Greek Papyri*, 36)

Little did Apion think that we would be reading his letter to his father some 2,000 years after he had written it. It shows how little human nature changes. The young man is hoping for promotion quickly. Who will Serenilla be but the girl he left behind? He sends the ancient equivalent of a photograph to the family and friends at home. Now, that letter falls into certain sections. (1) There is a greeting. (2) There is a prayer for the health of the recipients. (3) There is a thanksgiving to the gods. (4) There are the special contents. (5) Finally, there are the special salutations and the personal greetings. Practically every one of Paul's letters shows exactly the same sections, as we now demonstrate.

(1) *The greeting*: Romans 1:1; 1 Corinthians 1:1; 2 Corinthians 1:1; Galatians 1:1; Ephesians 1:1; Philippians 1:1; Colossians 1:1–2; 1 Thessalonians 1:1; 2 Thessalonians 1:1.

(2) *The prayer*: in every case, Paul prays for the grace of God on the people to whom he writes: Romans 1:7; 1 Corinthians 1:3; 2 Corinthians 1:2; Galatians 1:3; Ephesians

1:2; Philippians 1:3; Colossians 1:2; 1 Thessalonians 1:1; 2 Thessalonians 1:2.

(3) *The thanksgiving*: Romans 1:8; 1 Corinthians 1:4; 2 Corinthians 1:3; Ephesians 1:3; Philippians 1:3; 1 Thessalonians 1:3; 2 Thessalonians 1:3.

(4) *The special contents*: the main body of the letters.

(5) *The special salutations and personal greetings*: Romans 16; 1 Corinthians 16:19; 2 Corinthians 13:13; Philippians 4:21–2; Colossians 4:12–15; 1 Thessalonians 5:26.

When Paul wrote letters, he wrote them on the pattern which everyone used. The German theologian Adolf Deissmann says of them: 'They differ from the messages of the homely papyrus leaves of Egypt, not as letters but only as the letters of Paul.' When we read Paul's letters, we are reading things which were meant to be not academic exercises and theological treatises, but human documents written by a friend to his friends.

The Immediate Situation

With a very few exceptions, Paul's letters were written to meet an immediate situation. They were not systematic arguments which he sat down to write in the peace and silence of his study. There was some threatening situation in Corinth, or Galatia, or Philippi, or Thessalonica, and he wrote a letter to meet it. He was not in the least thinking of us when he wrote, but solely of the people to whom he was writing. Deissmann writes: 'Paul had no thought of adding a few fresh compositions to the already extant Jewish epistles; still less of enriching the sacred literature of his nation . . . He had no presentiment of the place his words would occupy in universal history; not so much that they would be in existence in the next generation, far less that one day people would look at them as Holy Scripture.' We must always remember that a thing need not be of only passing interest because it was written to meet an immediate situation. Every one of the great love songs of the world was written at a particular time for one person; but they live on for the benefit and enjoyment of all. It is precisely because Paul's letters were written to meet a threatening danger or a pressing need that they still throb with life. And it is because human need and the human situation do not change that God speaks to us through them today.

The Spoken Word

There is one other thing that we must note about these letters. Paul did what most people did in his day. He did not normally pen his own letters, but dictated them to a secretary and then added his own authenticating signature. (We actually know the name of one of the people who did the writing for him. In Romans 16:22, Tertius, the secretary, slips in his own greeting before the letter draws to an end.) In 1 Corinthians 16:21, Paul says in effect: 'This is my own signature, my autograph, so that you can be sure this letter comes from me' (cf. Colossians 4:18; 2 Thessalonians 3:17).

This explains a great deal. Sometimes Paul is hard to understand, because his sentences begin and never finish; his grammar breaks down and the construction becomes complicated. We must not think of him sitting quietly at a desk, carefully polishing each sentence as he writes. We must think of him striding up and down some little room, pouring out a torrent of words, while his secretary races to get them down. When Paul composed his letters, he had in his mind's eye a vision of the people to whom he was writing, and he was pouring out his heart to them in words that fell over each other in his eagerness to help.

7

Romans

The Essence of Paul's Thought

The Letter that is Different

There is an obvious difference between Paul's Letter to the Romans and his other letters. Anyone coming from, say, a reading of the Letters to the Corinthians will immediately feel that difference, both of atmosphere and of method. A very great part of this is due to one basic fact: when Paul wrote to the church at Rome, he was writing to a church with whose founding he had had nothing whatever to do and with which he had had no personal contact at all. That explains why in Romans there are so few of the details of practical problems which fill the other letters. That is why Romans, at first sight, seems so much more impersonal. As the German scholar Martin Dibelius put it, 'It is of all Paul's letters the least conditioned by the momentary situation.'

We may put that in another way. Romans, of all Paul's letters, comes nearest to being a theological treatise. In almost all his other letters, he is dealing with some immediate problem, some pressing situation, some current error, some threatening danger, which was causing trouble for the church to which he was writing. Romans is the nearest approach to a systematic exposition of Paul's own theological position, independent of any immediate set of circumstances.

Two Views of Paul's Letter

Because of that, two great scholars have applied two very illuminating adjectives to Romans. William Sanday called Romans '*testamentary*'. It is as if Paul was writing his theological last will and testament, as if into Romans he was distilling the very essence of his faith and belief. Rome was the greatest city in the world, the capital of the greatest empire the world had ever seen. Paul had never been there, and he did not know if he ever would get there. But, in writing to such a church in such a city, it was fitting that he should set down the very centre and core of his belief. Romans has been referred to by one scholar as '*prophylactic*'. A prophylactic is something which guards against infection. Paul had seen too often what harm and trouble could be caused by wrong ideas, twisted notions and misguided conceptions of Christian faith and belief. He therefore wished to send to the church in the city that was the centre of the world a letter which would so build up the structure of their faith that, if infections should ever come to them, they might have in the true word of Christian doctrine a powerful and effective defence. He felt that the best protection against the infection of false teaching was the antiseptic of the truth.

The Occasion of Paul's Writing to Rome

All his life, Paul had been haunted by the thought of Rome. It had always been one of his dreams to preach there. When he is in Ephesus, he is planning to go through Achaea and Macedonia again, and then he writes a sentence that comes quite obviously straight from the heart: 'After I have gone there, *I must also see Rome*' (Acts 19:21). When he was up against things in Jerusalem, and the situation looked threatening and the end seemed near, he had one of those visions which always lifted up his heart. In that vision, the Lord stood by him and said: 'Keep up your courage! For just as you have testified for me in Jerusalem, *so you must bear witness also in Rome*' (Acts 23:11). In the very first chapter of this letter, Paul's desire to see Rome breathes out. 'For I am longing to see you so that I may share with you some spiritual gift to strengthen you' (Romans 1:11). 'Hence my eagerness to proclaim the gospel to you also who are in Rome' (Romans 1:15). It might well be said that the name *Rome* was written on Paul's heart.

When he actually wrote the Letter to the Romans, the date was sometime in the year AD 58, and he was in Corinth. He was just about to bring to its completion a scheme that was very dear to his heart. The church at Jerusalem was the parent church of them all, but it was poor, and Paul had organized a collection throughout the younger churches for it (1 Corinthians 16:1ff.; 2 Corinthians 9:1ff.). That collection was two things. It was an opportunity for his younger converts to put Christian charity into Christian action, and it was a most practical way of impressing on all Christians the unity of the Christian Church, of teaching them that they were members not of isolated and independent congregations, but of one great Church, each part of which had a responsibility to all the rest. When Paul wrote Romans, he was just about to set out with that gift for the Jerusalem church. 'At present, however, I am going to Jerusalem in a ministry to the saints' (Romans 15:25).

The Object of Paul's Writing

Why, then, at such a moment should he write?

(1) Paul knew that the journey to Jerusalem was not without its dangers. He knew that he had enemies there, and that to go to Jerusalem was to take his life and liberty

in his hands. He needed the prayers of the Roman church before he set out on this expedition. 'I appeal to you brothers and sisters, by our Lord Jesus Christ and by the love of the Spirit, to join me in earnest prayer to God on my behalf, that I may be rescued from the unbelievers in Judea' (Romans 15:30–1). He was mobilizing the prayers of the Church before he embarked on this perilous undertaking.

(2) Paul had great schemes simmering in his mind. It has been said of him that he was 'always haunted by the regions beyond'. He never saw a ship at anchor but he wished to board it and to carry the good news to men and women across the sea. He never saw a range of mountains, blue in the distance, but he wished to cross them, and to bring the story of the cross to people who had never heard it. At this time, Paul was haunted by the thought of Spain. 'I desire, as I have for many years, to come to you when I go to Spain' (Romans 15:23–4). 'When I have completed this, and have delivered to them what has been collected, I will set out by way of you to Spain' (Romans 15:28).

Why this great desire to go to Spain? Rome had opened up that country. Some of the great Roman roads and buildings still stand there to this day. And it so happened that, just at this time, there was a blaze of greatness in Spain. Many of the great figures who were writing their names on Roman history and literature were Spaniards. There was Martial, the master of the epigram. There was Lucan, the epic poet. There were Columella and Pomponius Mela, great figures in Roman literature. There was Quintilian, the Roman orator. And, above all, there was Seneca, the greatest of the Roman Stoic philosophers, the tutor of the Emperor Nero, and the prime minister of the Roman Empire. It was most natural that Paul's thoughts should go out to this land which was producing such a scintillating galaxy of greatness.

What might happen if people like that could be touched for Christ? As far as we know, Paul never got to Spain. On that visit to Jerusalem, he was arrested and he was never freed again. But, when he was writing Romans, that was his dream.

Paul was a supreme strategist. He had an eye for the layout of territory like a great commander. He felt that, by this time, he could move on from Asia Minor and for the time being leave Greece behind. He saw the whole west lying in front of him, virgin territory to be won for Christ. But, if he was to launch a campaign in the west, *he needed a base for operations*. There was only one such base possible – *and that was Rome*.

That was why Paul wrote this letter to Rome. He had this great dream in his heart and this great plan in his mind. He needed Rome for a base for this new campaign. He was aware that the church in Rome must have heard of him. But he was also aware, for he was a realist, that the reports which reached Rome would be mixed. His opponents were not above spreading slanders and false accusations against him. So, he wrote this letter to set out for the church at Rome an account of the very essence of his belief, in order that, when the time came for action, he might find in Rome a sympathetic church from which the lines of communication might go out to Spain and the west. It was with such a plan and such an intention that, in Corinth in AD 58, Paul began to write his letter to the church at Rome.

The Layout of the Letter

Romans is both a very complicated and a very carefully constructed letter. It will therefore help us to find our way through it if we have in our minds an idea of its framework. It falls into four definite divisions.

(1) Chapters 1–8 deal with the problem of righteousness.

(2) Chapters 9–11 deal with the problem of the Jews, the chosen people.

(3) Chapters 12–15 deal with practical questions of life and living.

(4) Chapter 16 is a letter of introduction for Phoebe, and a list of final personal greetings.

(1) When Paul uses the word *righteousness*, he means *a right relationship with God*. The person who is righteous is someone who is in a right relationship with God, and whose life shows it.

Paul begins with a survey of the Gentile world. We have only to look at its decadence and corruption to know that it had not solved the problem of righteousness. He looks at the Jewish world. The Jews had sought to solve the problem of righteousness by meticulous obedience to the law. Paul had tried that way himself, and it had resulted in frustration and defeat, because no one on earth can ever fully obey the law, and, therefore, everyone must have the continual consciousness of being in debt to God and under his condemnation.

So, Paul finds the way to righteousness in the way of complete trust and total submission. The only way to a right relationship with God is to take him at his word, and to cast ourselves, just as we are, on his mercy and love. It is the way of faith. It is to know that the important thing is not what we can do for God but what he has done for us. For Paul, the centre of the Christian faith was that we can never earn or deserve the favour of God, nor do we need to. The whole matter is one of grace, and all that we can do is to accept in wondering love and gratitude and trust what God has done for us.

That does not free us, however, from obligations or entitle us to do as we like; it means that we must forever try to be worthy of the love which does so much for us. But we are no longer trying to fulfil the demands of stern and austere and condemnatory law; we are no longer like criminals before a judge; we are men and women who give and receive love and who have given all life in love to the one who first loved us.

(2) The problem of the Jews was a torturing one. In a real sense, they were God's chosen people; and yet, when his Son had come into the world, they had rejected him. What possible explanation could there be for this heartbreaking fact?

The only explanation that Paul could find was that, in the end, it was all God's doing. Somehow the hearts of the Jews had been hardened; but it was not all failure, for there had always been a faithful remnant. Nor was it for nothing, for the very fact that the Jews had rejected Christ opened the door to the Gentiles. Nor was it the end of the matter, for in the end the Gentiles would bring in the Jews and all would be saved.

Paul goes further. Every Jew had always claimed to be a member of the chosen people by virtue of being Jewish by birth. It was solely a matter of pure racial descent from Abraham. But Paul insists that the real Jew is not someone whose flesh-and-blood descent can be traced to Abraham but someone who has made the same decision of complete submission to God in loving faith that Abraham made. Therefore, Paul argues, there are many pure-blooded Jews who are not Jews in the real sense of the term at all; and there are many people of other nations who are really Jews in the true meaning of that word. The new Israel was not dependent on race at all; it was composed of those who had the same faith as Abraham had had.

(3) Chapter 12 of Romans is so great an ethical statement that it must always be set alongside the Sermon on the Mount. In it, Paul lays down the ethical character of the Christian faith. Chapters 14–15 deal with an ever-recurring problem. In the church, there was a narrower party who believed that they must abstain from certain foods and drinks, and who counted special days and ceremonies as of great importance. Paul thinks of them as the weaker Christians because their faith was dependent on these external matters. There was a more liberal party who had liberated themselves from these external rules and observances. He thinks of them as the Christians who are stronger in the faith. He makes it quite clear that his sympathies are with the more liberal party; but he lays down the great principle that no one must ever do anything to hurt the conscience of someone who is weaker or to put a stumbling-block in the way of someone whose beliefs are different. His whole point of view is that we must never do anything which makes it harder for someone else to be a Christian – and that that may well mean the giving up of something, which is right and safe for us, for the sake of the weaker brother or sister. Christian liberty must never be used in such a way that it injures another's life or conscience.

(4) The fourth section is a recommendation on behalf of Phoebe, a member of the church at Cenchreae, who is coming to Rome. The letter ends with a list of greetings and a final benediction.

Two Problems

Chapter 16 has always presented scholars with a problem. Many have felt that it does not really form part of the Letter to the Romans at all, and that it is really a letter to some other church which became attached to Romans when Paul's letters were collected. What are their grounds for suggesting this?

First and foremost, in this chapter Paul sends greetings to twenty-six different people, twenty-four of whom he mentions by name and all of whom he seems to know very well indeed. He can, for instance, say that the mother of Rufus has also been a mother to him. Is it likely that Paul knew twenty-six people so well in *a church which he had never visited*? He, in fact, greets far more people in this chapter than he does in any other letter; and yet he had never set foot in Rome. Here is something that needs explanation.

If this chapter was not written to Rome, what was its original destination? It is here that Prisca and Aquila come into the argument. We know that they left Rome in AD 52 when Claudius issued his edict banishing the Jews (Acts 18:2). We know that they went with Paul to Ephesus (Acts 18:18). We know that they were in Ephesus when Paul wrote his letter to Corinth, less than two years before he wrote Romans (1 Corinthians 16:19). And we know that they were still in Ephesus when the Pastoral Epistles were written (2 Timothy 4:19). It is certain that, if we had come across a letter sending greeting to Prisca and Aquila, we should have assumed that it was sent to Ephesus if no other address was given.

Is there any other evidence to make us think that chapter 16 may have been sent to Ephesus in the first place? There is the obvious reason that Paul spent longer in Ephesus than anywhere else, and it would be very natural for him to send greetings to many people there. Paul speaks of Epaenetus, *the first convert to Christ in Asia*. Ephesus is in Asia; and such a reference, too, would be very natural in a letter to Ephesus, but not so natural in a letter to Rome. Romans 16:17 speaks about *difficulties, in opposition to the doctrine which you have been taught*, which sounds as if Paul was speaking about possible disobedience to his own teaching – and he had never taught in Rome.

It can be argued that chapter 16 was originally addressed to Ephesus; but the argument is not as strong as it looks. For one thing, there is no evidence that the chapter was ever attached anywhere except to the Letter to the Romans. For another thing, the odd fact is that Paul does *not* send personal greetings to churches which he knew well. There are no personal greetings in Thessalonians, Corinthians, Galatians and Philippians, all of them letters to churches he knew well; whereas there *are* personal greetings in Colossians, although Paul had never set foot in Colossae.

The reason is really quite simple. If Paul had sent personal greetings to churches he knew well, jealousies might have arisen; on the other hand, when he was writing to churches he had never visited, he liked to establish as many personal links as possible. The very fact that Paul had never been in Rome makes it likely that he *would* try to establish as many personal connections as possible. Again, it is to be remembered that Prisca and Aquila *were banished by edict* from Rome. What is more likely than that, after the trouble was over, six or seven years later, they would return to Rome and pick up the threads of their business after their stay in other towns? And is it not most likely that many of the other names are names of people who shared in this banishment, who took up temporary residence in other cities, who met Paul there, and who, when the coast was clear, returned to Rome and their old homes? Paul would be delighted to have so many personal contacts in Rome and to hold on to them.

Further, as we shall see, when we come to study chapter 16 in detail, many of the names – the households of Aristobulus and Narcissus, Amplias, Nereus and others – fit in well with Rome as a location. In spite of the arguments for Ephesus, we may take it that there is no necessity to detach chapter 16 from the Letter to the Romans.

But there is a more interesting, and a much more important, problem. The early manuscripts show some very curious things with regard to chapters 14–16. The only natural place for a doxology is at *the very end*. Romans 16:25–7 is a doxology, and in most good manuscripts it comes at the end. But, in a number of manuscripts, it comes at the end of chapter 14; two good manuscripts have it in *both places*; one ancient manuscript has it at the end of chapter 15; and two manuscripts have it in *neither place*, but leave an empty space for it. One ancient Latin manuscript has a series of section summaries. The last two are as follows:

50: On the peril of him who grieves his brother by meat.

That is obviously Romans 14:15–23.

51: On the mystery of the Lord, kept secret before his passion but after his passion revealed.

That is equally clearly Romans 16:25–7, the doxology. Evidently, these summaries were made from a manuscript which did not contain chapters 15 and 16. Now, there is one thing which sheds a flood of light on this. In one manuscript, the mention of Rome in Romans 1:7 and 1:15 is *entirely omitted*. There is no mention of any destination.

All this goes to show that Romans circulated in two forms – one form as we have it with sixteen chapters, and one with fourteen chapters; and perhaps also one with fifteen chapters. The explanation must be this. As Paul wrote it *to Rome*, it had sixteen chapters; but chapters 15 and 16 are private and personal to Rome. Now, no other letter gives such a compendium of Paul's teaching. What must have happened was that Romans began to circulate among all the churches, *with the last two local chapters omitted*, except for the doxology. It must have been felt that Romans was too fundamental to be restricted to the church in Rome, and so the purely local references were removed and it was sent out to the Church at large. From very early times, the Church felt that Romans was so great an expression of the mind of Paul that it must become the possession not of one congregation but of the whole Church. We must remember, as we study it, that Christians have always looked on Romans as embodying the very essence of Paul's gospel.

8

1 & 2 Corinthians
Wisdom and Reconciliation

The Greatness of Corinth

A glance at the map will show that Corinth was made for greatness. The southern part of Greece is very nearly an island. On the west, the Corinthian Gulf deeply indents the land; and, on the east, the Saronic Gulf similarly cuts into the land. All that is left to join the two parts of Greece together is a little isthmus only four miles across. On that narrow neck of land stands Corinth. Such a position made it inevitable that it should be one of the greatest trading and commercial centres of the ancient world. All traffic from Athens and the north of Greece to Sparta and the Peloponnese had to be routed through Corinth, because it stood on the little neck of land that connected the two.

Not only did the north-to-south traffic of Greece pass through Corinth of necessity, but also by far the greater part of the east-to-west traffic of the Mediterranean passed through from choice. The extreme southern tip of Greece was known as Cape Malea (now called Cape Matapan). It was dangerous, and rounding Cape Malea was thought of in much the same way as rounding Cape Horn in later times. The Greeks had two sayings which showed what they thought of it: 'Let him who sails round Malea forget his home', and 'Let him who sails round Malea first make his will.'

The consequence was that mariners followed one of two courses. They sailed up the Saronic Gulf, and, if their ships were small enough, dragged them out of the water, set them on rollers, hauled them across the isthmus, and relaunched them on the other side. The isthmus was actually called the *Diolkos*, the place of dragging across. (The idea is reflected in the Scottish place names Tarbert and Tarbet, from the Gaelic *tairbeart*, which means a place where the land is so narrow that a boat can be dragged from loch to loch.) If that course was not possible because the ship was too large, the cargo was disembarked, carried by porters across the isthmus, and re-embarked on another ship at the other side. This four-mile journey across the isthmus, where the Corinth Canal now runs, saved a journey of about 200 miles round Cape Malea, the most dangerous cape in the Mediterranean.

It is easy to see how great a commercial city Corinth must have been. As already noted, the north-to-south traffic of Greece had no alternative but to pass through it; by far the greater part of the east-to-west trade of the Mediterranean world chose to pass through it. Round Corinth, there clustered three other towns: Lechaeum at the west end of the isthmus, Cenchrea at the east end and Schoenus just a short distance away. Dean Farrar, who wrote on the life and works of St Paul, writes: 'Objects of luxury soon found their way to the markets which were visited by every nation in the civilized world – Arabian balsam, Phoenician dates, Libyan ivory, Babylonian carpets, Cilician goats' hair, Lycaonian wool, Phrygian slaves.'

Farrar also calls Corinth the Vanity Fair of the ancient world. The city was called the Bridge of Greece, or even the Lounge of Greece. It has been said that anyone who stands long enough in Piccadilly Circus will in the end meet everyone in the country. Corinth was the Piccadilly Circus of the Mediterranean. To add to the throng which came to it, Corinth was the place where the Isthmian Games were held, which were second only to the Olympics. Corinth was a rich and populous city with one of the greatest commercial trades in the ancient world.

The Wickedness of Corinth

There was another side to Corinth. It had a reputation for commercial prosperity, but it was also a byword for evil living. The very word *korinthiazesthai*, to live like a Corinthian, had become a part of the Greek language, and meant to live with drunken and immoral debauchery. The word also entered the English language, and, in the early decades of the nineteenth century, in Regency times, a Corinthian was one of the wealthy young men who indulged in reckless and riotous living. Aelian, the third-century Greek writer, tells us that if ever a Corinthian was shown on the stage in a Greek play, he was shown drunk. The very name Corinth was synonymous with debauchery; and there was one source of evil in the city which was known all over the civilized world. Above the isthmus towered the hill of the Acropolis, and on it stood the great temple of Aphrodite, the goddess of love. To that temple, there were attached 1,000 priestesses who were sacred prostitutes, and in the evenings they came down from the Acropolis and plied their trade on the streets of Corinth. Eventually, it became the subject of a Greek proverb: 'It is not every man who can afford a journey to Corinth.' In addition to these cruder sins, there flourished far more subtle and little-known vices which had come in with the traders and the sailors from the ends of the earth, until Corinth became a synonym not only for wealth, luxury, drunkenness and debauchery, but also for filth.

The History of Corinth

The history of Corinth falls into two parts. It was a very ancient city. Thucydides, the Greek historian, claims that it was in Corinth that the first triremes, the Greek battleships, were built. Legend has it that it was in Corinth that they built the *Argo*, the ship in which Jason sailed the seas, searching for the golden fleece. But, in 146 BC, disaster befell the city. The Romans were engaged in conquering the world. When they sought to bring down Greece, Corinth was the leader of the opposition. But the Greeks could not stand against the disciplined Romans, and in 146 BC Lucius Mummius, the Roman general, captured Corinth and left it a desolate heap of ruins.

But any place with the geographical situation of Corinth could not remain in that devastated condition. Almost exactly 100 years later, in 46 BC, Julius Caesar rebuilt the city, and Corinth arose from the ruins. Now Corinth became a Roman colony. More, it became a capital city, the metropolis of the Roman province of Achaea, which included practically all Greece.

In those days, which were the days of Paul, Corinth's population was very mixed. (1) There were the Roman veterans whom Julius Caesar had settled there. When a Roman soldier had served his time, he was granted citizenship and was then sent out to some newly founded city and given a grant of land so that he might become a settler there. These Roman colonies were planted all over the world, and always the backbone of them was the contingent of veteran regular soldiers whose faithful service had won them the citizenship. (2) When Corinth was rebuilt, the merchants came back, for the city's situation still gave it commercial supremacy. (3) There were many Jews among the population. The rebuilt city offered them commercial opportunities which they were not slow to take. (4) There was a sprinkling of Phoenicians and Phrygians and people from the far east, with their exotic customs. Farrar spoke of 'this mongrel and heterogeneous population of Greek adventurers and Roman bourgeois, with a tainting infusion of Phoenicians; this mass of Jews, ex-soldiers, philosophers, merchants, sailors, freedmen, slaves, trades-people, hucksters and agents of every form of vice'. He characterizes Corinth as a colony 'without aristocracy, without traditions and without well-established citizens'.

Remember the background of Corinth, remember its name for wealth and luxury, for drunkenness and immorality and vice, and then read 1 Corinthians 6:9–10.

> Do you not know that wrongdoers will not inherit the kingdom of God? Do not be deceived! Fornicators, idolaters, adulterers, male prostitutes, sodomites, thieves, the greedy, drunkards, revilers, robbers – none of these will inherit the kingdom of God. *And this is what some of you used to be.*

In this hotbed of vice, in the most unlikely place in all the Greek world, some of Paul's greatest work was done, and some of the mightiest triumphs of Christianity were won.

Paul in Corinth

Paul stayed longer in Corinth than in any other city, with the single exception of Ephesus. He had left Macedonia with his life in peril and had crossed over to Athens. He had had little success there and had gone on to Corinth, where he remained for eighteen months. We realize how little we really know of his work when we see that the whole story of those eighteen months is compressed by Luke into seventeen verses (Acts 18:1–17).

When Paul arrived in Corinth, he took up residence with Aquila and Priscilla. He preached in the synagogue with great success. With the arrival of Timothy and Silas from Macedonia, he redoubled his efforts; but the Jews were so stubbornly hostile that he had to leave the synagogue. He took up residence with a man named Justus, who lived next door to the synagogue. His most notable convert was Crispus, who was actually the ruler of the synagogue, and among the general public he had much success.

In AD 52, there came to Corinth as its new governor a Roman called Gallio. He was famous for his charm and gentleness. The Jews tried to take advantage of his newness and good nature, and brought Paul to trial before him on a charge of teaching contrary to their law. But Gallio, with impartial Roman justice, refused to have anything to do with the case or to take any action. So, Paul completed his work in Corinth and moved on to Syria.

The Correspondence with Corinth

It was when he was in Ephesus in AD 55 that Paul, learning that things were not all well in Corinth, wrote to the church there. There is every possibility that the Corinthian correspondence as we have it is not in the correct order. We must remember that it was not until AD 90 or thereabouts that Paul's correspondence was collected. In many churches, it must have existed only on scraps of papyrus, and putting it together would have been a problem; and it seems that, when the Corinthian letters were collected, they were not all discovered and were not arranged in the right order. Let us see if we can reconstruct what happened.

(1) There was a letter which preceded 1 Corinthians. According to the Revised Standard Version, in 1 Corinthians 5:9 Paul writes: 'I wrote you in my letter not to associate

with immoral men.' This obviously refers to some previous letter. Some scholars believe that letter is lost without trace. Others think it is contained in 2 Corinthians 6:14–7:1. Certainly, that passage suits what Paul said he wrote about. It occurs rather awkwardly in its context, and, if we take it out and read straight on from 2 Corinthians 6:13 to 7:2, we get excellent sense and connection. Scholars call this letter 'the Previous Letter'. (In the original letters, there were no chapter or verse divisions. The chapters were not divided up until the thirteenth century and the verses not until the sixteenth century; and, because of that, the arranging of the collection of letters would be much more difficult.)

(2) News came to Paul, from various sources, of trouble at Corinth. (a) News came from members of the household of Chloe (1 Corinthians 1:11). They brought news of the disputes with which the church was torn. (b) News came with the visit of Stephanas, Fortunatus and Achaicus to Ephesus (1 Corinthians 16:17). By personal contact, they were able to fill in the gaps in Paul's information. (c) News came in a letter in which the Corinthian church had asked Paul's guidance on various problems. In 1 Corinthians 7:1, Paul begins: 'Now concerning the matters about which you wrote . . .' In answer to all this information, Paul wrote 1 Corinthians and despatched it to Corinth, apparently by the hand of Timothy (1 Corinthians 4:17).

(3) The result of the letter was that things became worse than ever; and, although we have no direct record of it, we can deduce that Paul paid a personal visit to Corinth. In 2 Corinthians 12:14, he writes: 'Here I am, ready to come to you this third time.' In 2 Corinthians 13:1–2, he says again that he is coming to them for the *third* time. Now, if there was a *third* time, there must have been a *second* time. We have the record of only one visit, the story of which is told in

Acts 18:1–17. We have no record at all of the second, but it only took two or three days to sail from Ephesus to Corinth.

(4) The visit did no good at all. Matters were only exacerbated, and the result was an exceedingly severe letter. We learn about that letter from certain passages in 2 Corinthians. In 2:4, Paul writes: 'I wrote to you out of much distress and anguish of heart and with many tears.' In 7:8, he writes: 'For even if I made you sorry with my letter, I do not regret it (though I did regret it, for I see that I grieved you with that letter, though only briefly).' It was a letter which was the product of anguish of mind, a letter so severe that Paul was almost sorry that he ever sent it.

Scholars call this 'the Severe Letter'. Have we got it? It obviously cannot be 1 Corinthians, because that is not a tear-stained and anguished letter. When Paul wrote it, it is clear enough that things were under control. Now, if we read through 2 Corinthians, we find an odd situation. In chapters 1–9, everyone has made up, there is complete reconciliation and all are friends again; but at chapter 10 comes the strangest break. Chapters 10–13 are the most heartbroken cry Paul ever wrote. They show that he has been hurt and insulted as he never was before or afterwards by any church. His appearance, his speech, his apostleship and his honesty have all been under attack.

Most scholars believe that chapters 10–13 are the severe letter, and that they became misplaced when Paul's letters were put together. If we want the real chronological course of Paul's correspondence with Corinth, we really ought to read chapters 10–13 of 2 Corinthians *before* chapters 1–9. We do know that this letter was sent off with Titus (2 Corinthians 2:13, 7:13).

(5) Paul was worried about this letter. He could not wait until Titus came back with an answer, so he set out to meet

him (2 Corinthians 2:13, 7:5, 7:13). Somewhere in Macedonia, he met him and learned that all was well; and, probably at Philippi, he sat down and wrote 2 Corinthians 1–9, the letter of reconciliation.

James Stalker of the United Church College in Aberdeen has said that the letters of Paul take the roof off the early churches and let us see what went on inside. Of none of them is that truer than the letters to Corinth. Here, we see what 'the care of all the churches' must have meant to Paul. Here, we see the heartbreaks and the joys. Here, we see Paul, the shepherd of his flock, bearing the sorrows and the problems of his people in his heart.

The Corinthian Correspondence

Before we read the letters in detail, let us list the progress of the Corinthian correspondence.

(1) 'The Previous Letter', which *may* be contained in 2 Corinthians 6:14–7:1.

(2) The arrival of Chloe's people, of Stephanas, Fortunatus and Achaicus, and of the letter to Paul from the Corinthian church.

(3) 1 Corinthians is written in reply and is despatched with Timothy.

(4) The situation grows worse, and Paul pays a personal visit to Corinth which is such a complete failure that it almost breaks his heart.

(5) The consequence is 'the Severe Letter', which is almost certainly contained in 2 Corinthians 10–13, and which was despatched with Titus.

(6) Unable to wait for an answer, Paul sets out to meet Titus. He meets him in Macedonia, learns that all is well and, probably from Philippi, writes 2 Corinthians 1–9, 'the Letter of Reconciliation'.

The first four chapters of 1 Corinthians deal with the divided state of the church of God at Corinth. Instead of being a unity in Christ, it was split into sects and parties who had attached themselves to the names of various leaders and teachers. It is Paul's teaching that these divisions had emerged because the Corinthians thought too much about human wisdom and knowledge and too little about the sheer grace of God. In fact, for all their so-called wisdom, they are really in a state of immaturity. They think that they are wise, but really they are no better than babies.

9

Galatians

Law and Grace

Paul under Attack

The letter to the Galatians has been likened to a sword flashing in a great warrior's hand. Both Paul and his gospel were under attack. If that attack had succeeded, Christianity might have become just another Jewish sect, dependent upon circumcision and on keeping the law, instead of being a thing of grace. It is strange to think that, if Paul's opponents had had their way, the gospel might have been kept for Jews and we might never have had the chance to know the love of Christ.

Paul's Apostleship Attacked

It is impossible to possess a vivid personality and a strong character as Paul did and not to encounter opposition; and it is equally impossible to lead such a revolution in religious thought as Paul did and not to be attacked. The first attack was on his apostleship. There were many who said that he was not an apostle at all.

From their own point of view, they were right. In Acts 1:21–2, we have the basic definition of an apostle. Judas the traitor had committed suicide; it was necessary to fill the gap made in the apostolic band. The one to be chosen is described as someone who must be 'one of the men who have accompanied us throughout the time that the Lord Jesus went in and out among us, beginning from the baptism of John until the day when he was taken up from us' and 'a witness with us to his resurrection'. To be an apostle, it was necessary to have kept company with Jesus during his earthly life and to have witnessed his resurrection. That qualification Paul obviously did not fulfil. Further, not so very long ago, he had been the chief persecutor of the Christian Church.

In the very first verse of the letter, Paul answers that challenge. Proudly, he insists that his apostleship is from no human source and that no human hand ordained him to that office, but that he received his call direct from God. Others might have the qualifications demanded when the first vacancy in the apostolic band was filled; but he had a unique qualification – he had met Christ face to face on the Damascus road.

Independence and Agreement

Further, Paul insists that for his message he was dependent on no one. That is why in chapters 1–2 he carefully details his visits to Jerusalem. He is insisting that he is not preaching some second-hand message which he received from a human source; he is preaching a message which he received direct from Christ. But Paul was no anarchist. He insisted that, although the message he received came to him in a unique and personal way, it had received the full approval of those who were the acknowledged leaders of the Christian Church (2:6–10). The gospel he preached came direct from God to him; but it was a gospel in full agreement with the faith delivered to the Church.

The Judaizers

But that gospel was under attack as well. It was a struggle which had to come and a battle which had to be fought. There were Jews who had accepted Christianity; *but* they believed that all God's promises and gifts were for Jews alone and that no Gentile could be admitted to these precious privileges. They therefore believed that Christianity was for Jews and Jews alone. If Christianity was God's greatest gift to men and women, that was all the more reason that only Jews should be allowed to enjoy it. In a way, that was inevitable. There were some Jews who arrogantly believed in the idea of the chosen people. They could say the most terrible things: 'God loves only Israel of all the nations he has made.' 'God will judge Israel with one measure and the Gentiles with another.' 'The best of the snakes crush; the best of the Gentiles kill.' 'God created the Gentiles to be fuel for the fires of Hell.' This was the spirit which made the law lay it down that it was illegal to help a Gentile mother in giving birth, for that would only be to bring another Gentile into the world. When these particular Jews saw Paul bringing the gospel to the despised Gentiles, they were appalled and infuriated.

The Law

There was a way out of this. If Gentiles wanted to become Christians, *let them become Jews first.* What did that mean? It meant that they must be circumcised and take on the whole burden of the law. That, for Paul, was the opposite of all that Christianity meant. It meant that a person's salvation was dependent on the ability to keep the law and could be won by an individual's unaided efforts, whereas, to Paul, salvation was entirely a thing of *grace.* He believed that no one could ever earn the favour of God. All that anyone could do was accept the love God offered by making an act of faith and appealing to God's mercy. A Jew would go to God saying: 'Look! Here is my circumcision. Here are my good deeds.

Give me the salvation I have earned.' Paul would say, as A. M. Toplady's great hymn 'Rock of Ages' expresses it so well:

> Not the labours of my hands
> Can fulfil thy law's demands;
> Could my zeal no respite know,
> Could my tears for ever flow,
> All for sin could not atone:
> Thou must save, and thou alone.

> Nothing in my hand I bring,
> Simply to thy cross I cling;
> Naked, come to thee for dress;
> Helpless, look to thee for grace;
> Foul, I to the fountain fly;
> Wash me, Saviour, or I die.

For him, the essential point was not what we could do for God, but what God had done for us.

'But', the Jews argued, 'the greatest thing in our national life is the law. God gave that law to Moses, and on it our very lives depend.' Paul replied: 'Wait a moment. Who is the founder of our nation? To whom were the greatest of God's promises given?' Of course, the answer is Abraham. 'Now,' Paul continued, 'how was it that Abraham gained the favour of God? He could not have gained it by keeping the law, because he lived 430 years before the law was given to Moses. *He gained it by an act of faith.* When God told him to leave his people and go out, Abraham made a sublime act of faith and went, trusting everything to him. It was faith that saved Abraham, not law; and,' Paul goes on, 'it is faith that must save every individual, not deeds of the law. The real child of Abraham is not someone racially descended from him but one who, irrespective of race, makes the same surrender of faith to God.'

The Law and Grace

If all this is true, one very serious question arises: what is the place of the law? It cannot be denied that it was given by God; does this emphasis on grace simply wipe it out?

The law has its own place in the scheme of things. First, it tells us what sin is. If there is no law, we cannot break it and there can be no such thing as sin. Second, and most important, the law really drives us to the grace of God. The trouble about the law is that, because we are all sinful, we can never keep it perfectly. Its effect, therefore, is to show us our weakness and to drive us to a despair in which we see that there is nothing left but to throw ourselves on the mercy and the love of God. The law convinces us of our own insufficiency and in the end compels us to admit that the only thing that can save us is the grace of God. In other words, the law is an essential stage on the way to that grace.

In this epistle, Paul's great theme is the glory of the grace of God and the necessity of realizing that we can never save ourselves.

10

Ephesians

The Supreme Letter

The Supreme Letter

By common consent, the Letter to the Ephesians ranks very high in the devotional and theological literature of the Christian Church. It has been called 'the Queen of the Epistles' – and rightly so. Many would hold that it is indeed the highest reach of New Testament thought. When the great Scottish Protestant reformer John Knox was very near to death, the book that was most often read to him was John Calvin's *Sermons on the Letter to the Ephesians*. The poet Samuel Taylor Coleridge said of Ephesians that it was 'the divinest composition'. He went on: 'It embraces first, those doctrines peculiar to Christianity, and, then, those precepts common with it in natural religion.' Ephesians clearly has a unique place in the Pauline correspondence.

And yet there are certain very real problems connected with it. These problems are not the product of the minds of over-critical scholars, but are plain for all to see. When, however, these problems are solved, Ephesians becomes a greater letter than ever and shines with an even more radiant light.

The Circumstances behind the Writing of Ephesians

Before we turn to the doubtful things, let us set down the certainties. First, it is clear that Ephesians was written when

Paul was in prison. He calls himself 'a prisoner for Christ' (3:1); it is as 'a prisoner for the Lord' that he begs them (4:1); he is 'an ambassador in chains' (6:20). It was in prison, and very near to the end of his life, that Paul wrote Ephesians.

Second, Ephesians clearly has a close connection with Colossians. It would seem that Tychicus was the bearer of both these letters. In Colossians, Paul says that Tychicus will tell them all his news (Colossians 4:7); and in Ephesians he says that Tychicus will tell them everything about what he is doing (Ephesians 6:21). Further, there is a close resemblance between the substance of the two letters, so close that more than fifty-five verses in the two letters are word for word the same. Either, as Coleridge held, Colossians is what might be called 'the overflow' of Ephesians, or Ephesians is a greater version of Colossians. We shall in the end come to see that it is this resemblance which gives us the clue to the unique place of Ephesians among the letters of Paul.

The Problem

So, it is certain that Ephesians was written when Paul was in prison for the faith and that it has in some way the closest possible connection with Colossians. The problem emerges when we begin to examine the question of *to whom Ephesians was written.*

In the ancient world, letters were written on rolls of papyrus. When finished, they were tied with thread, and, if they were especially private or important, the knots in the thread were then sealed. But it was rare for any address to be written on them, for the very simple reason that, for the ordinary individual, there was no postal system. There was a government post, but it was available only for official and imperial correspondence and not for the ordinary person. Letters in those days were delivered by hand, and therefore no address was necessary. So, the titles of the New Testament letters are not part of the original letters at all. They were inserted afterwards when the letters were collected and published for all the Church to read.

When we study Ephesians closely, we find that it is extremely unlikely that it was written to the church at Ephesus. There are *internal* reasons for arriving at that conclusion.

(1) The letter was written to Gentiles. The recipients were 'Gentiles by birth, called "the uncircumcision" by those who are called "the circumcision" . . . at that time without Christ, being aliens from the commonwealth of Israel, and strangers to the covenants of promise' (2:11–12). Paul urges that they 'no longer live as the Gentiles live' (4:17). The fact that they were Gentiles did not of itself mean that the letter could not have been written to Ephesus; but it is something to note.

(2) Ephesians is the most impersonal letter Paul ever wrote. It is entirely without personal greetings and without the intimate personal messages of which the other letters are so full. That is doubly surprising when we remember that Paul spent longer in Ephesus than in any other city – no less than three years (Acts 20:31). Further, there is no more intimate and affectionate passage in the whole New Testament than Acts 20:17–35, where we have Paul's farewell talk to the elders of Ephesus, before he left Miletus on his last journey. It is very difficult to believe in the light of all this that Paul would have sent a letter to Ephesus which was so impersonal.

(3) The indication of the letter is that Paul and the recipients did not know each other personally and that their knowledge of each other came by hearsay. In 1:15, Paul writes: 'I have *heard* of your faith in the Lord Jesus.' The loyalty of the people to whom he was writing was not

something he had experienced but something about which he had been told. In 3:2, he writes to them: 'For surely you have already heard of the commission of God's grace that was given to me for you.' That is to say: 'Surely you have heard that God gave me the special task and office of being the apostle to Gentiles such as you.' The Church's knowledge of Paul as the apostle to the Gentiles was something of which they had heard, but not something which they knew by personal contact with him. So, within itself, the letter bears signs that it does not fit the close and personal relationship which Paul had with the church at Ephesus.

These facts might be explained; but there is one *external* fact which settles the matter. In 1:1, none of the great early manuscripts of the Greek New Testament contains the words *in Ephesus*. They all read: 'Paul . . . to the saints who are also faithful in Christ Jesus.' And we know, from the way in which they comment on it, that that was the form in which the early Greek fathers knew the text.

Was Paul the Author?

Some scholars have gone on to find still another difficulty in Ephesians. They have doubted whether Paul was the author of the letter at all. On what grounds do they base their doubts?

They say that the *vocabulary* is different from the vocabulary of Paul; and it is true that there are some seventy words in Ephesians which are not found in any other letter written by Paul. That need not trouble us, for the fact is that in Ephesians Paul was saying things which he had never said before. He was travelling a road of thought along which he had not travelled before; and naturally he needed new words to express new thoughts. It would be ridiculous to demand that someone with a mind like Paul's should never add to his vocabulary and should always express himself in the same way.

They say that the *style* is not the style of Paul. It is true – we can see it even in the English, let alone in the Greek – that the style of Ephesians is different from that of the other letters. The other letters are all written to meet a definite situation. But, as the New Testament scholar A. H. McNeile has said, Ephesians is 'a theological tract, or rather a religious meditation'. Even the use of language is different. Another scholar, James Moffatt, puts it this way: generally speaking, Paul's language pours out like a torrent; but in Ephesians we have 'a slow, bright stream, flowing steadily along, which brims its high banks'. The length of the sentences in Ephesians is astonishing. In the Greek, Ephesians 1:3–14, 1:15–23, 2:1–9 and 3:1–7 are each one long, meandering sentence. McNeile very beautifully and rightly calls Ephesians 'a poem in prose'. All this is very unlike Paul's normal style.

What is to be said in response to this? There is first the general fact that no great writer always writes in the same style. Shakespeare can produce the very different styles of *Hamlet*, *A Midsummer Night's Dream*, *The Taming of the Shrew* and the sonnets. Any great stylist – and Paul was a great stylist – writes in a style to fit the aim and the circumstances at the time of writing. It is bad criticism to say that Paul did not write Ephesians simply because he has developed a new vocabulary and a new style.

But there is more. Let us remember how Paul wrote most of his letters. He wrote them in the middle of a busy ministry, when, for the most part, he was on the road. He wrote them to meet a pressing problem which had to be dealt with at that precise moment. That is to say, in most of his letters Paul was writing against time. Now, let us remember that, if Paul wrote

Ephesians, he wrote it *when he was in prison* and therefore had all the time in the world to consider what he wrote. Is it any wonder that the style of Ephesians is not the style of the earlier letters?

Moreover, this difference in style, this meditative, poetical quality, is most apparent in the first three chapters, and they are *one long prayer*, culminating in a great hymn of praise to God. There is, in fact, nothing like this in all Paul's letters. This is the language of lyrical prayer, not the language of argument or controversy or rebuke.

The differences are a long way from proving that Ephesians is not by Paul.

The Thought of the Epistle

Certain scholars want to go on to say that the thought of Ephesians is beyond the thought of any of the other letters of Paul. Let us see what that thought is. We have seen that Ephesians is intimately connected with Colossians, whose central thought is *the all-sufficiency of Jesus Christ*. In Jesus Christ were hidden all the treasures of wisdom and knowledge (Colossians 2:3); all the fullness of God dwelt in him (Colossians 1:19); in him the whole fullness of deity dwells bodily (Colossians 2:9); he alone is necessary and sufficient for our salvation (Colossians 1:14). The whole thought of Colossians is based on the complete sufficiency of Jesus Christ.

The thought of Ephesians is a development of that idea. It is summarized in two verses of the first chapter, in which Paul speaks of God as having 'with all wisdom and insight . . . made known to us the mystery of his will, according to his good pleasure that he set forth in Christ, as a plan for the fullness of time, to gather up all things in him, things in heaven and things on earth' (Ephesians 1:9–10).

The key thought of Ephesians is the gathering together of all things in Jesus Christ. In nature as it is, without Christ there is nothing but disunity and disharmony; it is, as Tennyson described it, 'red in tooth and claw'. The dominion that human beings hold has broken the social union which should exist between them and the natural world; we are divided from one another, class from class, nation from nation, ideology from ideology, Gentile from Jew. What is true of the world of outer nature is true of human nature. In every individual there is a tension; each one of us is a walking civil war, torn between the desire for good and the desire for evil; we hate our sins and love them at one and the same time. According to both Greek and Jewish thought in the time of Paul, this disharmony extends even to the heavenly places. A cosmic battle is raging between the powers of evil and the powers of good, between God and the demons. Worst of all, there is disharmony between God and human beings. Men and women, who were meant to be in fellowship with God, are estranged from him.

So, in this world without Christ, there is nothing but disunity. That disunity is not God's purpose, but it can become a unity only when all things are united in Christ. As E. F. Scott has it in his commentary: 'The innumerable broken strands were to be brought together in Christ, knotted again into one, as they had been in the beginning.' The central thought of Ephesians is the realization of the disunity in the universe and the conviction that it can become unity only when everything is united in Christ.

The Origin of Paul's Thought

How did Paul arrive at this great conception of the unity of all things in Jesus Christ? Most probably, he came to it in two ways. It is surely the inevitable outcome of his conviction, stated so vividly in Colossians, that Christ is all-sufficient. But it may well be that there was something else which moved Paul's mind in this direction. He was a Roman citizen and proud of it. In his journeys, Paul had seen a great deal of the Roman Empire, and now he was in Rome, the imperial city. In the Roman Empire, a new unity had come to the world. The *pax Romana*, the Roman peace, was a very real thing. Kingdoms and states and countries, which had struggled and been at war with each other, were gathered into a new unity in the empire which was Rome. It may well be that, in his imprisonment, Paul saw with new eyes how all this unity centred in Rome; and it may well have seemed to him a symbol of how all things must centre in Christ, if a disunited nature and world and humanity were ever to be gathered into a unity. Surely, far from being a conception that was beyond his thinking, all Paul's thinking and experience would lead him precisely to that.

The Function of the Church

It is in the first three chapters of the letter that Paul deals with this conception of the unity in Christ. In the last three chapters, he has much to say about the place of the Church in God's plan to bring about that unity. It is here that Paul produces one of his greatest phrases. The Church is the *body of Christ*. The Church is to be hands to do Christ's work, feet to run his errands, a mouth to speak for him. So, we have two lines of thought in Ephesians. First, Christ is God's instrument of reconciliation. Second, the Church is Christ's instrument of reconciliation. The Church must bring Christ to the world; and it is within the Church that all the middle walls of separation must be broken down. It is through the Church that the unity of all the discordant elements must be achieved. As the

New Testament scholar E. F. Scott has it: 'The Church stands for that purpose of worldwide reconciliation for which Christ appeared, and in all their intercourse with one another Christians must seek to realize this formative idea of the Church.'

Who but Paul?

This is the thought of Ephesians. As we have seen, there are some who, thinking of the vocabulary and the style and the thought of this letter, cannot believe that Paul wrote it. E. J. Goodspeed, the American scholar, has put forward an interesting – but unconvincing – theory. The probability is that it was in Ephesus about the year AD 90 that the letters of Paul were first collected and sent out to the Church at large. It is Goodspeed's theory that the person responsible for that collection, some disciple of Paul, wrote Ephesians as a kind of introduction to the whole collection. Surely that theory breaks down on one obvious fact. Any imitation is inferior to the original. But, far from being inferior, Ephesians might well be said to be the greatest of all the Pauline letters. If Paul did not write it himself, we have to suggest as its writer someone who was possibly greater than Paul. E. F. Scott very relevantly demands: 'Can we believe that in the Church of Paul's day there was an unknown teacher of this supreme excellence? The natural assumption is surely that an epistle so like the work of Paul at his best was written by no other man than by Paul himself.' No one ever had a greater vision of Christ than this. It sees in Christ the one centre in whom all the disunities of life are gathered into one. No one ever had a greater vision of the Church than this – a vision which sees in the Church God's instrument in that worldwide reconciliation. And we may well believe that no one other than Paul could rise to a vision like that.

The Destination of Ephesians

We must now return to the problem which earlier we left unsolved. If Ephesians was not written to Ephesus, to what church was it written?

The oldest suggestion is that it was written to *Laodicea.* In Colossians 4:16, Paul writes: 'And when this letter has been read among you, have it read also in the church of the Laodiceans; and see that you read also the letter from Laodicea.' That sentence makes certain that a letter had gone from Paul to the church at Laodicea. We possess no such letter among Paul's letters as they stand. Marcion was one of the first people to make a collection of Paul's letters, around the middle of the second century, and he actually calls Ephesians the Letter to the Laodiceans. So, from very early times, there must have been a feeling in the Church that Ephesians was actually sent in the first instance to Laodicea.

If we accept that interesting and attractive suggestion, we still have to explain how the letter lost its individual address to Laodicea and came to be connected with Ephesus. There could be two explanations.

It may be that, when Paul died, the church at Ephesus knew that the church at Laodicea possessed a wonderful letter from Paul, and wrote to Laodicea asking for a copy. A copy may have been made and sent off, omitting only the words *in Laodicea* in the first verse, and leaving a blank as the earliest manuscripts have a blank there. Almost thirty years later, the letters of Paul were collected for general publication. Laodicea was in a district which was notorious for earthquakes, and it may well have been that all its archives were destroyed and that therefore, when the collection was made, the only copy of the Letter to the Laodiceans was the one which survived in Ephesus. That letter may then have come to be known as the Letter to the Ephesians, because it was in Ephesus that the only surviving copy was held.

The second suggested explanation was put forward by Adolf von Harnack, the great German scholar. In later times, the church in Laodicea sadly fell from grace. In the book of Revelation, there is a letter to Laodicea which makes sad reading (Revelation 3:14–22). In that letter, the church of Laodicea is unsparingly condemned by the risen Christ, so much so that he says in that vivid phrase: 'I am about to spit you out of my mouth' (Revelation 3:16). Now, in the ancient world there was a custom called *damnatio memoriae*, the condemnation of a person's memory. An individual might have rendered great service to the state, for which the name of that person might occur in books, in the state registers, in inscriptions and on memorials. But, if such a person ended in some base act, something utterly dishonourable, the memory of that person was condemned. The person's name was erased from all books, obliterated from all inscriptions and chiselled out of all memorials. Harnack thinks it possible that the church of Laodicea underwent a *damnatio memoriae* so that the city's name was obliterated from the Christian records. If that were so, then the copies of the Letter to Laodicea would have no address at all; and, when the collection was made at Ephesus, the name of Ephesus might well have become attached to it.

The Circular Letter

Both these suggestions are possible; but still another suggestion is far more likely. We believe that *Ephesians was not in fact written to any one church, but was a circular letter to all Paul's Asian churches*. Let us look again at Colossians

4:16. He writes: 'And when this letter has been read among you, have it read also in the church of the Laodiceans; and see that you read also the letter from Laodicea.' Paul does not say that the Colossians must read the epistle *to* Laodicea; they must read the epistle *from* Laodicea. It is as if Paul said: 'There is a letter circulating; at the present moment it has reached Laodicea; when it is sent on to you from Laodicea, be sure to read it.' That sounds very much as if there was a letter circulating among the Asian churches – and we believe that letter was Ephesians.

The Essence of Paul's Message

If this is so, Ephesians is Paul's supreme letter. We have seen that Ephesians and Colossians are very close to each other. We believe that what happened was that Paul wrote Colossians to deal with a definite situation, an outbreak of heresy. In so doing, he stumbled on his great expression of the all-sufficiency of Christ. He said to himself: 'This is something that I must get across to everyone.' So, he took the material he had used in Colossians, removed all the local and temporary and controversial aspects, and wrote a new letter to tell everyone about the all-sufficient Christ. Ephesians, as we see it, is the one letter Paul sent to all the eastern churches to tell them that the destined unity of all people and of all things could never be found except in Christ, and to tell them of the supreme task of the Church – that of being Christ's instrument in the universal reconciliation of all men and women to one another and of their reconciliation to God. That is why Ephesians is the Queen of the Epistles.

11

Philippians

The Letter of Joy

We are fortunate in one thing in our study of Philippians – there are practically no critical problems involved, for no reputable New Testament critic has ever doubted its genuineness. We can accept Philippians as undoubtedly an authentic letter of Paul.

Philippi

When Paul chose a place in which to preach the gospel, he always did so with the eye of a strategist. He always chose one which was not only important in itself but was also the keypoint of a whole area. To this day, many of Paul's preaching centres are still great road centres and railway junctions. Such was Philippi, which had at least three great claims to distinction.

(1) In the neighbourhood, there were gold and silver mines, which had been worked as far back as the time of the Phoenicians. It is true that, by the time of the Christian era, these mines had been exhausted; but they had made Philippi a great commercial centre of the ancient world.

(2) The city had been founded by Philip, father of Alexander the Great; and it is his name that it bears. It was founded on the site of an ancient city called *Krēnidēs*, a name which means the Wells or Fountains. Philip had founded Philippi in 368 BC because there was no more strategic site in

all Europe. There is a range of hills which divides Europe from Asia, east from west; and at Philippi that chain of hills dips into a pass, so that the city commanded the road from Europe to Asia, since the road had to go through the pass. This was the reason that one of the great battles of history was fought at Philippi; for it was here that Antony defeated Brutus and Cassius, and thereby decided the future of the Roman Empire.

(3) Not very long after this, Philippi was raised to the status of a Roman colony. The Roman colonies were amazing institutions. They were not colonies in the sense of being outposts of civilization in unexplored parts of the world. They had begun by having a military significance. It was the custom of Rome to send out parties of veteran soldiers, who had served their time and been granted citizenship, to settle in strategic road centres. Usually, these parties consisted of 300 veterans with their wives and children. These colonies were the focal points of the great Roman road systems, which were so engineered that reinforcements could speedily be sent from one colony to another. They were founded to keep the peace and to command the strategic centres in Rome's far-flung empire. At first they had been founded in Italy, but soon they were scattered throughout the whole empire, as the empire grew. In later days, the title of colony was given by the government to any city which it wished to honour for faithful service.

Wherever they were, these colonies were little fragments of Rome, and their pride in their Roman citizenship was their dominating characteristic. The Roman language was spoken; Roman-style clothes were worn; Roman customs were observed; their magistrates had Roman titles, and carried out the same ceremonies as were carried out in Rome itself. They were stubbornly and unalterably Roman and would never have dreamt of becoming assimilated to the people among whom they were set. We can hear the Roman pride breathing through the charge against Paul and Silas in Acts 16:20–1: 'These men are Jews, and they are trying to teach and to introduce laws and customs which it is not right for us to observe – *for we are Romans.*'

'You are a colony of heaven' (Authorized Version), Paul wrote to the Philippian church (3:20). Just as the Roman colonists never forgot in any environment that they were Romans, so the Philippians must never forget in any society that they were Christians. Nowhere were people prouder of being Roman citizens than in these colonies; and Philippi was one such colony.

Paul and Philippi

It was on the second missionary journey, about the year AD 52, that Paul first came to Philippi. Urged on by the vision of the man of Macedonia with his appeal to come over and help them (cf. Acts 16:6–10), Paul had sailed from Alexandrian Troas in Asia Minor. He had landed at Neapolis in Europe, and made his way from there to Philippi.

The story of Paul's stay in Philippi is told in Acts 16; and an interesting story it is. It centres round three people – Lydia, the seller of purple; the demented slave girl, used by her masters to tell fortunes; and the Roman jailer. It is an extraordinary cross-section of ancient life. These three people were of different nationalities. Lydia was from *Asia*, and her name may well be not a proper name at all but simply 'the Lydian lady'. The slave girl was a native *Greek*. The jailer was a *Roman* citizen. The whole empire was being gathered into the Christian Church. But not only were these three individuals of different nationalities; they came from very different levels of society. Lydia was a dealer in purple, one of the most costly substances in the ancient world, and was the equivalent of a *merchant prince*. The girl was a *slave* and, therefore, in the eyes of the law not a person at all, but a living tool. The jailer was a Roman citizen, a member of the sturdy Roman *middle class*, from which the civil service was drawn. In these three, the top, the bottom and the middle of society are all represented. No chapter in the Bible shows so well the all-embracing faith which Jesus Christ brought to men and women.

Persecution

Paul had to leave Philippi after a storm of persecution and an illegal imprisonment. That persecution was inherited by the Philippian church. He tells them that they have shared in his imprisonment and in his defence of the gospel (1:7). He tells them not to fear their adversaries, for they are going through what he himself has gone through and is now enduring (1:28–30).

True Friendship

There had grown up between Paul and the Philippian church a bond of friendship closer than that which existed between him and any other church. It was his proud boast that he had never taken help from any individual or from any church, and that, with his own two hands, he had provided for his needs. It was from the Philippians alone that he had agreed to accept a gift. Soon after he left them and moved on to Thessalonica, they sent him a present (4:16). When he moved on and arrived in Corinth by way of Athens, once again they were the only ones who remembered him with their gifts (2 Corinthians 11:9). 'My brothers and sisters, whom I love and long for,' he calls them, 'my joy and crown . . . in the Lord' (4:1).

The Reasons for Writing the Letter

When Paul wrote this letter, he was in prison in Rome, and he wrote it with certain definite aims.

(1) It is a letter of thanks. The years have passed; it is now AD 63 or 64, and once again the Philippians have sent him a gift (4:10–11).

(2) It has to do with Epaphroditus. It seems that the Philippians had sent him not only as a bearer of their gift, but that he might stay with Paul and be his personal servant. But Epaphroditus had become ill. He was homesick, and he was worried because he knew that the people at home were worried about him. Paul sent him home; but he had the unhappy feeling that the people in Philippi might think of Epaphroditus as a quitter, so he goes out of his way to give him a testimonial: 'Welcome him then in the Lord with all joy, and honour such people, because he came close to death for the work of Christ' (2:29–30). There is something very moving in the sight of Paul, himself in prison and awaiting death, seeking to make things easier for Epaphroditus, when he was unexpectedly and unwillingly compelled to go home. Here is the height of Christian courtesy.

(3) It is a letter of encouragement to the Philippians in the trials which they are going through (1:28–30).

(4) It is an appeal for unity, from which rises the great passage which speaks of the selfless humility of Jesus Christ (2:1–11). In the church at Philippi, there were two women who had quarrelled and were endangering the peace (4:2); and there were false teachers who were seeking to lure the Philippians from the true path (3:2). This letter is an appeal to maintain the unity of the Church.

PHILIPPIANS

The Problem

It is at this point that the problem of Philippians arises. At 3:2, there is an extraordinary break in the letter. Up to 3:1, everything is serenity, and the letter seems to be drawing gently to its close; then without warning comes the outburst: 'Beware of dogs; beware of the evil workers; beware of the mutilation of the flesh.' There is no connection with what goes before. Further, 3:1 looks like the end. 'Finally, my brothers and sisters,' says Paul, 'rejoice in the Lord' – and, having said *finally*, he begins all over again! (That, of course, is not an unknown phenomenon in preaching.)

Because of this break, many scholars think that Philippians, as we possess it, is not one letter but two letters put together. They regard 3:2–4:3 as a letter of thanks and warning sent quite early after the arrival of Epaphroditus in Rome; and they regard 1:1–3:1 and 4:4–23 as a letter written a good deal later, and sent with Epaphroditus when he had to go home. That is perfectly possible. We know that Paul almost certainly did, in fact, write more than one letter to Philippi; for Polycarp, the second-century Bishop of Smyrna, in his letter to the Philippian church, says of him: 'when he was absent he wrote *letters* to you'.

The Explanation

And yet it seems to us that there is no good reason for splitting this letter into two. The sudden break between 3:1 and 3:2 can be otherwise explained in one of two ways.

(1) As Paul was writing, fresh news may have come of trouble at Philippi; and there and then he may have interrupted his line of thought to deal with it.

(2) The simplest explanation is this. Philippians is a personal letter, and a personal letter is never logically ordered

like the argument of a thesis. In such a letter, we put things down as they come into our heads; we chat on paper with our friends; and an association of ideas which may be clear enough to us may not be so obvious to anyone else. The sudden change of subject here is just the kind of thing which might occur in any such letter.

The Lovely Letter

For many of us, Philippians is the loveliest letter Paul ever wrote. It has been called by two titles. It has been called *the Epistle of Excellent Things* – and so indeed it is; and it has been called *the Epistle of Joy*. The words *joy* and *rejoice* are used again and again. 'Rejoice,' writes Paul, 'again I will say rejoice', even in prison directing the hearts of his friends – and ours – to the joy that no one can take from us.

12

Colossians

Resisting a Great Heresy

The Towns of the Lycus Valley

About 100 miles from Ephesus, in the valley of the River Lycus, near where it joins the Maeander, there once stood three important cities – Laodicaea, Hierapolis and Colosse. Originally they had been Phrygian cities, but now they were part of the Roman province of Asia. They stood almost within sight of each other. Hierapolis and Laodicaea stood on either side of the valley with the River Lycus flowing between, only six miles apart and in full view of each other; Colosse straddled the river twelve miles further up.

The Lycus Valley had two remarkable characteristics.

(1) It was notorious for earthquakes. The Greek geographer Strabo describes it by the curious adjective *euseistos*, which in English means *good for earthquakes*. More than once, Laodicaea had been destroyed by an earthquake; but it was a city so rich and so independent that it had risen from the ruins without the financial help which the Roman government had offered. As the John who wrote the Revelation was to say of Laodicaea, in its own eyes it was rich and had need of nothing (Revelation 3:17).

(2) The waters of the River Lycus and of its tributaries were impregnated with chalk. This chalk accumulated, and all over the countryside the most amazing natural formations built up. The biblical scholar J. B. Lightfoot writes of that

area: 'Ancient monuments are buried; fertile land is overlaid; river beds choked up and streams diverted; fantastic grottoes and cascades and archways of stone are formed, by this strange, capricious power, at once destructive and creative, working silently throughout the ages. Fatal to vegetation, these encrustations spread like a stony shroud over the ground. Gleaming like glaciers on the hillside, they attract the eye of the traveller at a distance of twenty miles, and form a singularly striking feature in scenery of more than common beauty and impressiveness.'

A Wealthy Area

In spite of these things, this was a wealthy area and famous for two closely related trades. Volcanic ground is always fertile, and what was not covered by the chalky encrustations was magnificent pasture land. On these pastures, there were large flocks of sheep; and the area was perhaps the greatest centre of the woollen industry in the world. Laodicaea was especially famous for the production of garments of the finest quality. The other trade was dyeing. There was some quality in those chalky waters which made them particularly suitable for dyeing cloth, and Colosse was so famous for this trade that a certain dye was named after it.

So, these three cities stood in a district of considerable geographical interest and of great commercial prosperity.

The Unimportant City

Originally the three cities had been of equal importance; but, as the years went on, their ways parted. Laodicaea became the political centre of the district and the financial headquarters of the whole area, a city of splendid prosperity. Hierapolis became a great trade centre and a notable spa. In that volcanic area, there were many chasms in the ground from which came hot vapours and springs, famous for their medicinal quality; and people came in their thousands to Hierapolis to bathe and to drink the waters.

Colosse at one time was as great as the other two. Behind it rose the Cadmus range of mountains, and it controlled the roads to the mountain passes. The Persian kings Xerxes and Cyrus had both halted there with their invading armies, and the Greek historian Herodotus had called Colosse 'a great city of Phrygia'. But, for some reason, the glory departed. How great that departure was can be seen from the fact that to this day Hierapolis and Laodicaea are both clearly discernible, because the ruins of some great buildings still stand; but there is not a stone to show where Colosse stood, and its site can only be guessed at. Even when Paul wrote, Colosse was a small town; and Lightfoot says that it was the most unimportant town to which Paul ever wrote a letter.

The fact remains that in this town of Colosse there had arisen a heresy which, if it had been allowed to develop unchecked, might well have been the ruination of the Christian faith.

The Jews in Phrygia

One other fact must be added to complete the picture. These three cities stood in an area in which there were many Jews. Many years before, Antiochus the Great had transported 2,000 Jewish families from Babylon and Mesopotamia into the regions of Lydia and Phrygia. These Jews had prospered; and, as always happens in such cases, more and more Jews had come into the area to share their prosperity. So many came that the stricter Jews of Palestine lamented the number of Jews who left the discipline of their ancestral land for 'the wines and baths of Phrygia'.

The number of Jews who lived there can be seen from the following historical incident. Laodicaea, as we have seen, was the administrative centre of the district. In the year 62 BC, Flaccus was the Roman governor resident there. He sought to put a stop to the Jewish practice of sending money out of the province to pay the Temple tax. He did so by placing an embargo on the export of currency; and in his own part of the province alone he seized an illegal shipment of no less than twenty pounds in weight of gold which was meant for the Temple at Jerusalem. That amount of gold would represent the Temple tax of no fewer than 11,000 people. Since women and children were exempt from the tax, and since many Jews would successfully evade the capture of their money, we may well put the Jewish population as high as almost 50,000.

The Church at Colosse

The Christian church at Colosse was one which Paul had not himself founded and which he had never visited. He classes the Colossians and the Laodicaeans with those who had never seen him face to face (2:1). But no doubt the founding of the church sprang from his instructions. During his three years in Ephesus, the whole province of Asia was evangelized, so that all its inhabitants, both Jews and Greeks, heard the word of the Lord (Acts 19:10). Colosse was about 100 miles from Ephesus, and it was no doubt in that campaign of expansion that the Colossian church was founded. We do not know who its founder was; but it may well have been Epaphras, who is described as Paul's fellow servant and the faithful minister of the Colossian church and who is later connected also with Hierapolis and Laodicaea (1:7, 4:12–13). If Epaphras was not the founder of the Christian church there, he was certainly the minister in charge of the area.

A Gentile Church

It is clear that the Colossian church was mainly Gentile. The phrase *estranged and hostile in mind* (1:21) is the kind of phrase which Paul regularly uses of those who had once been strangers to the covenant of promise. In 1:27, he speaks of making known the mystery of Christ among the Gentiles, when the reference is clearly to the Colossians themselves. In 3:5–7, he gives a list of their sins before they became Christians, and these are characteristically Gentile sins. We may confidently conclude that the membership of the church at Colosse was largely composed of Gentiles.

The Threat to the Church

It must have been Epaphras who brought to Paul, in prison in Rome, news of the situation which was developing in Colosse. Much of the news that he brought was good. Paul is grateful for news of their faith in Christ and their love for the saints (1:4). He rejoices at the Christian fruit which they are producing (1:6). Epaphras has brought him news of their love in the Spirit (1:8). He is glad when he hears of their order and steadfastness in the faith (2:5). There was trouble at Colosse, certainly; but it had not yet become an epidemic. Paul believed that prevention was better than cure; and in this letter he is grasping this evil before it has time to spread.

The Heresy at Colosse

What the heresy was which was threatening the life of the church at Colosse, no one can tell for certain. 'The Colossian Heresy' is one of the great problems of New Testament scholarship. All we can do is to go to the letter itself, list the characteristics we find indicated there and then see if we can find any general heretical tendency to fit the list.

(1) It was clearly a heresy which attacked the total adequacy and the unique supremacy of Christ. No Pauline letter has such a high view of Jesus Christ or such insistence on his completeness and finality. Jesus Christ is the image of the invisible God; in him all fullness dwells (1:15, 1:19). In him are hidden all the treasures of wisdom and of knowledge (2:2). In him dwells the fullness of the Godhead in bodily form (2:9).

(2) Paul goes out of his way to stress the part that Christ played in creation. By him, all things were created (1:16); in him, all things hold together (1:17). The Son was the Father's instrument in the creation of the universe.

(3) At the same time, he goes out of his way to stress the real humanity of Christ. It was in the body of his flesh that he did his redeeming work (1:22). The fullness of the Godhead dwells in him *sōmatikōs*, in bodily form (2:9). For all his deity, Jesus Christ was truly human flesh and blood.

(4) There seems to have been an astrological element in this heresy. In 2:8, as the Authorized Version has it, he says that they were walking after the *rudiments* of this world, and in 2:20 that they ought to be dead to the *rudiments* of this world. The word translated as *rudiments* is *stoicheia*, which has two meanings.

(a) Its basic meaning is *a row of things*; it can, for instance, be used for a line of soldiers. But one of its most common meanings is the A B C, the letters of the alphabet, set out, as it were, in a row. From that, it develops the meaning of *the elements of any subject*, the rudiments. It is in that sense that the Authorized Version takes it; and, if that is the correct sense, Paul means that the Colossians are slipping back to an elementary kind of Christianity when they ought to be going on to maturity.

(b) We think that the second meaning is more likely. *Stoicheia* can mean *the elemental spirits of the world*, and especially the spirits of the stars and planets. The ancient world was dominated by the thought of the influence of the stars; and even the greatest and the wisest people would not act without consulting them. It believed that all things were in the iron grip of a fatalism settled by the stars; and the science of astrology professed to provide men and women with the secret knowledge which would rid them of their slavery to the elemental spirits. It is most likely that the Colossian false teachers were teaching that it needed something more than Jesus Christ to rid people of their subjection to these elemental spirits.

(5) This heresy made much of the powers of demonic spirits. There are frequent references to *principalities* or *authorities*, which are Paul's names for these spirits (1:16, 2:10, 2:15). The ancient world believed implicitly in demonic powers. The air was full of them. Every natural force – the wind, the thunder, the lightning, the rain – had its demonic controller. Every place, every tree, every river, every lake had its spirit. They were in one sense intermediaries to God and in another sense barriers to him, for the vast majority of them were hostile to human beings. The ancient world lived in a demon-haunted universe. The Colossian false teachers were clearly saying that something more than Jesus Christ was needed to defeat the power of the demons.

(6) There was evidently what we might call a philosophical element in this heresy. The heretics are out to take people captive with philosophy and empty deceit (2:8). Clearly the Colossian heretics were saying that the simplicities of the gospel needed a far more elaborate and obscure knowledge added to them.

(7) There was a tendency in this heresy to insist on the observance of special days and rituals – festivals, new moons and Sabbaths (2:16).

(8) There was an element of self-denial in this heresy. It laid down laws about food and drink (2:16). Its slogans were: 'Touch not; taste not; handle not' (2:21). It was a heresy which was out to limit Christian freedom by insistence on all kinds of legalistic rules and regulations.

(9) Equally, this heresy had at least sometimes an antinomian streak in it, which ignored any respect for the moral law. It tended to make people neglect the chastity which Christians should have and to make them think lightly of the bodily sins (3:5–8).

(10) Apparently, this heresy gave at least some place to the worship of angels (2:18). Beside the demons, it introduced angelic intermediaries between human beings and God.

(11) Lastly, there seems to have been in this heresy something which can only be called spiritual and intellectual snobbery. In 1:28, Paul lays down his aim: it is to warn *everyone*, to teach *everyone* in *all* wisdom, and to present *everyone mature* in Jesus Christ. We see how the word *everyone* is reiterated and how the aim is to make all people *mature* in *all* wisdom. The clear implication is that the heretics limited the gospel to some chosen few and introduced a spiritual and intellectual aristocracy into the wide welcome of the Christian faith.

The Gnostic Heresy

Was there, then, any general heretical tendency of thought which would include all this? There was what was called *Gnosticism*. Gnosticism began with two basic assumptions about matter. First, it believed that spirit alone was good and that matter was essentially evil. Second, it believed that matter was eternal; and that the universe was created not out of nothing – which is orthodox belief – but out of this flawed matter. Now this basic belief had certain inevitable consequences.

(1) It had an effect on the doctrine of creation. If God was spirit, then he was altogether good and could not possibly work with this evil matter. Therefore God was *not* the creator of the world. He put out a series of emanations, each of which was a little more distant from God, until at the end of the series there was an emanation so distant that it could handle matter; and it was this emanation which created the world. The Gnostics went further. Since each emanation was more distant from God, it was also more ignorant of him. As the series went on, that ignorance turned to hostility. So the emanations most distant from God were both ignorant of him and hostile to him. It followed that he who created the world was both completely ignorant of, and at the same time utterly hostile to, the true God. It was to meet that Gnostic doctrine of creation that Paul insisted that the agent of God in creation was not some ignorant and hostile power, but the Son who perfectly knew and loved the Father.

(2) It had an effect on the doctrine of the person of Jesus Christ. If matter was altogether evil, and if Jesus was the Son of God, then Jesus could not have had a flesh-and-blood body – so the Gnostics argued. Jesus must have been a kind of spiritual phantom. So the Gnostic stories say that when Jesus walked, he left no footprints on the ground. This, of course, completely removed Jesus from humanity and made it impossible for him to be the Saviour of human beings. It was to meet this Gnostic doctrine that Paul insisted on the flesh-and-blood body of Jesus and insisted that Jesus saved men and women in the body of his flesh.

(3) It had an effect on the ethical approach to life. If matter was evil, then it followed that our bodies were evil. If our bodies were evil, one of two consequences followed. (a) We

must starve and beat and deny the body; we must practise a rigid regime of self-denial in which the body was suppressed, and in which every physical need and desire was refused. (b) It was possible to take precisely the opposite point of view. If the body was evil, it did not matter what was done with it; spirit was all that mattered. Therefore people could satisfy the body's desires to the full, and it would make no difference.

Gnosticism could, therefore, result in self-denial, with all kinds of laws and restrictions; or it could result in a rejection of the moral law, in which any immorality was justified. And we can see precisely both these tendencies at work in the false teachers at Colosse.

(4) One thing followed from all this – Gnosticism was a highly intellectual way of life and thought. There was this long series of emanations between human beings and God; people must fight their way up a long ladder to get to God. In order to do that, they would need all kinds of secret knowledge and private learning and hidden passwords. If they were to practise the self-denial of a rigid asceticism, they would need to know the rules; and so rigid would the asceticism be that it would be impossible for them to embark on the ordinary activities of life. The Gnostics were, therefore, quite clear that the higher levels of religion were open only to the chosen few. This conviction of the necessity of belonging to an intellectual religious aristocracy precisely suits the situation at Colosse.

(5) There remains one thing to fit into this picture. It is quite obvious that there was a Jewish element in the false teaching threatening the church at Colosse. The festivals and the new moons and the Sabbaths were characteristically Jewish; the laws about food and drink were essentially Jewish Levitical laws. Where then did the Jews come in?

It is a strange thing that many Jews were sympathetic to Gnosticism. They knew all about angels and demons and spirits. But, above all, they said: 'We know quite well that it takes special knowledge to reach God. We know quite well that Jesus and his gospel are far too simple – and that special knowledge is to be found nowhere else than in the Jewish law. It is our ritual and ceremonial law which is indeed the special knowledge which enables us to reach God.' The result was that there was not infrequently a strange alliance between Gnosticism and Judaism – and it is just such an alliance that we find in Colosse, where, as we have seen, there were many Jews.

It is clear that the false teachers of Colosse were tinged with Gnostic heresy. They were trying to turn Christianity into a philosophy and a theosophy, that is, a system for achieving knowledge of God through mysticism; and, if they had been successful, the Christian faith would have been destroyed.

The Authorship of the Letter

One question remains. Many scholars do not believe that Paul wrote this letter at all. They have three reasons.

(1) They say that in Colossians there are many words and phrases which do not appear in any other of Paul's letters. That is perfectly true. But it does not prove anything. We cannot demand that people should always write in the same way and with the same vocabulary. In Colossians, we may well believe that Paul had new things to say and found new ways to say them.

(2) They say that the development of Gnostic thought was, in fact, much later than the time of Paul, so that, if the Colossian heresy was connected with Gnosticism, the letter must be later than Paul. It is true that the great written Gnostic systems are later. But the idea of two worlds and the idea of

the evil of matter are deeply woven into both Jewish and Greek thought. There is nothing in Colossians which cannot be explained by long-standing Gnostic tendencies in ancient thought, although it is true that the systematization of Gnosticism came later.

(3) They say that the view of Christ in Colossians is far in advance of any of the letters known to have been written by Paul. There are two answers to that.

First, Paul speaks of the unsearchable riches of Christ. In Colosse, a new situation met him, and out of these unsearchable riches he drew new answers to meet it. It is true that the christology of Colossians is an advance on anything in the earlier letters of Paul; but that is far from saying that Paul did not write it, unless we are willing to argue that his thought remained completely static. It is true to say that people think out the implications of their faith only as circumstances compel them to do so; and, faced with a new set of circumstances, Paul thought out new implications of Christ.

Second, the germ of all Paul's thought about Christ in Colossians does, in fact, exist in one of his earlier letters. In I Corinthians 8:6, he writes of *one Lord Jesus Christ through whom are all things and through whom we exist*. In that phrase is the essence of all he says in Colossians. The seed was there in his mind, ready to blossom when a new climate and new circumstances called it into growth.

We need not hesitate to accept Colossians as a letter written by Paul.

The Great Letter

It remains a strange and wonderful fact that Paul wrote the letter which contains the highest point in his thinking to so unimportant a town as Colosse then was. But, in doing so, he halted a tendency which, had it been allowed to develop, would have wrecked Asian Christianity and might well have done irreparable damage to the faith of the whole Church.

13

1 & 2 Thessalonians

Advice and Reproof

Paul Comes to Macedonia

For anyone who can read between the lines, the story of Paul's coming to Macedonia is one of the most dramatic in the book of Acts. Luke, with supreme economy of words, tells it in Acts 16:6–10. Short as that narrative is, it gives the impression of a chain of circumstances inescapably culminating in one supreme event. Paul had passed through Phrygia and Galatia, and ahead of him lay the Hellespont. To the left lay the teeming province of Asia, to the right stretched the great province of Bithynia; but the Spirit would allow him to enter neither. There was something driving him relentlessly on to the Aegean Sea. So he came to Alexandrian Troas, still uncertain where he ought to go; and then there came to him a vision in the night of a man who cried: 'Come over into Macedonia and help us.' Paul set sail, and for the first time the gospel came to Europe.

One World

At that moment, Paul must have seen much more than a continent to be won for Christ. It was in Macedonia that he landed; and Macedonia was the kingdom of Alexander the Great, who had conquered the world and wept because there were no more worlds left to conquer. But Alexander was much more than a military conqueror. He was almost the first universalist. He was more a missionary than a soldier, and he dreamed of one world dominated and enlightened by the culture of Greece. Even so great a thinker as Aristotle had said that it was a plain duty to treat Greeks as free and all other peoples as slaves; but Alexander declared that he had been sent by God 'to unite, to pacify and to reconcile the whole world'. Deliberately, he had said that it was his aim 'to marry the east to the west'. He had dreamed of an empire in which there was neither Greek nor Jew, barbarian or Scythian, bond or free (Colossians 3:11). It is hard to see how Alexander could have failed to be in Paul's thoughts. Paul left from Alexandrian Troas, which was called after Alexander; he came to Macedonia, which was Alexander's original kingdom; he worked at Philippi, which was named after Philip, Alexander's father; he went on to Thessalonica, which was named after Alexander's half-sister. The whole territory was saturated with memories of Alexander; and Paul must surely have thought not of a country nor of a continent, but of a world for Christ.

Paul Comes to Thessalonica

This sense of the arms of Christianity stretching out far into the known world must have been accentuated when Paul came to Thessalonica. It was a great city. Its original name was Thermai, which means the Hot Springs, and it gave its name to the Thermaic Gulf on which it stood. Herodotus, 600 years earlier, had described it as a great city. It has always been a famous harbour. It was there that Xerxes, the Persian king, had his naval base when he invaded Europe; and even in Roman times it was one of the world's great dockyards. In 315 BC, Cassander, the king of Macedonia, had rebuilt the city and renamed it Thessalonica after his wife, who was a daughter of Philip of Macedon and a half-sister of Alexander the Great. It was a free city; that is to say, it had never suffered the indignity of having resident Roman troops within it. It had its own popular assembly and its own magistrates. Its population rose to 200,000, and for a time there was a question whether it or Constantinople would be recognized as the capital of the world.

But the supreme importance of Thessalonica lay in this – it straddled the Via Egnatia, the Egnatian Road, which stretched from Dyrrachium on the Adriatic to Constantinople on the Bosphorus and thence away to Asia Minor and the east. Its main street was part of the very road which linked Rome with the east. East and west converged on Thessalonica; it was said to be 'in the lap of the Roman Empire'. Trade poured into the city from east and west, so that it was said: 'As long as nature does not change, Thessalonica will remain wealthy and prosperous.'

It is impossible to overstress the importance of the arrival of Christianity in Thessalonica. If Christianity was established there, it was bound to spread east along the Egnatian Road until all Asia was conquered, and west until it stormed even the city of Rome. The coming of Christianity to Thessalonica was crucial in its development into a world religion.

Paul's Stay at Thessalonica

The story of Paul's stay at Thessalonica is in Acts 17:1–10. Now, for Paul, what happened at Thessalonica was of supreme importance. He preached in the synagogue for three Sabbaths (Acts 17:2), which means that his stay there could not have been much more than three weeks in length. He had such tremendous success that the Jews were enraged and raised so much trouble that he had to be smuggled out, in peril of his life, to Beroea. The same thing happened in Beroea (Acts 17:10–12), and Paul had to leave Timothy and Silas behind and make his escape to Athens. What exercised his mind was this. He had been in Thessalonica only three weeks. Was it possible to make such an impression on a place in the space of three weeks that Christianity was planted so deeply that it could never again be uprooted? If so, it was by no means an idle dream that the Roman Empire might yet be won for Christ. Or was it necessary to settle down and work for months, even years, before an impression could be made? If that was the case, no one could even dimly foresee when Christianity would penetrate all over the world. Thessalonica was a test case; and Paul was torn with anxiety to know how it would turn out.

News from Thessalonica

So anxious was Paul that, when Timothy joined him at Athens, he sent him back to Thessalonica to get the information without which he could not rest (1 Thessalonians 3:1–2, 3:5, 2:17). What news did Timothy bring back? There was good news. The affection of the Thessalonians for Paul was as strong as ever, and they were standing fast in the faith (1 Thessalonians 2:14, 3:4–6; 4:9–10). They were indeed 'his glory and joy' (1 Thessalonians 2:20). But there was worrying news.

(1) The preaching of the second coming had produced an unhealthy situation in which people had stopped working and had abandoned all ordinary activities to await the second coming with a kind of hysterical expectancy. So Paul tells them to calm down and to get on with their work (1 Thessalonians 4:11).

(2) They were worried about what was to happen to those who died before the second coming arrived. Paul explains that those who fall asleep in Jesus will miss none of the glory (1 Thessalonians 4:13–18).

(3) There was a tendency to despise all lawful authority; the argumentative Greeks were always in danger of producing a democracy run riot (1 Thessalonians 5:12–14).

(4) There was the ever-present danger that they would lapse into immorality. It was hard to unlearn the point of view of generations and to escape the contagion of the non-Christian world around them (1 Thessalonians 4:3–8).

(5) There was at least a section who slandered Paul. They hinted that he preached the gospel for what he could get out of it (1 Thessalonians 2:5, 2:9), and that he was something of a dictator (1 Thessalonians 2:6–7, 2:11).

(6) There was a certain amount of division in the church (1 Thessalonians 4:9, 5:13).

These were the problems with which Paul had to deal; and they show that human nature has not changed very much at all.

Why Two Letters?

We must ask why there are two letters. They are very much alike, and they must have been written within weeks – perhaps days – of each other. The second letter was written mainly to clear up a misconception about the second coming. The first letter insists that the day of the Lord will come like a thief in the night, and urges watchfulness (1 Thessalonians 5:2, 5:6). But this produced the unhealthy situation where people did nothing but watch and wait; and, in the second letter, Paul explains what signs must come first before the second coming arrives (2 Thessalonians 2:3–12). The Thessalonians had got their ideas about the second coming out of proportion. As so often happens to a preacher, Paul's preaching had been misunderstood, and certain phrases had been taken out of context and overemphasized; and the second letter seeks to put things back in their proper balance and to correct the thoughts of the excited Thessalonians regarding the second coming. Of course, Paul takes the opportunity in the second letter to repeat and to stress much of the good advice and rebuke he had given in the first: but its main aim is to tell them certain things which will calm their hysteria and make them wait, not in excited idleness, but in patient and diligent attention to each day's work. In these two letters, we see Paul solving the day-to-day problems which arose in the expanding Church.

14

1 & 2 Timothy and Titus

Hearing the Voice of Paul

Personal Letters

The two letters to Timothy and the letter to Titus have always been regarded as forming a separate group, different from the other letters of Paul. The most obvious difference is that they, along with the little letter to Philemon, are written to *individuals*, whereas all other Pauline letters are written to *churches*. The Muratorian Canon, which was the earliest official list of New Testament books, says that they were written 'from personal feeling and affection'. They are private rather than public letters.

Ecclesiastical Letters

But it very soon began to be seen that, though these are personal and private letters, they have a significance and a relevance far beyond the immediate. In 1 Timothy 3:15, their aim is set down. They are written to Timothy 'that you may know how one ought to behave in the household of God, which is the church of the living God'. So, it came to be seen that these letters have not only a personal significance but also what one might call an *ecclesiastical* significance. The Muratorian Canon says of them that, though they are personal letters written out of personal affection, 'they are still hallowed in the respect of the Catholic Church, and *in the arrangement of ecclesiastical discipline*'. The early Christian theologian

Tertullian said that Paul wrote 'two letters to Timothy and one to Titus, which were composed *concerning the state of the Church (de ecclesiastico statu)'*. It is not then surprising that the first name given to them was *Pontifical Letters*, that is, written by the *pontifex*, the priest, the controller of the church.

Pastoral Letters

Bit by bit, they came to acquire the name by which they are still known – the Pastoral Epistles. In writing about 1 Timothy, the philosopher and theologian Thomas Aquinas, as long ago as 1274, said: 'This letter is as it were *a pastoral rule* which the Apostle delivered to Timothy.' In his introduction to the second letter, he writes: 'In the first letter he gives Timothy instructions concerning ecclesiastical order; in this second letter he deals with a *pastoral care* which should be so great that it will even accept martyrdom for the sake of the care of the flock.' But this title, the Pastoral Epistles, really became attached to these letters in 1726 when a great scholar named Paul Anton gave a series of famous lectures on them under that title.

These letters, then, deal with the care and organization of the flock of God; they tell men and women how to behave within the household of God; and they give instructions as to how God's house should be administered, as to what kind of people the leaders and pastors of the Church should be, and as to how the threats which endanger the purity of Christian faith and life should be dealt with.

The Growing Church

The main interest of these letters is that in them we get a picture of the infant Church. In those early days, it was an island in a sea of idolatry. The people in it were only one remove from their origins in the ancient religions. It would have been so easy for them to lapse into the standards from which they had come; the tarnishing atmosphere was all around. It is most significant that missionaries have reported that, of all letters, the Pastoral Epistles speak most directly to the situation of the younger churches. The situation with which they deal has been re-enacted in India, in Africa and in China. They can never lose their interest, because in them we see, as nowhere else, the problems which continually confronted and pressed upon the growing Church.

The Ecclesiastical Background of the Pastorals

From the beginning, these letters have presented problems to New Testament scholars. There are many who have felt that, as they stand, they cannot have come directly from the hand and pen of Paul. That this is no new feeling may be seen from the fact that Marcion (a second-century heretic, who in spite of his unacceptable beliefs was the first person to draw up a list of New Testament books) did not include them among Paul's letters. Let us then see what makes people doubt their direct Pauline authorship.

In these letters, we are confronted with the picture of a church with a fairly highly developed ecclesiastical organization. There are *elders* (1 Timothy 5:17–19; Titus 1:5–6), there are *bishops*, superintendents or overseers (1 Timothy 3:1–7; Titus 1:7–16), and there are *deacons* (1 Timothy 3:8–13). From 1 Timothy 5:17–18, we learn that, by that time, elders were even paid officials. The elders who rule well are to be counted worthy of a double reward, and the Church is urged to remember that the labourer deserves to be paid. There is at least the beginning of the order of widows who became so prominent later on in the early Church (1 Timothy 5:3–

16). There is clearly here a quite elaborate structure within the Church – too elaborate, some would claim, for the early days in which Paul lived and worked.

The Days of Creeds

It is even claimed that in these letters we can see the days of creeds emerging. The word *faith* changed its meaning. In the earliest days, it is always *faith in a person*; it is the most intimate possible personal connection of love and trust and obedience with Jesus Christ. In later days, it became *faith in a creed*; it became the acceptance of certain doctrines. It is said that in the Pastoral Epistles we can see this change emerging.

In the later days, some will come who will depart from the *faith* and pay attention to teachings of demons (1 Timothy 4:1). A good servant of Jesus Christ must be nourished in the words of *faith and sound teaching* (1 Timothy 4:6). The heretics are people of corrupt minds and counterfeit *faith* (2 Timothy 3:8). The duty of Titus is to rebuke people that they may be sound in the *faith* (Titus 1:13).

This comes out particularly in an expression peculiar to the Pastorals. As the Revised Standard Version has it, Timothy is urged to keep hold of 'the truth that has been entrusted to you' (2 Timothy 1:14). The word for *that has been entrusted* is *parathēkē*. *Parathēkē* means a *deposit* which has been entrusted to a banker or someone else for safe-keeping. It is essentially something which must be handed back or handed on absolutely unchanged. That is to say, the stress is on *orthodoxy*. Instead of being a close, personal relationship to Jesus Christ, as it was in the thrilling, pulsating days of the early Church, faith has become the acceptance of a creed. It is even held that in the Pastorals we have echoes of the earliest creeds.

> He was revealed in flesh,
> vindicated in spirit,
> seen by angels,
> proclaimed among Gentiles,
> believed in throughout the world,
> taken up in glory. (1 Timothy 3:16)

That indeed sounds like the fragment of a creed which is to be recited.

> Remember Jesus Christ, raised from the dead, a descendant of David – that is my gospel. (2 Timothy 2:8)

That sounds like a reminder of a sentence from an accepted creed.

Within the Pastorals, there undoubtedly are indications that the time of insistence on acceptance of a creed has begun, and that the days of the first thrilling personal discovery of Christ are beginning to fade.

A Dangerous Heresy

It is clear that in the forefront of the situation against which the Pastoral Epistles were written there was a dangerous heresy which was threatening the welfare of the Christian Church. If we can distinguish the various characteristic features of that heresy, we may be able to go on to identify it.

It was characterized by *speculative intellectualism*. It produced questions (1 Timothy 1:4); those involved in it had a craving for questions (1 Timothy 6:4); it dealt in stupid and senseless questions (2 Timothy 2:23); its stupid questions are to be avoided (Titus 3:9). The word used in each case for *questions* is *ekzētēsis*, which means *speculative discussion*. This heresy was obviously one which was a playground of the intellectuals, or rather the pseudo-intellectuals of the Church.

It was characterized by *pride*. The heretics are proud, although in reality they know nothing (1 Timothy 6:4). There are indications that these intellectuals set themselves on a level above ordinary Christians; in fact, they may well have said that complete salvation was outside the grasp of the ordinary man or woman and open only to them. At times, the Pastoral Epistles stress the word *all* in a most significant way. The grace of God, which brings salvation, has appeared to *all* (Titus 2:11). It is God's will that *all* should be saved and come to a knowledge of the truth (1 Timothy 2:4). The intellectuals tried to make the greatest blessings of Christianity the exclusive possession of a chosen few; and, in complete contrast, the true faith stresses the all-embracing love of God.

There were within that heresy two opposite tendencies. There was a tendency to *self-denial*. The heretics tried to lay down special food laws, forgetting that everything God has made is good (1 Timothy 4:4–5). They listed many things as impure, forgetting that to the pure all things are pure (Titus 1:15). It is not impossible that they regarded sex as something unclean and belittled marriage, and even tried to persuade those who were married to renounce it, for in Titus 2:4 the simple duties of married life are stressed as being binding on Christians.

But this heresy also resulted in *immorality*. The heretics even went into private houses and led away weak and foolish women who were swayed by all kinds of desires (2 Timothy 3:6). They claimed to know God, but denied him by their actions (Titus 1:16). They were out to impose upon people and to make money out of their false teaching. To them, gain was godliness (1 Timothy 6:5); they taught and deceived for sordid gain (Titus 1:11).

On the one hand, this heresy produced an un-Christian self-denial, and on the other it produced an equally un-

Christian immorality. It was characterized, too, by *words* and *tales* and *genealogies*. It was full of godless chatter and useless controversies (1 Timothy 6:20). It produced endless genealogies (1 Timothy 1:4; Titus 3:9). It produced myths and fables (1 Timothy 1:4; Titus 1:14).

It was at least in some way and to some extent tied up with *Jewish legalism*. Among its devotees were those 'of the circumcision' (Titus 1:10). The aim of the heretics was to be teachers of the law (1 Timothy 1:7). It pressed on people Jewish myths and the commandments of those who reject the truth (Titus 1:14).

Finally, these heretics denied *the resurrection of the body*. They said that any resurrection that a Christian was going to experience had been experienced already (2 Timothy 2:18). This is probably a reference to those who held that the only resurrection Christians experienced was a spiritual one when they died with Christ and rose again with him in the experience of baptism (Romans 6:4).

The Beginnings of Gnosticism

Is there any heresy which fits all this material? There is, and its name is *Gnosticism*. The basic idea behind Gnosticism was that all matter is essentially evil and that spirit alone is good. That basic belief had certain consequences.

The Gnostics believed that matter is as eternal as God, and that when God created the world he had to use this essentially evil matter. That meant that, to them, God could not be the direct creator of the world. In order to touch this flawed matter, he had to send out a series of emanations or divine powers – they called them *aeons* – each one more and more distant from himself until at last there came an emanation or aeon so distant that it could deal with matter and create the world. Between human beings and God there stretched a series of these emanations, each one containing an individual's name and genealogy. So Gnosticism literally had endless myths and endless genealogies. If men and women were ever to get to God, they must, as it were, climb this ladder of emanations; and, to do that, they needed a very special kind of knowledge including all kinds of passwords to get them past each stage. Only a person of the highest intellectual ability could hope to acquire this knowledge and know these passwords and so get to God.

Further, if matter was totally evil, the body was altogether evil. From that, two opposite possible consequences sprang. Either the body must be held in check so that a rigorous self-discipline resulted, in which the needs of the body were as far as possible eliminated and its instincts, especially the sexual drive, as far as possible destroyed; or it could be held that, since it was evil, it did not matter what was done with the body, and its instincts and desires could be given full rein. The Gnostics therefore became either people who denied themselves all physical comforts or people to whom morality had ceased to have any relevance at all.

Still further, if the body was evil, clearly there could be no such thing as its resurrection. It was not the resurrection of the body but its destruction to which the Gnostics looked forward.

All this fits accurately the situation of the Pastoral Epistles. In Gnosticism, we see the intellectualism, the intellectual arrogance, the myths and the genealogies, the self-denial and the immorality, the refusal to contemplate the possibility of a bodily resurrection, which were part and parcel of the heresy against which the Pastoral Epistles were written.

One element in the heresy has not yet been fitted into place – the Judaism and the legalism of which the Pastoral Epistles speak. That too finds its place. Sometimes Gnosticism and Judaism joined hands. We have already said that the Gnostics insisted that to climb the ladder to God a very special knowledge was necessary, and that some of them insisted that for the good life a strict self-discipline was essential. It was the claim of certain of the Jews that it was precisely the Jewish law and the Jewish food regulations which provided that special knowledge and necessary self-discipline, and so there were times when Judaism and Gnosticism went hand in hand.

It is quite clear that the heresy behind the Pastoral Epistles was Gnosticism. Some have used that fact to try to prove that Paul could have had nothing to do with the writing of these letters, because, they say, Gnosticism did not emerge until much later than Paul. It is quite true that the great formal systems of Gnosticism, connected with such names as Valentinus and Basilides, did not arise until the second century; but these great figures only systematized what was already there. The basic ideas of Gnosticism were there in the atmosphere which surrounded the early Church, even in the days of Paul. It is easy to see their attraction, and also to see that, if they had been allowed to flourish unchecked, they could have turned Christianity into a speculative philosophy and wrecked it. In facing Gnosticism, the Church was facing one of the gravest dangers which ever threatened the Christian faith.

The Language of the Pastorals

The most impressive argument against the direct Pauline origin of the Pastorals is a fact which is quite clear in the Greek but not so clear in any English translation. The total number of words in the Pastoral Epistles is 902, of which fifty-four are proper names; and of these 902 words, no fewer than 306 never occur in any other of Paul's letters. That is to say, more than a third of the words in the Pastoral Epistles are totally absent from Paul's other letters. In fact, 175 words in the Pastoral Epistles occur nowhere else in the New Testament at all, although it is only fair to say that there are fifty words in the Pastoral Epistles which occur in Paul's other letters and nowhere else in the New Testament.

Further, when the other letters of Paul and the Pastorals say the same thing, they say it in different ways, using different words and different turns of speech to express the same idea.

Again, many of Paul's favourite words are entirely absent from the Pastoral Epistles. The words for the *cross* (*stauros*) and *to crucify* (*stauroun*) occur twenty-seven times in Paul's other letters, and never in the Pastorals. *Eleutheria* and the kindred words which have to do with *freedom* occur twenty-nine times in Paul's other letters, and never in the Pastorals. *Huios, son,* and *huiothesia, adoption,* occur forty-six times in Paul's other letters, and never in the Pastorals.

What is more, Greek has many more of those little words called *particles* and *enclitics* than English has. Sometimes they indicate little more than a tone of voice; every Greek sentence is joined to its predecessor by one of them; and they are often virtually untranslatable. Of these particles and enclitics, there are 112 which Paul uses altogether 932 times in his other letters that never occur in the Pastorals.

There is clearly something which has to be explained here. The vocabulary and the style make it hard to believe that Paul wrote the Pastoral Epistles in the same sense as he wrote his other letters.

Paul's Activities in the Pastorals

But perhaps the most obvious difficulty of the Pastorals is that they show Paul engaged in activities for which there is no room in his life as we know it from the Acts of the Apostles. He has clearly conducted a mission in Crete (Titus 1:5). And he proposes to spend a winter in Nicopolis, which is in Epirus (Titus 3:12). In Paul's life as we know it, that particular mission and that particular winter just cannot be fitted in. But it may well be that just here we have stumbled on the solution to the problem.

Was Paul Released from his Roman Imprisonment?

Let us sum up. We have seen that the church organization of the Pastorals is more elaborate than in any other Pauline letter. We have seen that the stress on orthodoxy sounds like second- or third-generation Christianity, when the thrill of the new discovery is wearing off and the Church is on the way to becoming an institution. We have seen that Paul is depicted as carrying out a mission or missions which cannot be fitted into the scheme of his life as we have it in Acts. But Acts leaves the question of what happened to Paul in Rome unresolved. It ends by telling us that he lived for two whole years in a kind of semi-captivity, preaching the gospel without hindrance (Acts 28:30–1). But it does not tell us how that captivity ended, whether in Paul's release or his execution. It is true that the general assumption is that it ended in his condemnation and death; but there is a by no means negligible stream of tradition which tells that it ended in his release, his liberty for two or three further years, his reimprisonment and finally his execution about the year AD 67.

Let us look at this question, for it is of considerable interest. First, it is clear that, when Paul was in prison in Rome, he did not regard release as impossible; in fact, it looks as if he expected it. When he wrote to the Philippians, he said that he was sending Timothy to them, and goes on: 'And I trust in the Lord that I will also come soon' (Philippians 2:24). When he wrote to Philemon, sending back the runaway Onesimus, he says: 'One thing more – prepare a guest room for me, for I am hoping through your prayers to be restored to you' (Philemon 22). Clearly he was prepared for release, whether or not it ever came.

Second, let us remember a plan that was very dear to Paul's heart. Before he went to Jerusalem on that journey on which he was arrested, he wrote to the church at Rome, and in that letter he is planning a visit to Spain. 'When I go to Spain . . . I do hope to see you on my journey', he writes. 'I will set out by way of you', he writes, 'to Spain' (Romans 15:24, 15:28). Was that visit ever paid?

The letter known as 1 Clement, which was sent from the Roman church to the Christians at Corinth in about AD 90, said of Paul that he preached the gospel in the east and in the west, that he instructed the whole world (that is, the Roman Empire) in righteousness, and that he went to the extremity (*terma*, the terminus) of the west before his martyrdom. What did Clement mean by *the extremity of the west*? There are many who argue that he meant nothing more than Rome. Now, it is true that someone writing some distance away in the east in Asia Minor would probably think of Rome as *the extremity of the west. But Clement was writing from Rome*, and it is difficult to see that for anyone in Rome *the extremity of the west* could be anything other than Spain. It certainly seems that Clement believed that Paul reached Spain.

The greatest of all the early Church historians was Eusebius, who was writing early in the fourth century. In his account of Paul's life, he writes: 'Luke, who wrote the Acts of the Apostles, brought his history to a close at this point, after stating that Paul had spent two whole years at Rome as a prisoner at large, and preached the word of God without constraint. Thus, after he had made his defence, it is said that the Apostle was sent again on the ministry of preaching, and that on coming to the same city a second time he suffered martyrdom' (*Ecclesiastical History*, 2:22:2). Eusebius has nothing to say about Spain, but he did know the story that Paul had been released from his first Roman imprisonment.

The Muratorian Canon, that first list of New Testament books, describes Luke's scheme in writing Acts: 'Luke related to Theophilus events of which he was an eyewitness, as also, in a separate place, he evidently declares the martyrdom of Peter [he probably refers to Luke 22:31–2]; but omits the journey of Paul from Rome to Spain.'

In the fifth century, two of the great Christian fathers are definite about this journey. John Chrysostom in his sermon on 2 Timothy 4:20 says: 'Saint Paul after his residence in Rome departed to Spain.' Jerome in his *Catalogue of Writers* says that Paul 'was dismissed by Nero that he might preach Christ's gospel in the west'.

Beyond doubt, there was a stream of tradition which held that Paul journeyed to Spain.

This is a matter on which we will have to come to our own decision. The one thing which makes us doubt the historicity of that tradition is that in Spain itself there is not, and never was, any tradition that Paul had worked and preached there – no stories about him, no places connected with his name. It would be very strange if the memory of such a visit had become totally obliterated. It could well be that the whole story of Paul's release and journey to the west arose simply as a deduction from his expressed intention to visit Spain (Romans 15). Most New Testament scholars do not think that Paul was released from his imprisonment; the general consensus of opinion is that his only release was by death.

1 & 2 TIMOTHY AND TITUS

Paul and the Pastoral Epistles

What then shall we say of Paul's connection with these letters? If we can accept the tradition of his release, and of his return to preaching and teaching, and of his death as late as AD 67, we might well believe that as they stand they came from his hand. But, if we cannot believe that – and the evidence is on the whole against it – are we to say that they have no connection with Paul at all?

We must remember that the ancient world did not think of these things as we do. It would see nothing wrong in issuing a letter under the name of a great teacher if it was sure that the letter said the things which that teacher would say under the same circumstances. To the ancient world, it was natural and entirely appropriate that a disciple should write in his master's name. No one would have seen anything wrong in one of Paul's disciples meeting a new and threatening situation with a letter under Paul's name. To regard that as forgery is to misunderstand the thinking in the ancient world. Are we then to swing completely to the other extreme and say that one of Paul's disciples issued these letters in Paul's name years after he was dead, and at a time when the Church was much more highly organized than it ever was during his lifetime?

As we see it, the answer is no. It is incredible that any disciple would put into Paul's mouth a claim to be the chief of sinners (1 Timothy 1:15); the tendency would be to stress Paul's holiness, not to talk about his sin. It is incredible that anyone writing in the name of Paul would give Timothy the homely advice to drink a little wine for the sake of his health (1 Timothy 5:23). The whole of 2 Timothy 4 is so personal and so full of intimate, loving details that no one but Paul could have written it.

Where can we find the solution? It may well be that something like this happened. It is quite obvious that many letters of Paul were lost. Apart from his great public letters, he must have had a continuous private correspondence, and of that we possess only the little letter to Philemon. It may well be that in the later days there were some fragments of Paul's correspondence in the possession of some Christian teacher. This teacher saw the church of his day and his locality in Ephesus threatened on every side. It was threatened with heresy from outside and from within. It was threatened with a fall away from its own high standards of purity and truth. The quality of its members and the standard of its office-bearers were degenerating. He had in his possession little letters of Paul which said exactly the things that should be said; but, as they stood, they were too short and too fragmentary to publish. So he amplified them and made them supremely relevant to the contemporary situation and sent them out to the church.

In the Pastoral Epistles, we are still hearing the voice of Paul, and often hearing it speak with a unique personal intimacy; but we think that the form of the letters is the work of a Christian teacher who summoned the help of Paul when the church of the day needed the guidance which only he could give.

15

Philemon

More than a Slave

The Unique Letter

In one respect, this little letter to Philemon is unique. It is the only *private letter* of Paul which we possess. Doubtless Paul must have written many private letters; but, of them all, only Philemon has survived. Quite apart from the grace and the charm which pervade it, this fact gives it a special significance.

Onesimus, the Runaway Slave

There are two possible reconstructions of what happened. One is quite straightforward; the other, connected with the name of the American scholar E. J. Goodspeed, is rather more complicated and certainly more dramatic. Let us take the simple view first.

Onesimus was a runaway slave and very probably a thief into the bargain. 'If he has wronged you in any way', Paul writes, 'or owes you anything, charge that to my account' (verses 18–19). Somehow the runaway had found his way to Rome, to lose himself in the crowded and busy streets of that great city; somehow he had come into contact with Paul, and somehow he had become a Christian, the child to whom Paul had become a father during his imprisonment (verse 10).

Then something happened. It was obviously impossible for Paul to go on harbouring a runaway slave, and something brought the problem to a head. Perhaps it was the coming of Epaphras. It may be that Epaphras recognized Onesimus as a slave he had seen at Colosse, and at that point the whole wretched story came out; or it may be that, with the coming of Epaphras, Onesimus' conscience moved him to make a clean breast of all his discreditable past.

Paul Sends Onesimus Back

In the time that he had been with him, Onesimus had made himself very nearly indispensable to Paul; and Paul would have liked to keep him beside him. 'I wanted to keep him with me', he writes (verse 13). But he will do nothing without the consent of Philemon, Onesimus' master (verse 14). So he sends Onesimus back. No one knew better than Paul how great a risk he was taking. A slave was not a person but a living tool. A master had absolute power over his slaves. 'He can box their ears or condemn them to hard labour – making them, for instance, work in chains upon his lands in the country, or in a sort of prison-factory. Or, he may punish them with blows of the rod, the lash or the knot; he can brand them upon the forehead, if they are thieves or runaways, or, in the end, if they prove irreclaimable, he can crucify them.' The Roman lawyer and satirist Juvenal draws the picture of the mistress who will beat her maid servant at her whim and of the master who 'delights in the sound of a cruel flogging, deeming it sweeter than any siren's song', who is never happy 'until he has summoned a torturer and he can brand someone with a hot iron for stealing a couple of towels', 'who revels in clanking chains'. Slaves were continually at the mercy of the whims of a master or a mistress.

What made it worse was that the slaves were deliberately repressed. There were in the Roman Empire 60,000,000 of them, and the danger of revolt was constantly to be guarded against. A rebellious slave was promptly eliminated. And, if a slave ran away, at best he would be branded with a red-hot iron on the forehead, with the letter F – standing for *fugitivus, runaway* – and at the worst he would be put to death by crucifixion. Paul was well aware of all this and that slavery was so ingrained into the ancient world that even to send Onesimus back to the Christian Philemon was a considerable risk.

Paul's Appeal

So Paul gave Onesimus this letter. He makes a pun on Onesimus' name. *Onesimus* in Greek literally means *profitable*. Once Onesimus was a useless fellow, but now he is useful (verse 11). Now, as we might say, he is not only Onesimus by name, he is also Onesimus by nature. Maybe Philemon lost him for a time in order to have him forever (verse 15). He must take him back, not as a slave but as a Christian brother (verse 16). He is now Paul's son in the faith, and Philemon must receive him as he would receive Paul himself.

Emancipation

Such, then, was Paul's appeal. Many people have wondered why Paul says nothing in this letter about the whole matter of slavery. He does not condemn it; he does not even tell Philemon to set Onesimus free; it is still as a slave that he would have him taken back. There are those who have criticized Paul for not seizing the opportunity to condemn the slavery on which the ancient world was built. The New Testament scholar J. B. Lightfoot says: 'The word *emancipation* seems to tremble on his lips, but he never utters it.' But there are reasons for his silence.

Slavery was an integral part of the ancient world; the whole of society was built on it. Aristotle held that it was in the nature of things that certain men should be slaves, hewers of wood and drawers of water, to serve the higher classes. It may well be that Paul accepted the institution of slavery because it was almost impossible to imagine society without it. Further, if Christianity had, in fact, given the slaves any encouragement to revolt or to leave their masters, nothing but tragedy could have followed. Any such revolt would have been savagely crushed; slaves who took their freedom would have been mercilessly punished; and Christianity would itself have been branded as revolutionary and subversive. Given the Christian faith, liberation was bound to come – but the time was not ripe; and to have encouraged slaves to hope for it, and to seize it, would have done infinitely more harm than good. There are some things which cannot be achieved suddenly, and for which the world must wait, until the leaven works.

The New Relationship

What Christianity did was to introduce a new relationship between individuals in which all external differences were abolished. Christians are one body whether Jews or Gentiles, slaves or free (1 Corinthians 12:13). In Christ there is neither Jew nor Greek, slave or free, male or female (Galatians 3:28). In Christ there is neither Greek nor Jew, circumcised or uncircumcised, barbarian, Scythian, slave or free (Colossians 3:11). It was as a slave that Onesimus ran away, and it was as a slave that he was coming back; but now he was not only a slave, he was a beloved brother in the Lord. When a relationship like that enters into life, social grades and classes cease to matter. The very names, master and slave, become irrelevant. If masters treat slaves as Christ would have treated them, and if slaves serve the masters as they would serve Christ, then the terms *master* and *slave* do not matter; their relationship does not depend on any human classification, for they are both in Christ.

In the early days, Christianity did not attack slavery; to have done so would have been disastrous. But it introduced a new relationship in which the human divisions in society ceased to matter. It is to be noted that this new relationship never gave slaves the right to take advantage of it; rather, it made them better slaves and more efficient servants, for now they had to do things in such a way that they could offer them to Christ. Nor did it mean that the master must be soft and easy-going, willing to accept bad work and inferior service; but it did mean that he no longer treated any servant as a thing, but as a person and a brother or sister in Christ.

There are two passages in which Paul sets out the duties of slaves and masters – Ephesians 6:5–9 and Colossians 3:22–4:1. Both were written when Paul was in prison in Rome, and most likely when Onesimus was with him; and it is difficult not to think that they owe much to long talks that Paul had with the runaway slave who had become a Christian.

On this view, Philemon is a private letter, sent by Paul to Philemon, when he sent back his runaway slave; and it was written to urge Philemon to receive back Onesimus, not as a master who was not a Christian would, but as a Christian receives a brother.

Archippus

Let us now turn to the other view of this letter.

We may begin with a consideration of the place of Archippus. He appears in both Colossians and Philemon. In Philemon, greetings are sent to Archippus, *our fellow soldier* (verse 2); and such a description might well mean that Archippus is the minister of the Christian community in question. He is also mentioned in Colossians 4:17: 'And say to Archippus, "See that you complete the task that you have received in the Lord."' Now, that instruction comes after a whole series of very definite references, not to Colosse, but to *Laodicaea* (Colossians 4:13, 4:15, 4:16). Might not the fact that he appears among the messages sent to Laodicaea imply that Archippus must be at Laodicaea too? Why in any event should he get this personal message? If he was at Colosse, he would hear the letter read, as everyone else would. Why has this verbal order to be sent to him? It is surely possible that the answer is that he is not in Colosse at all, but in Laodicaea.

If that is so, it means that Philemon's house is in *Laodicaea* and that Onesimus was a runaway *Laodicaean* slave. This must mean that the letter to Philemon was, in fact, written to Laodicaea. And, if so, the missing letter to Laodicaea, mentioned in Colossians 4:16, is none other than the letter to Philemon. This indeed solves problems.

Let us remember that in ancient society, with its view of slavery, Paul took a considerable risk in sending Onesimus back at all. So, it can be argued that Philemon is not really only a personal letter. It is indeed written to Philemon *and to the church in his house*. And, further, it has also to be read at Colosse. What, then, is Paul doing? Knowing the risk that he takes in sending Onesimus back, he is mobilizing church opinion both in Laodicaea and in Colosse in his favour. The decision about Onesimus is not to be left to Philemon; it is to be the decision of the whole Christian community. It so happens that there is one little, but important, linguistic point, which is very much in favour of this view. In verse 12, the Revised Standard Version makes Paul write that he has *sent back* Onesimus to Philemon. The verb is *anapempein*; this is the regular verb – it is more common in this sense than in any other – for officially referring a case to someone for decision. And verse 12 should most probably be translated: 'I am referring his case to you' – that is, not only to Philemon but also to the church in his house.

There is a lot to be said for this view. There is only one difficulty. In Colossians 4:9, Onesimus is referred to as *one of you*, which certainly looks as if he is a Colossian. But E. J. Goodspeed, who states this view with such scholarship and persuasiveness, argues that Hierapolis, Laodicaea and Colosse were so close together, and so much a single church, that they could well be regarded as one community, and that, therefore, *one of you* need not mean that Onesimus came from Colosse, but simply that he came from that closely connected group. If we are prepared to accept this, the last obstacle to the theory is removed.

The Continuation of the Story

Goodspeed does not stop there. He goes on to reconstruct the history of Onesimus in a most moving way.

In verses 13–14, Paul makes it quite clear that he would very much have liked to keep Onesimus with him. 'I wanted to keep him with me, so that he might be of service to me in your place during my imprisonment for the gospel; but I preferred to do nothing without your consent, in order that your good deed might be voluntary and not something forced.' He reminds Philemon that he owes him his very soul (verse 19). He says, with charming wit: 'Let me have this benefit from you in the Lord!' (verse 20). He says: 'Confident of your obedience, I am writing to you, knowing that you will do even more than I say' (verse 21). Is it possible that Philemon could have resisted this appeal? Spoken to in such a way, could he do anything other than send Onesimus back to Paul with his blessing? Goodspeed regards it as certain that Paul got Onesimus back and that he became Paul's helper in the work of the gospel.

The Bishop of Ephesus

Let us move on about fifty years. Ignatius, one of the great Christian martyrs, is being taken to execution from Antioch to Rome. As he goes, he writes letters – which still survive – to the churches of Asia Minor. He stops at Smyrna and writes to the church at Ephesus, and in the first chapter of that letter he has much to say about their wonderful bishop. And what is the bishop's name? It is *Onesimus*; and Ignatius makes exactly the same pun as Paul made – he is Onesimus by name and Onesimus by nature, the one who is profitable to Christ. It may well be that, with the passing years, the runaway slave had become the great Bishop of Ephesus.

What Christ did for Me

If all this is true, we have still another explanation. Why did this little slip of a letter, this single papyrus sheet, survive; and how did it ever get itself into the collection of Pauline letters? It deals with no great doctrine; it attacks no great heresy; it is the only one of the letters universally accepted as having been written by Paul that is addressed to an individual. It is practically certain that the first collection of Paul's letters was made at *Ephesus*, about the turn of the century. It was just then that Onesimus was Bishop of Ephesus; and it may well be that it was he who insisted that this letter be included in the collection, short and personal as it was, in order that all might know what the grace of God had done for him. Through it, the bishop tells the world that once he was a runaway slave and that he owed his life to Paul and to Jesus Christ.

Did Onesimus come back to Paul with Philemon's blessing? Did the young man who had been the runaway slave become the great Bishop of Ephesus? Did he insist that this little letter be included in the Pauline collection to tell what Christ, through Paul, had done for him? We can never tell for certain; but it is a lovely story of God's grace in Christ – and we hope that it is true!

16

Hebrews

Access to God

God Fulfils Himself in Many Ways

Religion has never been the same thing to everyone. 'God', as Tennyson said in *Mort d'Arthur*, 'fulfils himself in many ways.' The Irish writer George Russell said: 'There are as many ways of climbing to the stars as there are people to climb.' There is a saying which tells us very truly and very beautifully that 'God has his own secret stairway into every heart.' Broadly speaking, there have been four great conceptions of religion.

(1) To some, it is *inward fellowship with God*. It is a union with Christ so close and so intimate that Christians can be said to live in Christ and Christ to live in them. That was Paul's conception of religion. To him, it was something which mystically united him with God.

(2) To some, religion is what gives us *a standard for life and a power to reach that standard*. On the whole, that is what religion was to James and to Peter. It was something which showed them what life ought to be and which enabled them to attain it.

(3) To some, religion is *the highest satisfaction of their minds*. Their minds seek and seek until they find that they can rest in God. It was Plato who said that 'the unexamined life is the life not worth living'. There are some people who have to understand things in order to make sense of life. On

the whole, that is what religion was to John. The first chapter of his gospel is one of the greatest attempts in the world to state religion in a way that really satisfies the mind.

(4) To some, religion is *access to God.* It is that which removes the barriers and opens the door to his living presence. That is what religion was to the writer of the Letter to the Hebrews. His mind was dominated with that idea. He found in Christ the one person who could take him into the very presence of God. His whole idea of religion is summed up in the great passage in Hebrews 10:19–22:

> Therefore, my friends, since we have confidence to enter the sanctuary by the blood of Jesus, by the new and living way that he opened for us through the curtain (that is, through his flesh) . . . let us approach with a true heart in full assurance of faith.

If the writer to the Hebrews had one text, it was: '*Let us draw near.*'

The Double Background

The writer to the Hebrews had a double background, and this idea fitted into both sides. He had a *Greek background.* Ever since the time of Plato, 500 years before, the Greeks had been occupied in their thinking by the contrast between the real and the unreal, the seen and the unseen, things that exist in time and things that are eternal. It was the Greek idea that somewhere there was a real world of which this was only a shadowy and imperfect copy. Plato had the idea that somewhere there was a world of perfect *forms* or *ideas* or *patterns,* of which everything in this world was an imperfect copy. To take a simple instance, somewhere there was laid up the pattern of a perfect chair of which all the chairs in this world were inadequate copies. Plato said: 'The Creator of the world had designed and carried out his work according to an unchangeable and eternal pattern of which the world is only a copy.' The Jewish thinker Philo, who took his ideas from Plato, said: 'God knew from the beginning that a fair copy could never come into being apart from a fair pattern; and that none of the objects perceivable by sense could be flawless which was not modelled after an archetype and spiritual idea, and thus, when he prepared to create this visible world, he shaped beforehand the ideal world in order to constitute the corporeal after the incorporeal and godlike pattern.' When the Roman statesman Cicero was talking of the laws that people know and use on earth, he said: 'We have no real and life-like likeness of real law and genuine justice; all we enjoy is a shadow and a sketch.'

The thinkers of the ancient world all had this idea that somewhere there is a real world of which this one is only a kind of imperfect copy. Here, we can only guess and feel our way; here, we can work only with copies and imperfect things. But, in the unseen world, there are the real and perfect things. When the great churchman John Henry Newman died, they erected a statue to him, and on the pedestal of it are the Latin words: *Ab umbris et imaginibus ad veritatem*, 'Away from the shadows and the semblances to the truth.' If that is so, clearly the great task of this life is to get away from the shadows and the imperfections and to reach *reality*. This is exactly what the writer to the Hebrews claims that Jesus Christ can enable us to do. To the Greeks, the writer to the Hebrews said: 'All your lives, you have been trying to get from the shadows to the truth. That is just what Jesus Christ can enable you to do.'

The Jewish Background

But the writer to the Hebrews also had a *Jewish background*. To the Jews, it was always dangerous to come too near to

God. 'No one', said God to Moses, 'shall see me and live' (Exodus 33:20). It was Jacob's astonished exclamation at Peniel: 'I have seen God face to face, and yet my life is preserved' (Genesis 32:30). When Manoah realized who his visitor had been, he said in terror to his wife: 'We shall surely die, for we have seen God' (Judges 13:23). The great day of Jewish worship was the Day of Atonement. That was the one day of the whole year when the high priest entered the Holy of Holies where the very presence of God was held to dwell. No one ever entered in except the high priest, and he only on that day. When he did, the law laid it down that he must not linger in the Holy Place for long 'lest he put Israel in terror'. It was dangerous to enter the presence of God; and, if anyone stayed there too long, that person might be struck dead.

In view of this, the idea of a *covenant* entered into Jewish thought. God, in his grace and in a way that was quite unmerited, approached the nation of Israel and offered them a special relationship with himself. But this unique access to God was conditional on the observance by the people of the law that he gave to them. We can see this relationship being entered into and this law being accepted in the dramatic scene in Exodus 24:3–8.

So, Israel had access to God, *but only if the people kept the law.* To break the law was sin, and sin put up a barrier which stopped the way to God. It was to take away that barrier that the system of the Levitical priesthood and sacrifices was constructed. The law was given; the people sinned; the barrier was up; the sacrifice was made; and the sacrifice was designed to open the way to God that had been closed. But the experience of life was that this was precisely what sacrifice could not do. It was proof of the ineffectiveness of the whole system that sacrifice had to go on and on and on. It was a losing and ineffective battle to remove the barrier that sin had erected between men and women and God.

The Perfect Priest and the Perfect Sacrifice

What was needed was a *perfect priest* and a *perfect sacrifice*, someone who could bring to God a sacrifice that once and for all opened the way of access to him. That, said the writer to the Hebrews, is exactly what Christ did. He is the perfect priest because he is both perfectly human and perfectly God. In his humanity, he can take us to God; and in his Godhead, he can take God to us. He has no sin. The perfect sacrifice he brings is the sacrifice of himself, a sacrifice so perfect that it never needs to be made again. To the Jews, the writer to the Hebrews said: 'All your lives, you have been looking for the perfect priest who can bring the perfect sacrifice and give you access to God. You have him in Jesus Christ and in him alone.'

To the Greeks, the writer to the Hebrews said: 'You are looking for the way from the shadows to reality; you will find it in Jesus Christ.' To the Jews, the writer to the Hebrews said: 'You are looking for that perfect sacrifice which will open the way to God which your sins have closed; you will find it in Jesus Christ.' Jesus was the one person who gave access to reality and access to God. That is the key thought of this letter.

The Riddle of the New Testament

So much is clear; but, when we turn to the other questions of introduction, Hebrews is wrapped in mystery. The New Testament scholar E. F. Scott wrote: 'The Epistle to the Hebrews is in many respects the riddle of the New Testament.' When it was written, to whom it was written, and who wrote it are questions at which we can only guess. The very history of the letter shows how its mystery is to be treated with a certain reserve and suspicion. It was a long time before it became an unquestioned New Testament book. The first list of New Testament books, the Muratorian Canon, compiled about AD 170, does not mention it at all. The great Alexandrian scholars of the second and third centuries, Clement and Origen, knew it and loved it but agreed that its place as Scripture was disputed. Of the great African fathers of the same period, Cyprian never mentions it and Tertullian knows that its place was disputed. Eusebius, the early church historian, says that it ranked among the disputed books. It was not until the time of Athanasius, in the middle of the fourth century, that Hebrews was definitely accepted as a New Testament book, and even the founder of the Reformation, Martin Luther, was not too sure about it. It is strange to think how long this great book had to wait for full recognition.

When was it Written?

The only information we have comes from the letter itself. Clearly, it is written for what we might call second-generation Christians (2:3). The story was transmitted to its recipients by those who had heard the Lord. The members of the community to whom it was written were not new to the Christian faith; they ought to have been mature (5:12). They must have had a long history, for they are called to look back on the former days (10:32). They had a great history behind them and heroic martyr figures on which they ought to look back for inspiration (13:7).

The thing that will help us most in dating the letter is its references to persecution. It is clear that at one time their leaders had died for their faith (13:7). It is clear that they themselves had not yet suffered persecution, for they had not yet resisted to the point of shedding their blood (12:4). It is also clear that they have had ill-treatment to suffer, for they have had to undergo the looting of their goods (10:32–4). And it is clear from the outlook of the letter that there is a risk of persecution about to come. From all that, it is safe to say that this letter must have been written between two persecutions, in days when Christians were not actually persecuted but were nonetheless unpopular. Now, the first persecution was in the time of Nero in the year AD 64; and the next was in the time of Domitian about AD 85. Somewhere between these dates, this letter was written – most likely nearer to Domitian's rule. If we take the date as AD 80, we shall not be far wrong.

To Whom was it Written?

Once again, we have to be dependent on such hints as we get from the letter itself. One thing is certain: it cannot have been written to any of the great churches, or the name of the place could not have so completely vanished. Let us set down what we know. The letter was written to a long-established church (5:12). It was written to a church which had at some time in the past suffered persecution (10:32–4). It was written to a church which had had great days and great teachers and leaders (13:7). It was written to a church which had not been directly founded by the apostles (2:3). It was written to a church which had been marked by generosity and liberality (6:10).

We do have one direct hint. Among the closing greetings, we find the sentence, as the Revised Standard Version translates it: 'Those who come from Italy send you greetings' (13:24). Taken by itself, that phrase could mean either that the letter was written *from* Italy or that it was written *to* Italy; but the greater likelihood is that it was written *to* Italy. Suppose I am in Glasgow and am writing to some place abroad. I would not be likely to say: 'All the people from Glasgow greet you.' I would be much more likely to say:

'All the people in Glasgow greet you.' But suppose I am somewhere abroad where there is a little colony of Glaswegians, I might well say: 'All the people from Glasgow send you their greetings.' So, we may say that the letter was written *to Italy*; and, if it was written to Italy, it was almost certainly written to Rome.

But, quite certainly, it was not written to the church at Rome as a whole. If it had been, it would not have lost its title. Furthermore, it gives the unmistakable impression that it was written to a small body of like-minded individuals. Moreover, it was obviously written to a scholarly group. From 5:12, we can see that they had been under instruction for some time and were preparing themselves to become teachers of the Christian faith. Still further, Hebrews demands such a knowledge of the Old Testament that it must always have been a book written by a scholar for scholars.

When we sum it all up, we can say that Hebrews is a letter written by a great teacher to a little group or college of Christians in Rome. He was their teacher; at the time he was separated from them and was afraid that they were drifting away from the faith; and so he wrote this letter to them. It is not so much a letter as a talk. It does not begin like Paul's letters do, although it ends with greetings as a letter does. The writer himself calls it 'a word of exhortation' (13:22).

By Whom was it Written?

Perhaps the most insoluble problem of all is the problem of its authorship. It was precisely that uncertainty which kept it so long on the fringes of the New Testament. The title in the earliest days was simply: 'To the Hebrews'. No author's name was given; no one connected it directly with the name of Paul. Clement of Alexandria used to think that Paul might have written it in Hebrew and that Luke translated it, for the style is quite different from that of Paul. Origen made a famous remark: 'who wrote the Letter to the Hebrews only God knows for certain'. Tertullian thought that Barnabas wrote it. Jerome said the Latin Church did not receive it as Paul's and, speaking of the author, said: 'the writer to the Hebrews whoever he was'. St Augustine felt the same way about it. Luther declared that Paul could never have written it because the thought was not his. The reformer John Calvin said that he could not bring himself to think that this letter was a letter of Paul.

At no time in the history of the Church did anyone ever really think that Paul wrote Hebrews. How then did it get attached to his name? It happened very simply. When the New Testament came into its final form, there was of course argument about which books were to be included and which were not. To settle it, one test was used. Was a book the work of an apostle or at least the work of one who had been in direct contact with the apostles? By this time, Hebrews was known and loved throughout the Church. Most people felt, like Origen, that God alone knew who wrote it; but they wanted it. They felt it *must* go into the New Testament, and the only way to ensure that this happened was to include it with the thirteen letters of Paul. Hebrews won its way into the New Testament on the grounds of its own greatness; but, to get in, it had to be included with the letters of Paul and come under his name. People knew quite well that it was not Paul's, but they included it among his letters because no one knew who wrote it and yet it had to go in.

The Author of Hebrews

Can we guess who the author was? Many candidates have been put forward. We can only glance at three of the many suggestions.

(1) Tertullian thought that Barnabas wrote it. Barnabas was a native of Cyprus; the people of Cyprus were famous for the excellence of the Greek they spoke; and Hebrews is written in the best Greek in the New Testament. Barnabas was a Levite (Acts 4:36) and, of all people in the New Testament, he would have had the closest knowledge of the priestly and sacrificial system on which the whole thought of the letter is based. He is called a son of *encouragement*; the Greek word is *paraklēsis*; and Hebrews calls itself a word of *paraklēsis* (13:22). He was one of the few people acceptable to both Jews and Greeks and at home in both worlds of thought. It might be that Barnabas wrote this letter; but, if so, it is strange that his name should vanish in connection with it.

(2) Luther was sure that Apollos was the author. Apollos, according to the New Testament mention of him, was a Jew, born at Alexandria, an eloquent man and well versed in the Scriptures (Acts 18:24ff.; 1 Corinthians 1:12, 3:4). The person who wrote this letter knew the Scriptures, was eloquent, and thought and argued in the way that a cultured Alexandrian would. The person who wrote Hebrews was certainly someone like Apollos in thought and in background.

(3) The most romantic of all conjectures is that of Adolf von Harnack, the great German scholar. He thought that maybe Aquila and Priscilla wrote it between them. Aquila was a teacher (Acts 18:26). Their house in Rome was a church in itself (Romans 16:5). Harnack thought that that is why the letter begins with no greetings and why the writer's name has vanished – because the main author of Hebrews was a woman, and a woman was not allowed to teach.

But, when we come to the end of conjecture, we are compelled to say, as Origen said 1,800 years ago, that only God knows who wrote Hebrews. To us, the author must remain a voice and nothing more; but we can be thankful to God for the work of this great nameless individual who wrote with incomparable skill and beauty about the Jesus who is the way to reality and the way to God.

17

James

An Early Christian Sermon

James is one of the books which had a very hard fight to get into the New Testament. Even when it did come to be regarded as Scripture, it was spoken of with a certain reserve and suspicion, and even as late as the sixteenth century the reformer Martin Luther would gladly have banished it from the New Testament altogether.

The Doubts of the Early Christian Fathers

In the Latin-speaking part of the Church, it is not until the middle of the fourth century that James emerges in the writings of the fathers. The first list of New Testament books ever to be compiled is the Muratorian Canon, which dates to about AD 170 – and James is absent from it. Tertullian, writing in the middle of the third century, is an immense quoter of Scripture; he has 7,258 quotations from the New Testament, but never one from James. The first appearance of James in Latin is in a Latin manuscript called the Codex Corbeiensis, which dates to about AD 350. This manuscript attributes the authorship of the book to James the son of Zebedee, and includes it, not with the universally acknowledged New Testament books, but with a collection of religious tracts written by the early fathers. James has now emerged, but it is accepted with a certain reservation. The first Latin writer to quote James verbatim is Hilary of Poitiers in a work *On the Trinity*, written about AD 357.

If, then, James was so late in emerging in the Latin church, and if, when it did emerge, it was still regarded with some uncertainty, how did it become integrated into the New Testament? The moving influence was that of the biblical scholar Jerome, for he unhesitatingly included James in his Latin version of the New Testament, the Vulgate, completed early in the fifth century. But even then there is an accent of doubt. In his book *On Famous Men*, Jerome writes: 'James, who is called the brother of the Lord . . . wrote only one epistle, which is one of the seven catholic epistles, and which, some people say, was issued by someone else under James' name.' Jerome fully accepted the letter as Scripture, but he felt that there was some doubt as to who the writer was. The doubt was finally set at rest by the fact that Augustine fully accepted James and was not in doubt that the James in question was the brother of our Lord.

James was late in emerging in the Latin church; for a long time there was a kind of question mark against it, but in the end, and only after a struggle, Jerome's inclusion of it in the Vulgate and Augustine's full acceptance of it brought it full recognition.

The Syrian Church

One would have thought that the Syrian church would have been the first to accept James, if it was really written in Palestine and was really the work of the brother of our Lord; but in the Syrian church there was the same wavering and swinging of opinion. The official New Testament of the Syrian church is called the Peshitto. This was to the Syrian church what the Vulgate was to the Latin church. It was made by Rabbula, the Bishop of Edessa, about AD 412, and in it for the first time James was translated into Syriac. Up to that time there was no Syriac version of the book, and up to AD 451 there is no trace of James in Syriac religious literature. After that, James was widely enough accepted, but as late as AD 545 Paul of Nisibis was still questioning its right to be in the New Testament. It was not, in fact, until mid-way through the eighth century that the great authority of the Greek theologian John of Damascus did for James in the Syrian church what Augustine had done for it in the Latin.

The Greek Church

Although James emerged sooner in the Greek-speaking church than it did in the Latin and Syrian, it was nonetheless late in making a definite appearance. The first writer to quote it by name is Origen, head of the school of Alexandria. Writing almost mid-way through the third century, he says: 'If faith is called faith, but exists apart from works, such a faith is dead, as we read in the letter which is currently reported to be by James.' It is true that in other works he quotes it as being without doubt by James and shows that he believes James to be the brother of our Lord, but once again there is the accent of doubt. Eusebius, the great scholar of Caesarea, investigated the position of the various books in the New Testament or on its fringe mid-way through the fourth century. He classes James among the books which are 'disputed', and he writes of it: 'The first of the epistles called Catholic is said to be his [James']; but it must be noted that some regard it as spurious; and it is certainly true that very few of the ancient writers mention it.' Here again, there is evidence of doubt. Eusebius himself accepted James, but he was well aware that there were those who did not. The turning point in the Greek-speaking church came in AD 367. In that year, Athanasius, the theologian and Bishop of Alexandria, issued his famous Easter Letter in Egypt. Its purpose was to inform his people what books were Scripture and what were not, because apparently their reading had become too wide, or, at least, too many books were being regarded as holy writ. In that Letter, James was included without qualification, and its position from that point onwards was safe.

So, in the early Church, no one really questioned the value of James, but in every branch of it the letter was late in emerging and had to go through a period when its right to be considered a New Testament book was under dispute.

In fact, the history of James is still to be seen in its position in the Roman Catholic Church. In 1546, the Council of Trent once and for all laid down the Roman Catholic Bible. A list of books was given to which none could be added and from which none could be subtracted, and which had to be read in the Vulgate version and in no other. The books were divided into two classes: those which were *proto-canonical*, that is to say, those which had been unquestioningly accepted from the beginning; and those which were *deutero-canonical*, that is to say, those which only gradually won their way into the New Testament. Although the Roman Catholic Church never had any doubts about James, it is nonetheless in the second class that it is included.

Luther and James

In our own day, it is true to say that James, at least for most people, does not occupy a position in the forefront of the New Testament. Few would mention it in the same breath as John or Romans, or Luke or Galatians. There is still for many a kind of reservation about it. Why should that be? It cannot have to do with the doubt about James in the early Church, for the history of the New Testament books in those distant days is not known to many people in the modern Church. The reason lies in this. In the Roman Catholic Church, the position of James was finally settled by the Edict of the Council of Trent; but in the Protestant Church its history continued to be troubled, and indeed became even more troubled, because Luther attacked it and would have removed it from the New Testament altogether. In his printing of the German New Testament, Luther had a contents page with the books set out and numbered. At the end of the list, there was a little group, separate from the others and with no numbers assigned to them. That group consisted of James, Jude, Hebrews and Revelation. These were books which Luther held to be secondary.

Luther was especially severe on James – and the adverse judgment of a great scholar on any book can be a millstone round its neck forever. It is in the concluding paragraph of his *Preface to the New Testament* that Luther's famous verdict on James can be found:

> In sum: the gospel and the first epistle of St John, St Paul's epistles, especially those to the Romans, Galatians and Ephesians; and St Peter's first epistle, are the books which show Christ to you. They teach everything you need to know for your salvation, even if you were never to see or hear any other book or hear any other teaching. In comparison with these, the epistle of James is an *epistle full of straw*, because it contains nothing evangelical. But more about this in other prefaces.

As he promised, Luther developed this verdict in the *Preface to the Epistles of St James and St Jude*. He begins: 'I think highly of the epistle of James, and regard it as valuable although it was rejected in early days. It does not expound human doctrines, but lays much emphasis on God's law. Yet to give my own opinion, without prejudice to that of anyone else, I do not hold it to be of apostolic authorship.' He then goes on to give his reasons for this rejection.

First, in direct opposition to Paul, and the rest of the Bible, it ascribes justification to works, quoting Abraham wrongly as one who was justified by his works. This in itself proves that the epistle cannot be of apostolic origin.

Second, not once does it give to Christians any instruction or reminder of the passion, resurrection or Spirit of Christ. It mentions Christ only twice. Then Luther goes on to state his own principle for testing any book: 'The true touchstone for testing any book is to discover whether it emphasises the prominence of Christ or not . . . What does not teach Christ is not apostolic, not even if taught by Peter or Paul. On the other hand, what does preach Christ is apostolic, even if Judas, Annas, Pilate, or Herod does it.' On that test, James fails. So Luther goes on: 'The epistle of James however only drives you to the law and its works. He mixes one thing to another to such an extent that I suspect some good and pious man assembled a few things said by disciples of the apostles, and put them down in black and white; or perhaps the epistle was written by someone else who made notes of a sermon of his. He calls the law a law of freedom (James 1:25, 2:12), although St Paul calls it a law of slavery, wrath, death, and sin' (Galatians 3:23–4; Romans 4:15, 7:10–11).

So Luther comes to his conclusion: 'In sum: he wishes to guard against those who depended on faith without going on to works, but he had neither the spirit, nor the thought, nor the eloquence equal to the task. He does violence to Scripture and so contradicts Paul and all Scripture. He tries to accomplish by emphasizing law what the apostles bring about by attracting man to love. I therefore refuse him a place among the writers of the true canon of my Bible; but I would not prevent anyone else placing him or raising him where he likes, for the epistle contains many excellent passages. One man does not count as a man even in the eyes of the world; how then shall this single and isolated writer count against Paul and all the rest of the Bible?'

Luther does not spare James, and it may be that once we have studied the book we may think that for once he allowed personal prejudice to injure sound judgment.

Such, then, is the troubled history of James. Now we must try to answer the questions it poses regarding authorship and date.

The Identity of James

The author of this letter gives us practically no information about himself. He calls himself simply: 'James, a servant of God and of the Lord Jesus Christ' (James 1:1). So who is he? In the New Testament, there are apparently at least five people who bear that name.

(1) There is the James who was the father of the member of the Twelve called Judas, not Iscariot (Luke 6:16). He is no more than a name and cannot have had any connection with this letter.

(2) There is James, the son of Alphaeus, who was a member of the Twelve (Matthew 10:3; Mark 3:18; Luke 6:15; Acts 1:13). A comparison of Matthew 9:9 with Mark 2:14 makes it certain that Matthew and Levi were one and the same person. Levi was also a son of Alphaeus, and therefore Matthew and this James must have been brothers. But of James, the son of Alphaeus, nothing else is known; and he also can have had no connection with this letter.

(3) There is the James who is called James the younger and is mentioned in Mark 15:40 (cf. Matthew 27:56; John 19:25). Again nothing is known of him, and he cannot have had any connection with this letter.

(4) There is James, the brother of John, and the son of Zebedee, a member of the Twelve (Matthew 10:2; Mark 3:17; Luke 6:14; Acts 1:13). In the gospel story, James never appears independently of his brother John (Matthew 4:21, 17:1; Mark 1:19, 1:29, 5:37, 9:2, 10:35, 10:41, 13:3, 14:33; Luke 5:10, 8:51, 9:28, 9:54). He was the first of the apostolic band to be martyred, for he was beheaded on the orders of Herod Agrippa I in the year AD 44. He has been connected with the letter. The fourth-century Latin Codex Corbeiensis, at the end of the epistle, has a note quite definitely attributing it to James the son of Zebedee. The only place where this view on the authorship was taken seriously was in the Spanish church, in which, down to the end of the seventeenth century, he was often held to be the author. This was due to the fact that St James of Compostella, the patron saint of Spain, is identified with James the son of Zebedee; and it was natural that the Spanish church should be predisposed to wish that their country's patron saint should be the author of a New Testament letter. But the martyrdom of James came too early for him to have written the letter, and in any case there is nothing beyond the Codex Corbeiensis to connect him with it.

(5) Finally, there is James, who is called the brother of Jesus. Although the first definite connection of him with this letter does not emerge until Origen in the first half of the third century, it is to him that it has always been traditionally attributed. The Roman Catholic Church agrees with this view, for in 1546 the Council of Trent laid it down that James is canonical and is written by an apostle.

Let us then collect the evidence about this James. From the New Testament, we learn that he was one of the brothers of Jesus (Mark 6:3; Matthew 13:55). We shall later discuss in what sense the word 'brother' is to be taken. During Jesus' ministry, it is clear that his family did not understand or sympathize with him and would have wished to restrain him (Matthew 12:46–50; Mark 3:21, 3:31–5; John 7:3–9). John says bluntly: 'For not even his brothers believed in him' (John 7:5). So, during Jesus' earthly ministry, James was numbered among his opponents.

With the Acts of the Apostles, there comes a sudden and unexplained change. When Acts opens, Jesus' mother and his brothers are there with the little group of Christians (Acts 1:14). From there onwards, it becomes clear that James has become the leader of the Jerusalem church, although how that came about is never explained. It is to James that Peter sends the news of his escape from prison (Acts 12:17). James presides over the Council of Jerusalem, which agreed to the entry of the Gentiles into the Christian Church (Acts 15). It is James and Peter whom Paul meets when he first goes to Jerusalem, and it is with Peter, James and John, the pillars of the Church, that he discusses and settles his sphere of work (Galatians 1:19, 2:9). It is to James that Paul comes with his collection from the Gentile churches on the visit to Jerusalem which is destined to be his last and which leads to his imprisonment (Acts 21:18–25). This last episode is important, for it shows James very sympathetic to the Jews who still observe the Jewish law, and so eager that their scruples should not be offended that he actually persuades Paul to demonstrate his loyalty to the law by assuming responsibility for the expenses of certain Jews who are fulfilling a Nazirite vow, a vow taken in gratitude for some special blessing from God.

Plainly, then, James was the leader of the Jerusalem church. As might be expected, this was something which tradition greatly developed. Hegesippus, the second-century Church historian, says that James was the first bishop of the church at Jerusalem. The early Christian theologian Clement of

Alexandria goes further and says that he was chosen for that office by Peter and John. Jerome, in his book *On Famous Men*, says: 'After the passion of the Lord, James was immediately ordained bishop of Jerusalem by the apostles . . . He ruled the church of Jerusalem for thirty years, that is, until the seventh year of the reign of Nero.' *The Clementine Recognitions* take the final step in the development of the legend, for they say that James was ordained Bishop of Jerusalem by none other than Jesus himself. Clement of Alexandria relates a strange tradition: 'To James the Just, and John and Peter, after the resurrection, the Lord committed knowledge; they committed it to the other apostles; and the other apostles to the seventy.' The later developments are not to be accepted, but the basic fact remains that James was the undisputed head of the church at Jerusalem.

James and Jesus

Such a change must have some explanation. It may well be that we have it in a brief sentence in the New Testament itself. In 1 Corinthians 15, Paul gives us a list of the resurrection appearances of Jesus and includes the words: 'Then he appeared to James' (1 Corinthians 15:7). It so happens that there is a strange reference to James in the Gospel according to the Hebrews, which was one of the early gospels which did not gain admittance to the New Testament but which, to judge from its surviving fragments, had much of value in it. The following passage from it is handed down by Jerome:

> Now the Lord, when he had given the linen cloth unto the servant of the high priest, went unto James and appeared to him (for James had sworn that he would not eat bread from that hour, wherein he had drunk the Lord's cup, until he should see him risen again from among them that sleep). And again after a little, 'Bring

> ye', saith the Lord, 'a table and bread', and immediately
> it is added: 'He took bread and blessed and brake it and
> gave it unto James the Just and said unto him: "My
> brother, eat thy bread, for the Son of Man is risen from
> among them that sleep."'

That passage is not without its difficulties. The beginning
seems to mean that Jesus, when he rose from the dead and
emerged from the tomb, handed the linen shroud, which he
had been wearing in death, to the servant of the high priest
and went to meet his brother James. It also seems to imply
that James was present at the Last Supper. But although the
passage has its obscurities, one thing is clear. Something about
Jesus in the last days and hours had fastened on James' heart,
and he had vowed that he would not eat until Jesus had risen
again; and so Jesus came to him and gave him the assurance
for which he waited. That there was a meeting of James and
the risen Christ is certain. What happened at that moment we
shall never know. But we do know this, that after it the James
who had been hostile and unsympathetic to Jesus became his
servant for life and his martyr in death.

James the Martyr of Christ

That James died a martyr's death is the consistent statement
of early tradition. The accounts of the circumstances vary,
but the fact that he was martyred remains constant. The Jewish
historian Josephus' account is very brief (*Antiquities*, 20:9:1):

> So Ananus, being that kind of man, and thinking that
> he had got a good opportunity because Festus was dead
> and Albinus not yet arrived, holds a judicial council;
> and he brought before it the brother of Jesus, who was
> called Christ – James was his name – and some others,
> and on the charge of violating the law he gave them
> over to be stoned.

Ananus was a Jewish high priest; Festus and Albinus were procurators of Palestine, holding the same position as Pilate had held. The point of the story is that Ananus took advantage of the interregnum, the period between the death of one procurator and the arrival of his successor, to eliminate James and other leaders of the Christian Church. This, in fact, fits well with the character of Ananus as it is known to us, and would mean that James was martyred in AD 62.

A much longer account is given in the history of Hegesippus. Hegesippus' history is itself lost, but his account of the death of James has been preserved in full by the Church historian Eusebius, who wrote early in the fourth century (*Ecclesiastical History*, 2:23). It is lengthy, but it is of such interest that it must be quoted in its entirety.

> To the government of the Church in conjunction with the apostles succeeded the Lord's brother, James, he whom all from the time of the Lord to our own day call the Just, as there were many named James. And he was holy from his mother's womb; wine and strong drink he drank not, nor did he eat flesh; no razor touched his head, he anointed himself not with oil, and used not the bath. To him alone was it permitted to enter the Holy Place, for neither did he wear wool, but linen clothes. And alone he would enter the Temple, and be found prostrate on his knees beseeching pardon for the people, so that his knees were callous like a camel's in consequence of his continual kneeling in prayer to God and beseeching pardon for the people. Because of his exceeding righteousness he was called the Just, and Oblias, which is in Greek Bulwark of the People, and Righteousness, as the prophets declare concerning him.
>
> Therefore, certain of the seven sects among the people, already mentioned by me in the *Memoirs*, asked him: 'What is the door of Jesus?' and he said that He

was the Saviour – of whom some accepted the faith
that Jesus is the Christ. Now the aforesaid sects were
not believers either in a Resurrection or in One who
should come to render to every man according to his
deeds; but as many as believed did so because of James.
So, since many of the rulers, too, were believers, there
was a tumult of the Jews and scribes and Pharisees, for
they said there was danger that all the people would
expect Jesus the Christ. Accordingly they said, when
they had met together with James: 'We entreat thee
restrain the people since it has gone astray unto Jesus,
holding him to be the Christ. We entreat thee to persuade
concerning Jesus all those who come to the day of the
Passover, for we all listen to thee. For we and all the
people testify to thee that thou art just and that thou
respectest not persons. So thou, therefore, persuade the
people concerning Jesus not to go astray, for all the
people and all of us listen to thee. Take thy stand,
therefore, on the pinnacle of the Temple, that up there
thou mayest be well seen, and thy words audible to all
the people. For because of the Passover all the tribes
have come together and the gentiles also.'

So the aforesaid scribes and Pharisees set James on
the pinnacle of the Temple and called to him: 'O thou,
the Just, to whom we all ought to listen, since the people
is going astray after Jesus the crucified, tell us what is
the door of Jesus?' And with a loud voice he answered:
'Why do you ask me concerning the Son of Man? He
sitteth himself in heaven on the right hand of the great
Power, and shall come on the clouds of heaven.' And
when many were convinced and gave glory for the
witness of James, and said: 'Hosanna to the Son of
David', then again the same scribes and Pharisees said
to one another: 'We were wrong to permit such a testimony to Jesus; but let us go up and cast him [James]
down, that through fear they may not believe him.' And

they cried out saying: 'Ho, Ho! even the Just has gone astray', and they fulfilled the Scriptures written in Isaiah: 'Let us away with the Just, because he is troublesome to us; therefore they shall eat the fruits of their doings.'

Accordingly they went up and cast the Just down. And they said to one another: 'Let us stone James the Just', and they began to stone him, since he was not killed by the fall, but he turned and knelt down saying: 'I beseech thee, Lord God Father, forgive them, for they know not what they do.' And so, as they were stoning him, one of the Priests of the sons of Rechab, the son of Rechabim, mentioned by Jeremiah the prophet, cried out saying: 'Stop! what are ye doing? The Just prays for you.' And a certain one of them, one of the fullers, taking the club with which he pounds clothes, brought it down on the head of the Just; and so he suffered martyrdom.

And they buried him there on the spot, near the Temple. A true witness has he become both to Jews and Greeks that Jesus is Christ. And immediately Vespasian besieges them.

The last sentence shows that Hegesippus had a different date for the death of James. Josephus makes it AD 62; but, if this happened just before the siege of Vespasian, the date is perhaps about AD 66.

Much in the story of Hegesippus may well be legendary; but, from it, two things emerge. First, it is again evidence that James died a martyr's death. Second, it is evidence that, even after James became a Christian, he remained in complete loyalty to the orthodox Jewish law, so loyal that the Jews regarded him as one of themselves. This would fit well with what we have already noted of James' attitude to Paul when he came to Jerusalem with the collection for the Jerusalem church (Acts 21:18–25).

The Brother of our Lord

There is one other question about the person of James which we must try to solve. In Galatians 1:19, Paul speaks of him as *the Lord's brother*. In Matthew 13:55 and in Mark 6:3, he is named among the brothers of Jesus; and in Acts 1:14, although no names are given, the brothers of Jesus are said to be among his followers in the earliest Church. The question of the meaning of *brother* is one which must be faced, for the Roman Catholic Church in particular attaches a great deal of importance to the answer. Ever since the time of Jerome, there has been continuous argument in the Church on this question. There are three theories of the relationship of these 'brothers' to Jesus, and we shall consider them one by one.

The Hieronymian Theory

The Hieronymian Theory takes its name from Jerome, whose name in Greek is Hieronymos. It was he who worked out the theory which declares that the 'brothers' of Jesus were in fact his *cousins*; and this is the belief of the Roman Catholic Church, for which it is an article of faith. It was put forward by Jerome in AD 383, and the best way to grasp his complicated argument is by setting it out in a series of steps.

(1) James the brother of our Lord is included among the apostles. Paul writes: 'But I did not see any other apostle except James the Lord's brother' (Galatians 1:19).

(2) Jerome insists that the word *apostle* can be used only of the Twelve. If that is so, we must look for James among them. He cannot be identified with James, brother of John and son of Zebedee, who, apart from anything else, was martyred by the time of Galatians 1:19, as Acts 12:2 plainly tells us. Therefore, he must be identified with the only other James among the Twelve, James the son of Alphaeus.

(3) Jerome proceeds to make another identification. In Mark 6:3, we read: 'Is not this the carpenter, the son of Mary and brother of James and Joses?'; and in Mark 15:40 we find beside the cross Mary the mother of James the younger and of Joses. Since James the younger is the brother of Joses and the son of Mary, he must therefore be the same person as the James of Mark 6:3, who is the brother of our Lord. Therefore, according to Jerome, James the brother of the Lord, James the son of Alphaeus and James the younger are all the same person described in different ways.

(4) Jerome bases the next and final step of his argument on a deduction made from the lists of the women who were there when Jesus was crucified. Let us set down that list as given by the three gospel writers.

In Mark 15:40, it is:

> Mary Magdalene, Mary the mother of James the younger and Joses, and Salome.

In Matthew 27:56, it is:

> Mary Magdalene, Mary the mother of James and of Joseph, and the mother of the sons of Zebedee.

In John 19:25, it is:

> Jesus' mother, his mother's sister, Mary the wife of Clopas, and Mary Magdalene.

Now let us analyse these lists. In each of them, Mary Magdalene appears by name. It is safe to identify Salome and the mother of the sons of Zebedee. But the real problem is: *how many women are there in John's list?* Is the list to be read like this:

(1) Jesus' mother;
(2) Jesus' mother's sister;

(3) Mary the wife of Clopas;

(4) Mary Magdalene?

Or is the list to be read like this:

(1) Jesus' mother;

(2) Jesus' mother's sister, Mary the wife of Clopas;

(3) Mary Magdalene?

Jerome insists that the second way is correct and that Jesus' mother's sister and Mary, the wife of Clopas, are one and the same person. If that is so, she must also be the Mary who in the other lists is the mother of James and Joses. This James who is her son is the man who is variously known as James the younger and as James the son of Alphaeus and as James the apostle who is known as the brother of our Lord. This means that James is the son of Mary's sister and therefore is Jesus' cousin.

There, then, is Jerome's argument. Against it, at least four criticisms can be levelled.

(1) Again and again, James is called the *brother* of Jesus or is numbered among the *brothers* of Jesus. The word used in each case is *adelphos*, the normal word for *brother*. True, it can describe people who belong to a common fellowship, just as the Christians called each other *brother* and *sister*. True, it can be used as a term of endearment, and we may call someone to whom we are very close a *brother*. But when it is used of those who are kin, it is, to say the least of it, very doubtful that it can mean *cousin*. If James was the *cousin* of Jesus, it is extremely unlikely – perhaps impossible – that he would be called the *adelphos* of Jesus.

(2) Jerome was quite wrong in assuming that the term *apostle* could be used only of the Twelve. Paul was an apostle (Romans 1:1; 1 Corinthians 1:1; 2 Corinthians 1:1; Galatians 1:1). Barnabas was an apostle (Acts 14:14; 1 Corinthians 9:6).

Silas was an apostle (Acts 15:22). Andronicus and Junia were apostles (Romans 16:7). It is impossible to limit the word *apostle* to the Twelve. Since, therefore, it is not necessary to look for James the Lord's brother among the Twelve, Jerome's whole argument collapses.

(3) It is, on the face of it, much more likely that John 19:25 is a list of four women, not three, for, if Mary the wife of Clopas were the sister of Mary, Jesus' mother, it would mean that there were two sisters in the same family both called Mary, which is extremely unlikely.

(4) It must be remembered that the Church knew nothing of this theory until AD 383, when Jerome produced it; and it is quite certain that it was produced for no other reason than to preserve the doctrine of the perpetual virginity of Mary.

The theory that those called Jesus' brothers were, in fact, his cousins must be dismissed. The facts of the case do not support it.

The Epiphanian Theory

The second of the great theories concerning the relationship of Jesus and his 'brothers' holds that these 'brothers' were, in fact, his half-brothers, sons of Joseph by a previous marriage. This is called the Epiphanian Theory after Epiphanius, who argued strongly for it in about AD 370. He did not construct it. It existed long before this and may indeed be said to be the most usual opinion in the early Church.

The substance of it already appears in an apocryphal book called the Book of James or the Protevangelium, which dates back to the middle of the second century. That book tells how there was a devout husband and wife called Joachim and Anna. Their great grief was that they did not have children. To their great joy, in their old age a child was born to them, and this too, apparently, was regarded as a virgin birth. The child, a girl, was called Mary and was to be the mother of Jesus. Joachim and Anna dedicated their child to the Lord, and when she reached the age of three they took her to the Temple and left her there in the charge of the priests. She grew up in the Temple, and when she reached the age of twelve the priests began to consider her marriage. They called together the widowers of the people, telling each man to bring his rod with him. Among those who came was Joseph the carpenter. The high priest took the rods, and Joseph's was last. To the other rods nothing happened, but from the rod of Joseph there flew a dove which came and settled on Joseph's head. In this way, it was revealed that Joseph was to take Mary as his wife. Joseph at first was very unwilling. 'I have sons,' he said, 'and I am an old man, but she is a girl: lest I become a laughing-stock to the children of Israel' (Protevangelium 9:1). But in the end he took her in obedience to the will of God, and in due course Jesus was born. The material of the Protevangelium is, of course, simply legend, but it shows that by the middle of the second century the theory which was one day to bear the name of Epiphanius was widely held.

There is no direct evidence for this theory whatsoever, and all the support produced in its favour is of an indirect character.

(1) It is asked: would Jesus have handed the care of his mother to John, if she had other sons besides himself (John 19:26–7)? The answer is that, as far as we know, Jesus' family were quite out of sympathy with him, and it would hardly have been possible to hand the care of his mother to them.

(2) It is argued that the behaviour of Jesus' 'brothers' towards him is that of elder brothers towards a younger brother. They questioned his sanity and wanted to take him home (Mark 3:21, 3:31–5); they were actively hostile to him (John 7:1–5). But it could just as well be argued that their

behaviour was due to the simple fact that they found him an embarrassment to the family in a way that had nothing to do with age.

(3) It is argued that Joseph must have been older than Mary because he vanishes completely from the gospel story and, therefore, probably had died before Jesus' public ministry began. The mother of Jesus was at the wedding feast at Cana of Galilee, but there is no mention of Joseph (John 2:1). Jesus is called, at least sometimes, the son of Mary, and the implication is that Joseph was dead and Mary was a widow (Mark 6:3; but cf. Matthew 13:55). Further, Jesus' long stay in Nazareth until he was thirty years old (Luke 3:23) is most easily explained by the assumption that Joseph had died and that Jesus had become responsible for the support of the household. But the fact that Joseph was older than Mary does not by any means prove that he had no other children by her, and the fact that Jesus stayed in Nazareth as the village carpenter in order to support the family would much more naturally indicate that he was the eldest, and not the youngest, son.

But basically this theory springs from the same origin as the Hieronymian theory. Its aim is to preserve the perpetual virginity of Mary. There is no direct evidence whatsoever for it, and no one would ever have thought of it had it not been for the desire to think that Mary never ceased to be a virgin.

The Helvidian Theory

The third theory is called the Helvidian Theory. It states quite simply that the brothers and sisters of Jesus were in the full sense of the term his brothers and sisters – that, to use the technical term, they were his uterine brothers and sisters. Nothing whatever is known of the Helvidius with whose name this theory is connected except that he wrote a treatise to support it, which Jerome strongly opposed. What may be said in favour of it?

(1) No one reading the New Testament story without theological presuppositions would ever think of anything else. On the face of it, that story does not think of Jesus' brothers and sisters as anything other than his brothers and sisters in the full sense of the term.

(2) The birth narratives in both Matthew and Luke presuppose that Mary had other children. Matthew writes: 'When Joseph awoke from sleep, he did as the angel of the Lord commanded him; he took her as his wife, but had no marital relations with her until she had borne a son' (Matthew 1:24-5). The clear implication is that Joseph entered into a normal married relationship with Mary after the birth of Jesus. Tertullian, in fact, uses this passage to prove that both virginity and the married state are consecrated in Christ by the fact that Mary was first a virgin and then a wife in the full sense of the term. Luke, in writing of the birth of Jesus, says: 'She gave birth to her *firstborn* son' (Luke 2:7). To call Jesus a first-born son is plainly to indicate that other children followed.

(3) As we have already said, the fact that Jesus remained in Nazareth as the village carpenter until the age of thirty is at least an indication that he was the eldest son and had to take upon himself the responsibility of the support of the family after the death of Joseph.

We believe that the brothers and sisters of Jesus really were his brothers and sisters. Any other theory ultimately springs from the glorification of self-denial and from a wish to regard Mary as forever a virgin. It is surely a far more lovely thing to believe in the sanctity of the home than to insist that celibacy is to be valued more than married love.

So, we believe that James, called the Lord's brother, was in every sense the brother of Jesus.

James as the Author

Can we then say that this James was also the author of this letter? Let us collect the evidence in favour of that view.

(1) If James wrote a letter at all, it would most naturally be a general letter, as this is. James was not, like Paul, a traveller and a man of many congregations. He was the leader of the Jewish section of the Church, and the kind of letter we would expect him to write would be a general letter directed to all Jewish Christians.

(2) There is scarcely anything in the letter that a good Jew could not accept – so much so that there are those who think that it is actually a Jewish ethical tract which has found its way into the New Testament. The New Testament scholar A. H. McNeile has pointed out that in instance after instance there are phrases in James which can be read equally well in a Christian or a Jewish sense. The twelve tribes of the Dispersion (1:1) could be taken to refer either to the exiled Jews scattered all over the world or to the Christian Church, the new Israel of God. 'The Lord' can again and again in this letter be understood equally well of Jesus or of God (1:7; 4:10, 15; 5:7, 8, 10, 11, 14, 15). Our bringing forth by God by the word of his truth to be the first fruits of his creation (1:18) can equally well be understood of God's first act of creation or of his re-creation of men and women in Jesus Christ. The perfect law and the royal law (1:25, 2:8) can equally well be understood of the ethical law of the Ten Commandments or of the new law of Christ. The elders of the church, the *ekklēsia* (5:14), can equally well be understood as meaning the elders of the Christian Church or the Jewish elders – for in the Septuagint, the Greek edition of the

traditional Hebrew Scriptures that was most widely used in the synagogues in New Testament times, *ekklēsia* is the title of the chosen nation of God. In 2:2, 'your *assembly*' is spoken of. The word there used for assembly is *sunagōgē*, which can mean the synagogue even more readily than it can mean the Christian congregation. The habit of addressing its readers as brothers is thoroughly Christian, but it is equally thoroughly Jewish. The coming of the Lord and the picture of the Judge standing at the door (5:7, 5:9) are just as common in Jewish thought as in Christian thought. The accusation that they have murdered the righteous one (5:6) is a phrase which occurs again and again in the prophets; but a Christian could read it as a statement of the crucifixion of Christ. There is nothing in this letter which orthodox Jews could not heartily accept, if they read it in their own terms.

It could be argued that all this perfectly suits James. He was the leader of what might be called Jewish Christianity; he was the head of that part of the Church which remained centred in Jerusalem. There must have been a time when the Church was very close to Judaism and it was more a reformed Judaism than anything else. There was a kind of Christianity which did not have the width or the universality which the mind of Paul put into it. Paul himself said that the task of preaching to the Gentiles had been allocated to him and the task of taking the good news to the Jews was given to Peter, James and John (Galatians 2:9). The letter of James may well represent a kind of Christianity that had remained in its earliest form. This would explain two things.

First, it would explain the frequency with which James repeats the teaching of the Sermon on the Mount. We may, out of many instances, compare James 2:12–13 and Matthew 6:14–15; James 3:11–13 and Matthew 7:16–20; James 5:12 and Matthew 5:34–7. Any Jewish Christian would be supremely interested in the ethical teaching of the Christian faith.

Second, it would help to explain the relationship of this letter to the teaching of Paul. At a first reading, James 2:14–26 reads like a direct attack on Paulinism. 'A person is justified by works and not by faith alone' (James 2:24) seems a flat contradiction of the Pauline teaching of justification by faith. But what James is attacking is a so-called faith which has no ethical results, and one thing is quite clear – anyone who charges Paul with preaching such a faith cannot possibly have read his letters. They are full of ethical demands, as, for instance, a chapter like Romans 12 illustrates. Now James died in AD 62 and, therefore, could not have read Paul's letters, which did not become the common property of the Church until at least AD 90. Therefore, what James is attacking is either a misunderstanding of what Paul said or a distortion of it, and nowhere was such a misunderstanding or distortion more likely to arise than in Jerusalem, where Paul's stress on faith and grace and his attack on the law were likely to be regarded with more suspicion than anywhere else.

(3) It has been pointed out that James and the letter of the Council of Jerusalem to the Gentile churches have at least two rather curious similarities. Both begin with the word *Greeting* (James 1:1; Acts 15:23). The Greek is *chairein*. This was the normal Greek beginning to a letter, but nowhere else in all the New Testament is it found other than in the letter of Claudius Lysias, the military officer, to the governor of the province quoted in Acts 23:26–30. Second, Acts 15:17 has a phrase in the letter of the Council of Jerusalem in which, as the Revised Standard Version has it, it speaks of the Gentiles *who are called by my name*. This phrase occurs nowhere else in the New Testament other than in James 2:7, where it is translated as *the name by which you are called*. Although

these translations differ slightly, the Greek is exactly the same. It is curious that the letter of the Council of Jerusalem presents us with two unusual phrases which recur only in James, when we remember that the letter of the Council of Jerusalem must have been drafted by James.

There is, then, evidence which supports the belief that the Letter of James was the work of James, the Lord's brother and head of the Jerusalem church.

On the other hand, there are facts which make us a little doubtful whether he was, after all, the author.

(1) If the writer was the brother of our Lord, we would have expected him to make some reference to that fact. All he calls himself is 'a servant of God and of the Lord Jesus Christ' (1:1). Such a reference would not have been in any sense for his own personal glory, but simply to lend authority to his letter. And such authority would have been especially useful outside Palestine, in countries where James could hardly have been known. If the author was indeed the Lord's brother, it is surprising that he makes no reference, direct or indirect, to that fact.

(2) Failing a reference to his relationship to Jesus, we would have expected a reference to the fact that he was an apostle. It was Paul's regular custom to begin his letters with a reference to his apostleship. Again, it is not a question of personal prestige but simply a guarantee of the authority by which he writes. If this James was indeed the Lord's brother and the head of the Jerusalem church, we should have expected some reference at the beginning of the letter to his apostolic status.

(3) The most surprising fact of all is that which made Luther question the right of this letter to a place in the New Testament – the almost complete absence of any references to Jesus Christ. Only twice in the whole letter is his name

mentioned, and these mentions are almost incidental (1:1, 2:1).

There is no reference at all to his resurrection. We know well that the early Church was built on faith in the risen Christ. If this letter is the work of James, it is contemporary with the events of Acts in which the resurrection is mentioned no fewer than twenty-five times. What makes it still more surprising is that James had a personal reason for writing about the appearance of Jesus which may well have been what changed the direction of his life. It is surprising that anyone writing at such a time in the Church's history should write without reference to the resurrection of Jesus, and it is doubly surprising if the writer should be James, the brother of our Lord.

Further, there is no reference to Jesus as Messiah. If James, the leader of the Jewish church, was writing to Jewish Christians in these very early days, one would have thought his main aim would have been to present Jesus as Messiah, or that at least he would have made his belief in that fact plain; but the letter does not mention it.

(4) It is plain that the writer of this letter is steeped in the Old Testament. It is also plain that he is intimately acquainted with the Wisdom Literature; and that in James is only to be expected. There are in his letter twenty-three apparent quotations from the Sermon on the Mount; that too is easy to understand, because from the very beginning, long before the gospels were written, compendiums of Jesus' teaching must have circulated. It is argued by some that he must have known Paul's letters to the Romans and to the Galatians in order to write as he does about faith and works, and it is argued rightly that a Jew who had never been outside Palestine and who died in AD 62 could not have known these letters. As we have seen, this argument will not stand, because the criticism of

Paul's teaching in James is criticism which could have been offered only by someone who had not read the letters of Paul at first hand and who is dealing with a misunderstanding or a distortion of Pauline doctrine. But the phrase in 1:17, 'Every generous act of giving, with every perfect gift', is a hexameter line (a line with six accented beats) and clearly a quotation from some Greek poet; and the phrase in 3:6: 'the cycle of nature', may be an Orphic phrase from the mystery religions. How could James of Palestine pick up quotations like these?

There are things which are difficult to account for on the assumption that James, the brother of our Lord, was the author of this letter.

The evidence for and against James' authorship of this letter is extraordinarily evenly balanced. For the moment, we must leave the matter unresolved and turn to certain other questions.

The Date of the Letter

When we turn to the evidence for the date of the letter, we find this same even balance. It is possible to argue that it is very early, and equally possible to argue that it is rather late.

(1) When James was writing, it is clear that the hope of the second coming of Jesus Christ was still very real (5:7–9). Now the expectation of the second coming never left the Christian Church, but it did to some extent fade from the foreground of its thought as it was unexpectedly delayed for longer and longer. This would suggest an early date.

(2) In the early chapters of Acts and in the letters of Paul, there is a continuous background of Jewish controversy against acceptance of the Gentiles into the Church on the basis of faith alone. Wherever Paul went, the Judaizers followed him, and the acceptance of the Gentiles was not a battle which was easily won. In James, there is not even a

hint of this Jewish–Gentile controversy, a fact which is doubly surprising when we remember that James, the Lord's brother, took a leading part in settling the matter at the Council of Jerusalem. That being so, this letter could be either very early and written before that controversy emerged, or it could be late and written after the last echo of the controversy had died away. The fact that there is no mention of the Jewish–Gentile controversy can be used as an argument either way.

(3) The evidence from the church order reflected in the letter is equally conflicting. The meeting place of the Church is still called the *sunagōgē* (2:2). That points to an early date; later, an assembly of Christians would definitely be called the *ekklēsia*, for the Jewish term was soon dropped. The elders of the Church are mentioned (5:14), but there is no mention of either deacons or bishops. This again indicates an early date, and possibly a Jewish connection, for the eldership was a Jewish institution before it was a Christian one. James is worried about the existence of *many teachers* (3:1). This could well indicate a very early situation, before the Church had systematized its ministry and introduced some kind of order; or it could indicate a late date, when many false teachers had arisen to plague the Church.

There are two general facts which seem on the whole to indicate that James is late. First, as we have seen, there is hardly any mention of Jesus at all. The subject of the letter is, in fact, the inadequacies and the imperfections, the sins and the mistakes of the members of the church. This seems to point to a fairly late date. The early preaching was ablaze with the grace and the glory of the risen Christ; later preaching became, as it so often is today, a tirade against the imperfections of the members of the church. The second general fact is the condemnation of the rich (2:1–3, 5:1–6). The flattery of the rich and the arrogance of the rich seem to have been real problems when this letter was written. Now in the very early Church there were few, if any, rich people (1 Corinthians 1:26–7). James seems to indicate a later time when the once poor Church was being threatened with a spirit of worldliness in its members.

The Preachers of the Ancient World

It will help us to date this so-called letter of James, and may also help us to identify its author, if we place it in its context in the ancient world.

The sermon is identified with the Christian Church, but it was by no means its invention. It had roots in both the Hellenistic and the Jewish world, and when we set James beside the Hellenistic and the Jewish sermons we cannot fail to be struck by the resemblances.

1. Let us look first at the Greek preachers and their sermons. The wandering philosopher was a common figure in the ancient world. Sometimes he was a Stoic; far more often he was a Cynic. Wherever people were gathered together, you would find him there calling them to virtue. You would find him at the street corner and in the city squares; you would find him at the vast concourses which gathered for the games; you would even find him at the gladiatorial games, sometimes even directly addressing the emperor, rebuking him for luxury and tyranny, and calling him to virtue and justice. The ancient preacher, the philosopher-missionary, was a regular figure in the ancient world. There was a time when philosophy had been chiefly the concern of the schools; but now its voice and its ethical demands were to be heard daily in the public places.

These ancient sermons had certain characteristics. The method was always the same; and that method had deeply influenced Paul's presentation of the gospel, and James followed the same tradition. We will list some of the tricks of the trade of these ancient preachers, noting how they occur in James and bearing in mind the way in which Paul writes to his churches. The main aim of these ancient preachers, it must be remembered, was not to investigate new truth; it was to awaken sinners to the error of their ways and compel them to look at truths, which they knew but were deliberately neglecting or had forgotten. Their aim was to confront people with the good life in the midst of the looseness of their living and their forgetfulness of the gods.

(1) They frequently carried on imaginary conversations with imaginary opponents, speaking in what has been called a kind of 'truncated dialogue'. James also uses that method in 2:18–19 and 5:13–14.

(2) They habitually made the transition from one part of the sermon to another by way of a question which introduced the new subject. Again, James does that in 2:14 and 4:1.

(3) They were very fond of imperatives, direct orders, in which they commanded their hearers to right action and to the abandoning of their errors. In James' 108 verses, there are almost sixty imperatives.

(4) They were very fond of the rhetorical question flung out at their audience. James frequently employs such questions (cf. James 2:4–5, 2:14–16, 3:11–12, 4:4).

(5) They frequently used vivid direct addresses, known by the term 'apostrophes', to particular sections of the audience. So James speaks pointedly to the merchants out for gain and to the arrogant rich (4:13, 5:6).

(6) They were fond of personifying virtues and vices, sins and graces. So James personifies sin (1:15), mercy (2:13) and rust (5:3).

(7) They sought to awaken the interest of their audience by pictures and figures from everyday life. The figures of the

bridle, the rudder and the forest fire are standard figures in the ancient sermons (cf. James 3:3–6). Among many other illustrations, James vividly uses the picture of the farmer and his patience (5:7).

(8) They frequently used the example of famous men and women as illustrations for their moral. So James uses the examples of Abraham (2:21–3), Rahab (2:25), Job (5:11) and Elijah (5:17).

(9) It was the custom of the ancient preachers to begin their sermons with a paradox which would hold the attention of their hearers. James does that by telling his readers to consider it nothing but joy when they are involved in trials (1:2). In the same way, the ancient preachers often pointed out how true goodness meant the reversal of all popular verdicts on life. So James insists that the happiness of the rich lies in their being 'brought low' (1:10). They used the weapon of irony as James does (2:14–19, 5:1–6).

(10) The ancient preachers could speak with harshness and with sternness. So James addresses his reader as a 'senseless person' and calls those who listen to him adulterers (2:20, 4:4). The ancient preachers had sharp tongues, and so has James.

(11) The ancient preachers had certain standard ways of constructing their sermons.

(a) They often concluded a section with a vivid antithesis, a pairing of stark opposites, setting the right beside the wrong way. James follows the same custom (cf. 2:13, 2:26).

(b) They often made their point by means of a searching question fired at the hearer, and so does James (4:12).

(c) They often used quotations in their preaching. James also does this (5:20, 1:11, 1:17, 4:6, 5:11).

It is true that we do not find in James the bitterness, the scolding, the frivolous and often broad humour that the Greek preachers used; but it is plain to see that he uses all the other methods which the wandering Hellenistic preachers used in order to win their way into the minds and hearts of men and women.

2. The Jewish world also had its tradition of preaching. That preaching was done mainly by the Rabbis at the services of the synagogue. It had many of the characteristics of the preaching of the Greek wandering philosophers. It had its rhetorical questions and its imperatives and its pictures taken from life, and its quotations and its citations of the heroes of the faith. But Jewish preaching had one curious characteristic. It was deliberately disconnected. The Jewish masters instructed their pupils never to linger for any length of time on any one subject, but to move quickly from one subject to another in order to maintain the interest of listeners. Hence one of the names for preaching was *charaz*, which literally means *stringing beads*. The Jewish sermon was frequently a string of moral truths and exhortations coming one after another. This is exactly what the Letter of James is. It is difficult, if not impossible, to extract from it a continuous and coherent plan. Its sections follow each other with a certain disconnectedness. The American scholar E. J. Goodspeed writes: 'The work has been compared to a chain, each link related to the one before and the one after it. Others have compared its contents to beads on a string . . . And, perhaps, James is not so much a chain of thoughts or beads as it is a handful of pearls dropped one by one into the hearer's mind.'

James, whether looked at from the Hellenistic or from the Jewish point of view, is a good example of an ancient sermon. And here is, perhaps, the clue we need to its authorship. With all this in mind, let us now turn to ask who the author is.

The Author of James

There are five possibilities.

(1) We begin with a theory worked out in detail by the German New Testament scholar Heinrich Meyer in the early years of the twentieth century and revived by B. S. Easton in the *Interpreter's Bible*. One of the most common things in the ancient world was for books to be published in the name of some great figure of the past. Jewish literature between the Testaments is full of writings like that, ascribed to Moses, the Twelve Patriarchs, Baruch, Enoch, Isaiah and people of similar standing in order that the added authority might give greater encouragement to their readers. This was an accepted practice. One of the best-known books in the Apocrypha is the Wisdom of Solomon, in which the later sage attributes new wisdom to the wisest of the kings.

Let us remember three things about James. (a) There is nothing in it which an orthodox Jew could not accept if the two references to Jesus in 1:1 and 2:1 are removed, as they easily may be. (b) The Greek for James is in fact *Iakōbos*, which of course is the Old Testament *Jacob*. (c) The book is addressed to 'the twelve tribes in the Dispersion'. This theory holds that James is nothing other than a Jewish writing, written under the name of Jacob and meant for the Jews who were scattered throughout the world to encourage them in faith and belief amid the trials through which they might be passing in Gentile lands.

This theory is further elaborated in this way. In Genesis 49, we have Jacob's last address to his sons. The address consists of a series of short descriptions in which each son is in turn characterized. Meyer professed to be able to find in James allusions to the descriptions of each of the patriarchs and, therefore, of each of the twelve tribes, in Jacob's address. Here are some of his identifications.

Asher is the worldly rich man; James 1:9–11; Genesis 49:20.

Issachar is the doer of good deeds; James 1:12; Genesis 49:14–15.

Reuben is the first fruits; James 1:18; Genesis 49:3.

Simeon stands for anger; James 1:19–20; Genesis 49:5–7.

Levi is the tribe which is specially connected with religion and is alluded to in James 1:26–7.

Naphtali is characterized by peace; James 3:18; Genesis 49:21.

Gad stands for wars and fightings; James 4:1–2; Genesis 49:19.

Dan represents waiting for salvation; James 5:7; Genesis 49:18.

Joseph represents prayer; James 5:13–18; Genesis 49:22–6.

Benjamin stands for birth and death; James 5:20; Genesis 49:27.

That is a most ingenious theory. No one can either finally prove it or disprove it, and it certainly would explain in the most natural way the reference in 1:1 to the twelve tribes in the Dispersion, the tribes scattered abroad. It would hold that some Christian came upon this Jewish tract, written under the name of Jacob to all the exiled Jews, and was so impressed with its moral worth that he made certain adjustments and additions to it and issued it as a Christian book. There is no doubt that this is an attractive theory – but it is possible for a theory to be too ingenious.

(2) Just as the Jews did, the Christians also wrote many books under the names of the great figures of the Christian faith. There are gospels issued under the name of Peter and Thomas and James himself; there is a letter under the name of Barnabas; there are gospels of Nicodemus and

Bartholomew; and there are Acts of John, Paul, Andrew, Peter, Thomas, Philip and others. The technical title for these books is *pseudonymous*, that is, written under a *false name*.

It has been suggested that James was a letter written by someone else under the name of the Lord's brother. That is apparently what Jerome thought when he said that this letter 'was issued by someone under James' name'. But, whatever else this work is, it cannot be that – because, whenever such a book was written, the author was careful to make quite clear who was supposed to have written it. If this had been pseudonymous, no possible doubt would have been left that the author was supposed to be James *the brother of our Lord*; but this fact is not mentioned at all.

(3) The New Testament scholar James Moffatt inclined to the theory that the writer was not the brother of our Lord, or any other well-known James, but simply a teacher called James of whose life and story we have no information whatever. That is by no means impossible, for the name James was just as common then as it is now; but it would be rather difficult to understand how such a book gained entry into the New Testament, and how it came to be connected with the name of the Lord's brother.

(4) The traditional view is that the book was written by James, the Lord's brother. We have already seen that it seems strange that such a book should have only two incidental references to Jesus, and none at all to the resurrection or to Jesus as the Messiah. A further and most serious difficulty is this. The book is written in good Greek. In his commentary, J. H. Ropes says that Greek must have been the native language of the man who wrote it; and J. B. Mayor, himself one of the greatest of Greek scholars, says: 'I should be inclined to rate the Greek of this epistle as approaching more nearly to the standard of classical purity than that of any other

book in the New Testament with the exception perhaps of the Epistle to the Hebrews.' Quite certainly, James' native language was Aramaic and not Greek, and quite certainly he would not be an expert in classical Greek. His orthodox Jewish upbringing would make him despise and avoid it as a hated Gentile language. It is next to impossible to think of James actually writing this letter.

(5) So we come to the fifth possibility. Let us remember how closely the Letter of James resembles a sermon. It is possible that this is, in substance, a sermon preached by James, taken down by someone else, translated into Greek, added to and decorated a little and then issued to the wider church so that everyone could benefit from it. That explains its form and how it came to be attached to the name of James. It even explains the scarcity of the references to Jesus, to the resurrection and to the messiahship of Jesus – for, in one single sermon, James could not go through the whole range of orthodoxy and is, in fact, pressing moral duty upon men and women, and not talking about theology. It seems to us that this is the one theory that explains the facts.

One thing is certain – we may approach this little letter feeling that it is one of the lesser books of the New Testament; but, if we study it faithfully, we will lay it down thanking God that it was preserved for our instruction and inspiration.

18

1 Peter

The Lovely Letter

The Catholic or General Epistles

First Peter belongs to that group of New Testament letters which are known as the Catholic or General Epistles. Two explanations of that title have been offered.

(1) It is suggested that these letters were so called because they were addressed to the wider Church, as distinct from the Pauline letters which were addressed to individual churches. But that is not so. James is addressed to a definite, though widely scattered, community. It is written to the twelve tribes in the Dispersion, the tribes that are scattered throughout the world (James 1:1). It needs no argument that 2 and 3 John are addressed to definite communities; and, although 1 John has no specific address, it is clearly written with the needs and perils of a particular community in mind. First Peter itself is written to the strangers scattered abroad through Pontus, Galatia, Cappadocia, Asia and Bithynia (1 Peter 1:1). It is true that these General Epistles have a wider range than the letters of Paul; at the same time, they all have a definite community in mind.

(2) So we must turn to the second explanation – that these letters were called Catholic or General because they were accepted as Scripture by the whole Church as distinct from that large number of letters which enjoyed a local and

temporary authority but which were never universally accepted as Scripture. At the time when these letters were being written, there was an outbreak of letter-writing in the Church. We still possess many of the letters which were written then – the letter of Clement of Rome to Corinth, the letter of Barnabas, the letters of Ignatius and the letters of Polycarp. All were regarded as very precious in the churches to which they were written but were never regarded as having authority throughout the Church; on the other hand, the Catholic or General Epistles gradually won a place in Scripture and were accepted by the whole Church. Here is the true explanation of their title.

The Lovely Letter

Of all the General Epistles, it is probably true that 1 Peter is the best known and loved, and the most read. No one has ever been in any doubt about its charm. In his commentary on these letters, James Moffatt writes of it: 'The beautiful spirit of the pastoral shines through any translation of the Greek text. "Affectionate, loving, lowly, humble," are Izaak Walton's quaternion of adjectives for the Epistles of James, John and Peter, but it is 1 Peter which deserves them pre-eminently.' It is written out of the love of a pastor's heart to help people who were experiencing troubled times and for whom worse things still lay ahead. 'The key-note', says Moffatt, 'is steady encouragement to endurance in conduct and innocence in character.' It has been said that its distinctive characteristic is *warmth*. The biblical scholar E. J. Goodspeed wrote: '1 Peter is one of the most moving pieces of persecution literature.' Even today, it is one of the easiest letters in the New Testament to read, for it has never lost its captivating appeal to the human heart.

The Modern Doubt

Until a comparatively short time ago, few would have raised any doubts about the authenticity of 1 Peter. The nineteenth-century French theologian Joseph Ernest Renan, who was by no means a conservative critic, wrote of it: 'The First Epistle is one of the writings of the New Testament which are most anciently and most unanimously cited as genuine.' But more recently the Petrine authorship of the letter has been widely questioned. The commentary by F. W. Beare, published in 1947, goes as far as saying: 'There can be no possible doubt that "Peter" is a pseudonym.' That is to say, Beare has no doubt that someone else wrote this letter under the name of Peter. In fairness, we shall go on to investigate that view; but first we shall set out the traditional view – which we ourselves unhesitatingly accept – of the date and authorship of this letter. This is that 1 Peter was written from Rome by Peter himself, about the year AD 67, in the days immediately following the first persecution of the Christians by Nero, to the Christians in those parts of Asia Minor named in the address. What is the evidence for this early date and, therefore, for the Petrine authorship?

The Second Coming

When we go to the letter, we find that expectation of the second coming of Christ is in the very forefront of its thought. Christians are being kept for the salvation which is to be revealed at the last time (1:5). Those who keep the faith will be saved from the coming judgment (1:7). Christians are to hope for the grace which will come at the revelation of Jesus Christ (1:13). The day of visitation is expected (2:12). The end of all things is at hand (4:7). Those who suffer with Christ will also rejoice with Christ when his glory is revealed (4:13).

Judgment is to begin at the household of God (4:17). The writer himself is sure that he will be a sharer in the glory to come (5:1). When the chief shepherd shall appear, the faithful Christian will receive a crown of glory (5:4).

From beginning to end of the letter, the second coming is in the forefront of the writer's mind. It is the motive for steadfastness in the faith, for the loyal living of the Christian life and for gallant endurance amid the sufferings that have come and will come upon them.

It would be untrue to say that the second coming ever dropped out of Christian belief; but it did recede from the forefront of Christian belief as the years passed and Christ did not return. It is, for instance, significant that in Ephesians, one of Paul's later letters, there is no mention of it. On this basis, it is reasonable to suppose that 1 Peter is early and comes from the days when the Christians vividly expected the return of their Lord at any moment.

Simplicity of Organization

It is clear that 1 Peter comes from a time when the organization of the Church is very simple. There is no mention of deacons, nor of the *episkopos*, the bishop, who begins to emerge in the Pastoral Epistles and becomes prominent in Ignatius' letters in the first half of the second century. The only church officials mentioned are the elders. 'As an elder myself . . . I exhort the elders among you' (5:1). For this reason, also, it is reasonable to suppose that 1 Peter comes from an early date.

The Theology of the Early Church

What is most significant of all is that the theology of 1 Peter is the theology of the very early Church. E. G. Selwyn has made a detailed study of this in his commentary, and he has proved beyond all question that the theological ideas of

1 Peter are exactly the same as those we meet in the recorded sermons of Peter in the early chapters of Acts.

The preaching of the early Church was based on five main ideas. One of the greatest contributions of C. H. Dodd to New Testament scholarship was his formulation of these. They form the framework of all the sermons of the early Church, as recorded in Acts, and they are the foundation of the thought of all the New Testament writers. The summary of these basic ideas has been given the name *kērugma*, which means the announcement or the proclamation of a herald.

These are the fundamental ideas which the Church in its first days proclaimed. We shall take them one by one and shall set down after each, first, the references in the early chapters of Acts and, second, the references in 1 Peter; and we will make the significant discovery that the basic ideas of the sermons of the early Church and the theology of 1 Peter are precisely the same. We are not claiming, of course, that the sermons in Acts are word-for-word reports of what was actually preached, but we believe that they give correctly the *substance* of the message of the first preachers.

(1) The age of fulfilment has dawned; the messianic age has begun. This is God's last word. A new order is being inaugurated, and the elect are summoned to join the new community (Acts 2:14–16, 3:12–26, 4:8–12, 10:34–43; 1 Peter 1:3, 1:10–12, 4:7).

(2) This new age has come through the life, death and resurrection of Jesus Christ, all of which are in direct fulfilment of the prophecies of the Old Testament and are, therefore, the result of the definite plan and foreknowledge of God (Acts 2:20–31, 3:13–14, 10:43; 1 Peter 1:20–1).

(3) By virtue of the resurrection, Jesus has been exalted to the right hand of God and is the messianic head of the

new Israel (Acts 2:22–6, 3:13, 4:11, 5:30–1, 10:39–42; 1 Peter 1:21, 2:7, 2:24, 3:22).

(4) These messianic events will shortly reach their fulfilment in the return of Christ in glory and the judgment of the living and the dead (Acts 3:19–23, 10:42; 1 Peter 1:5, 1:7, 1:13, 4:5, 4:13, 4:17–18, 5:1, 5:4).

(5) These facts are made the grounds for an appeal for repentance, and the offer of forgiveness and of the Holy Spirit, and the promise of eternal life (Acts 2:38–9, 3:19, 5:31, 10:43; 1 Peter 1:13–25, 2:1–3, 4:1–5).

These declarations are the five main building blocks in the structure of early Christian preaching, as recorded for us in the sermons of Peter in the early chapters of Acts. They are also the dominant ideas in 1 Peter. The correspondence is so close and so consistent that we are almost certainly looking at the same hand and mind in both.

Quotations from the Fathers

We may add another point to our evidence that 1 Peter is an early work. Very early on, the fathers and preachers of the Church begin to quote it. The first person to quote 1 Peter by name is Irenaeus, who lived from AD 130 until well into the next century. He twice quotes 1 Peter 1:8: 'Although you have not seen him, you love him; and even though you do not see him now, you believe in him and rejoice with an indescribable and glorious joy.' And he once quotes 1 Peter 2:16, with its command not to use liberty as a pretext for evil. But, even before this, the fathers of the Church are quoting Peter without mentioning his name. Clement of Rome, writing about AD 95, speaks of 'the precious blood of Christ', an unusual phrase which may well come from Peter's statement that we are redeemed by the precious blood of Christ (1:19). Polycarp, who was martyred in AD 155, repeatedly quotes Peter without using his name. We may select three passages to show how closely he gives Peter's words.

> Wherefore, girding up your loins, serve God in fear . . . believing on him who raised up our Lord Jesus Christ from the dead, and gave him glory (Polycarp, *To the Philippians*, 2:1).

> Therefore, gird up your minds . . . through him you have confidence in God, who raised him from the dead and gave him glory (1 Peter 1:13, 1:21).

> Christ Jesus who bore our sins in his own body on the tree, who did no sin, neither was guile found in his mouth (Polycarp, *To the Philippians*, 8:1).

> He committed no sin; no guile was found on his life . . . He himself bore our sins in his body on the tree (1 Peter 2:22, 2:24).

> Having your conversation blameless among the Gentiles (Polycarp, *To the Philippians*, 10:2).

> Maintain good conduct among the Gentiles (1 Peter 2:12).

There can be no doubt that Polycarp is quoting Peter, although he does not name him. It takes some time for a book to acquire such an authority and familiarity that it can be quoted almost unconsciously, its language woven into the language of the Church. Once again, we see that 1 Peter must be a very early book.

The Excellence of the Greek

If, however, we are defending the Petrine authorship of this letter, there is one problem we must face – and that is the excellence of the Greek. It seems impossible that it could be the work of a Galilaean fisherman. New Testament scholars are at one in praising the Greek of this letter. F. W. Beare writes: 'The epistle is quite obviously the work of a man of letters, skilled in all the devices of rhetoric, and able to draw on an extensive, and even learned, vocabulary. He is a stylist of no ordinary capacity, and he writes some of the best Greek in the whole New Testament, far smoother and more literary than that of the highly-trained Paul.' James Moffatt speaks of this letter's 'plastic language and love of metaphor'. J. B. Mayor says that 1 Peter has no equal in the New Testament for 'sustained stateliness of rhythm'. Charles Bigg has likened certain of 1 Peter's phrases to the writing of the Greek historian Thucydides. In his commentary, E. G. Selwyn has spoken of 1 Peter's 'Euripidean tenderness' and of its ability to coin compound words as the poet and dramatist Aeschylus might have done. The Greek of 1 Peter is not entirely unworthy to be set beside that of the masters of the language. It is difficult, if not impossible, to imagine Peter using the Greek language like that.

The letter itself supplies the solution to this problem. In the concluding short section, Peter himself says: 'Through Silvanus . . . I have written this short letter' (1 Peter 5:12). *Through Silvanus – dia Silouanou –* is an unusual phrase. The Greek means that Silvanus was Peter's agent in the writing of the letter; it means that he was more than merely Peter's secretary, taking down word for word what Peter said.

Let us approach this from two angles. First, let us inquire what we know about Silvanus. (The evidence is set out more fully in our study section on 1 Peter 5:12.) In all probability, he is the same person as the Silvanus of Paul's letters and the Silas of Acts, Silas being a shortened and more familiar form of Silvanus. When we examine these passages, we find that Silas or Silvanus was no ordinary person but a leading figure in the life and counsels of the early Church.

He was a prophet (Acts 15:32); he was one of the 'leaders among the brothers' at the Council of Jerusalem and one of the two chosen to deliver the decisions of the Council to the church at Antioch (Acts 15:22, 15:27). He was Paul's chosen companion in the second missionary journey, and was with Paul both in Philippi and in Corinth (Acts 15:37–40, 16:19, 16:25, 16:29, 18:5; 2 Corinthians 1:19). He was associated with Paul in the initial greetings of 1 and 2 Thessalonians (1 Thessalonians 1:1; 2 Thessalonians 1:1). He was a Roman citizen (Acts 16:37).

Silvanus, then, was a notable man in the early Church; he was not so much the assistant as the colleague of Paul; and, since he was a Roman citizen, there is at least a possibility that he was a man who had an education and culture such as Peter could never have enjoyed.

Now let us add our second line of thought. In a missionary situation, when missionaries can speak a language well enough but cannot write it very well, it is quite common for them to do one of two things in order to send a message to the people. They either write it out in as good a style as they can, and then get a native speaker of the language to correct mistakes and to polish the style; or, if they have a reliable native-speaking colleague, they explain what they want to say, leave the colleague to put the message into written form and then vet the result.

We can well imagine that this was the part Silvanus played in the writing of 1 Peter. Either he corrected and polished Peter's inevitably inadequate Greek, or he wrote in his own words what Peter wanted said, with Peter vetting the final product and adding the last personal paragraph to it.

The thought is that of Peter, but the style is that of Silvanus. And so, although the Greek is excellent, there is no need to deny that the letter comes from Peter himself.

The Recipients of the Letter

The recipients of the letter are the exiles (a Christian is always a temporary resident on the earth) scattered throughout Pontus, Galatia, Cappadocia, Asia and Bithynia.

Almost all of these words had a double significance. They stood for ancient kingdoms, and they stood for Roman provinces to which the ancient names had been given; and the ancient kingdoms and the new provinces did not always cover the same territory. Pontus was never a province. It had originally been the kingdom of Mithradates, and part of it was incorporated in Bithynia and part of it in Galatia. Galatia had originally been the kingdom of the Gauls in the area of the three cities Ancyra, Pessinus and Tavium, but the Romans had expanded it into a much larger unit of administration, including sections of Phrygia, Pisidia, Lycaonia and Isauria. The kingdom of Cappadocia had become a Roman province in AD 17 in practically its original form. Asia was not the continent of Asia as we use the term. It had been an independent kingdom, whose last king, Attalus III, had bequeathed it as a gift to Rome in 133 BC. It included the centre of Asia Minor and was bounded on the north by Bithynia, on the south by Lycia, and on the east by Phrygia and Galatia. In popular language, it was that part of Asia Minor which lay along the shores of the Aegean Sea.

We do not know why these particular districts were picked out, but this much is certain – they covered a large area with a very large population, and the fact that they are all mentioned is one of the greatest proofs of the immense missionary activity of the early Church, quite apart from the missionary activities of Paul.

All these districts lie in the north-east corner of Asia Minor. Why they are named as a group and why they are named in this particular order, we do not know. But a glance at the map will show that, if the bearer of this letter – who may well have been Silvanus – sailed from Italy and landed at Sinope in north-east Asia Minor, a journey through these provinces would be a circular tour which would take him back to Sinope. From Sinope in Bithynia, he would go south to Galatia, further south to Cappadocia, west to Asia, north again to Bithynia, and then east to arrive back in Sinope.

It is clear from the letter itself that its recipients were mainly Gentiles. There is no mention of any question of the law, a question which always arose when there was a Jewish background. Their previous condition had been one of physical passions (1:14, 4:3–4) which fits Gentiles far better than Jews. At one time, they were not a people – Gentiles outside the covenant – but now they are the people of God (2:9–10).

The form of his name which Peter uses also shows that this letter was intended for Gentiles, for Peter is a Greek name. Paul calls him Cephas (1 Corinthians 1:12, 3:22, 9:5, 15:5; Galatians 1:18, 2:9, 2:11, 2:14); among his fellow Jews, he was known as Simeon (Acts 15:14), which is the name by which he is called in 2 Peter (1:1). Since he uses his Greek name here, it is likely that he was writing to Greek people.

The Circumstances behind the Letter

That this letter was written in a time when persecution threatened is abundantly clear. They are going through various trials (1:6). They are likely to be falsely accused as evildoers (3:16). A fiery ordeal is going to try them (4:12). When they suffer, they are to commit themselves to God (4:19). They may well have to suffer for doing what is right (3:14). They are sharing in the afflictions which Christians throughout the world are called upon to endure (5:9). Behind this letter lie fiery trial, a campaign of slander and suffering for the sake of Christ. Can we identify this situation?

There was a time when the Christians had little to fear from the Roman government. In Acts, it is repeatedly the Roman magistrates and the Roman soldiers and officials who save Paul from the fury of Jews and Gentiles alike. As the author of *The Decline and Fall of the Roman Empire*, Edward Gibbon, had it, the tribunal of the Roman magistrate proved the most assured refuge against the fury of the synagogue. The reason was that in the early days the Roman government was not able to distinguish between Jews and Christians. Within the empire, Judaism was what was called a *religio licita*, a permitted religion, and Jews were completely free to worship in their own way. It was not that the Jews did not try to enlighten the Romans as to the true facts of the situation; they did so in Corinth, for example (Acts 18:12–17). But, for some time, the Romans simply regarded the Christians as a Jewish sect and, therefore, did not molest them.

The change came in the days of Nero, and we can trace almost every detail of the story. On 19th July, AD 64, the great fire of Rome broke out. Rome, a city of narrow streets and high wooden tenements, was in real danger of being wiped out. The fire burned for three days and three nights, was halted, and then broke out again with redoubled violence. The Roman populace had no doubt who was responsible, and put the blame on the emperor. Nero had a passion for building, and they believed that he had deliberately taken steps to obliterate Rome so that he could rebuild it. Nero's responsibility must remain forever in doubt; but it is certain that he watched the raging inferno from the tower of Maecenas and expressed himself as charmed with the flower and loveliness of the flames. It was freely said that those who tried to extinguish the fire were deliberately hindered and that men were seen to rekindle it again when it was likely to subside. The people were overwhelmed. The ancient landmarks and the ancestral shrines had vanished; the Temple of Luna, the Ara Maxima, the great altar, the Temple of Jupiter Stator, the shrine of Vesta, their very household gods were gone. They were homeless; and, in the phrase of the Dean of Canterbury, F. W. Farrar, there was 'a hopeless brotherhood of wretchedness'.

The resentment of the people was bitter. Nero had to divert suspicion from himself; a scapegoat had to be found. The Christians were made the scapegoat. Tacitus, the Roman historian, tells the story (*Annals*, 15:44):

> Neither human assistance in the shape of imperial gifts, nor attempts to appease the gods, could remove the sinister report that the fire was due to Nero's own orders. And, so, in the hope of dissipating the rumour, he falsely diverted the charge on to a set of people to whom the vulgar gave the name of Chrestians, and who were detested for the abominations they perpetrated. The founder of the sect, one Christus by name, had been executed by Pontius Pilate in the reign of Tiberius; and the dangerous superstition, though put down for the moment, broke out again, not only in Judaea, the original home of the pest, but even in Rome, where everything shameful and horrible collects and is practised.

Clearly, Tacitus had no doubt that the Christians were not to blame for the fire and that Nero was simply choosing them to be the scapegoats for his own crime.

Why did Nero pick on the Christians, and how was it possible even to suggest that they were responsible for the fire of Rome? There are two possible answers.

(1) The Christians were already the victims of certain slanders.

(a) In popular opinion, they were connected with the Jews. Anti-semitism is no new thing, and it was easy for the Roman mob to attach any crime to the Jews and, therefore, to the Christians.

(b) The Lord's Supper was secret, at least in a sense. It was open only to the members of the Church. And certain phrases connected with it were fruitful sources of slanders. There were phrases about eating someone's body and drinking someone's blood. That was enough to produce a rumour that the Christians were cannibals. In time, the rumour grew until it became a story that the Christians killed and ate a Gentile, or a newly born child. At the Lord's table, the Christians gave each other the kiss of peace (1 Peter 5:14). Their meeting was called the *Agape*, the Love Feast. That was enough for stories to spread that the Christian meetings were orgies of vice.

(c) It was always a charge against the Christians that they 'tampered with family relationships'. There was some truth in such a charge, for Christianity did indeed become a sword to split families, when some members of a family became Christian and some did not. A religion which split homes was bound to be unpopular.

(d) It was the case that the Christians spoke of a coming day when the world would dissolve in flames. Many Christian preachers must have been heard preaching of the second coming and the fiery dissolution of all things (Acts 2:19–20). It would not be difficult to put the blame for the fire on people who spoke like that.

There was abundant material which could be distorted into false charges against the Christians by anyone maliciously disposed to victimize them.

(2) The Jewish faith had always appealed especially to women because of its moral standards in a world where

chastity did not exist. There were, therefore, many women of the aristocracy who had embraced Judaism. The Jews did not hesitate to work upon these women to influence their husbands against the Christians. We get a definite example of that in what happened to Paul and his company in Antioch of Pisidia. There, it was through such women that the Jews stirred up action against Paul (Acts 13:50). Two of Nero's court favourites were Jewish converts. There was Aliturus, his favourite actor, and there was Poppaea, his mistress. It is very likely that through them the Jews influenced Nero to take action against the Christians.

In any event, the blame for the fire was attached to the Christians, and a savage outbreak of persecution occurred. Nor was it simply persecution by legal means. What the Roman historian Tacitus called an *ingens multitudo*, a huge multitude, of Christians perished in the most sadistic ways. Nero rolled the Christians in pitch, set light to them and used them as living torches to light his gardens. He sewed them up in the skins of wild animals and set his hunting dogs on them, to tear them limb from limb while they were still alive. Tacitus writes (*Annals*, 15:44):

> Mockery of every sort was added to their deaths. Covered with the skins of beasts, they were torn by dogs and perished, or were nailed to crosses, or were doomed to the flames and burned, to serve as a nightly illumination, when daylight had expired. Nero offered his gardens for the spectacle and was exhibiting a show in the circus, while he mingled with the people in the dress of a charioteer or stood aloft on a car. Hence, even for criminals who deserve extreme and exemplary punishment, there arose a feeling of compassion; for it was not, as it seemed, for the public good, but to glut one man's cruelty that they were being destroyed.

The same terrible story is told by the later Christian historian, Sulpicius Severus, in his *Chronicle*:

> In the meantime, the number of Christians being now very large, it happened that Rome was destroyed by fire, while Nero was stationed at Antium. But the opinion of all cast the odium of causing the fire upon the emperor, and he was believed in this way to have sought for the glory of building a new city. And, in fact, Nero could not, by any means he tried, escape from the charge that the fire had been caused by his orders. He, therefore, turned the accusation against the Christians and the most cruel tortures were accordingly inflicted upon the innocent. Nay, even new kinds of death were invented so that, being covered in the skins of wild beasts, they perished by being devoured by dogs, while many were crucified, or slain by fire, and not a few were set apart for this purpose, that, when the day came to a close, they should be consumed to serve for light during the night. In this way, cruelty first began to be manifested against the Christians. Afterwards, too, their religion was prohibited by laws which were enacted; and by edicts openly set forth it was proclaimed unlawful to be a Christian.

It is true that this persecution was confined originally to Rome; but the gateway to persecution had been opened, and in every place they were ready victims for the mob.

The New Testament scholar James Moffatt writes:

> After the Neronic wave had passed over the capital, the wash of it was felt on the far shores of the provinces; the dramatic publicity of the punishment must have spread the name of Christian *urbi et orbi*, far and wide, over the entire empire; the provincials would soon hear of it, and when they desired a similar outburst at the

expense of the loyal Christians, all that they needed was
a proconsul to gratify their wishes and some outstanding
disciple to serve as a victim.

Forever after, the Christians were to live under threat. The
mobs of the Roman cities knew what had happened in Rome,
and the slanderous stories against the Christians persisted.
There were times when the mob loved blood, and there were
many governors ready to pander to their blood lust. It was
not Roman law but lynch law which threatened the Christians.

From now on, Christians were in peril of their lives. For
years, nothing might happen; then some spark might set off
the explosion, and the terror would break out. That is what
lies behind I Peter; and it is confronted by that situation that
Peter calls his people to hope and to courage and to that lovely
Christian living which alone can give the lie to the slanders
with which they are attacked and which are the grounds for
taking measures against them. First Peter was not written to
meet theological heresy; it was written to strengthen men
and women who were in danger of losing their lives.

The Doubts

We have set out in full the arguments which go to prove that
Peter is really the author of the first letter which bears his
name. But, as we have said, a number of first-class scholars
have felt that it cannot have been his work. We ourselves
accept the view that Peter is the author of the letter; but in
fairness we set out the other side, largely as it is presented in
the chapter on I Peter in *The Primitive Church* by B. H.
Streeter.

Strange Silences

Charles Bigg writes in the introduction to his commentary:
'There is no book in the New Testament which has earlier,

better, or stronger attestation [than I Peter].' It is true that Eusebius, the great fourth-century scholar and historian of the Church, classes I Peter among the books universally accepted in the early Church as part of Scripture (Eusebius, *Ecclesiastical History*, 3:25:2). But certain things are to be noted.

(a) Eusebius cites certain quotations from earlier writers to prove his contention that I Peter was universally accepted. This he never does in connection with the gospels or the letters of Paul; and the very fact that he feels called upon to produce his evidence in the case of I Peter might be held to indicate that in it he felt the need to prove his point, a need which did not exist in connection with the other books. Was there a doubt in Eusebius' own mind? Or were there people who had to be convinced? Was the universal acceptance of I Peter not so unanimous after all?

(b) In his book, *The Canon of the New Testament*, B. F. Westcott noted that, although no one in the early Church questions the right of I Peter to be part of the New Testament, surprisingly few of the early fathers quote it and, still more surprising, very few of the early fathers in the west and in Rome quote it. Tertullian is a frequent quoter of Scripture. In his writings, there are 7,258 quotations from the New Testament, but only two of them are from I Peter. If Peter wrote this letter and wrote it in Rome, we would expect it to be well known and largely used in the Church of the west.

(c) The earliest known official list of New Testament books is the Muratorian Canon, so called after Cardinal Muratori who discovered it. It is the official list of New Testament books as accepted in the church at Rome about the year AD 170. It is an extraordinary fact that I Peter does not appear at all. It can be fairly argued that the Muratorian Canon, as we possess it, is defective and that it may originally have contained a reference to I Peter. But that argument is seriously weakened by the next consideration.

(d) It is a fact that I Peter was still not in the New Testament of the Syrian church as late as AD 373. It did not get in until the Syriac version of the New Testament known as the Peshitto was made about AD 400. We know that it was the Christian scholar Tatian who brought the New Testament books to the Syriac-speaking church, and he brought them to Syria from Rome when he went to Edessa and founded the church there in AD 172. It could, therefore, be argued that the Muratorian Canon is correct as we possess it and that I Peter was not part of the Roman church's New Testament as late as AD 170. This would be a very surprising fact if Peter wrote it – and actually wrote it at Rome.

When all these facts are put together, it does seem that there are some strange silences in regard to I Peter and that the evidence supporting it may not be as strong as is usually assumed.

First Peter and Ephesians

Further, there is definitely some connection between I Peter and Ephesians. There are many close parallels of thought and expression between the two, and we select the following specimens of this similarity.

> Blessed be the God and Father of our Lord Jesus Christ! By his great mercy he has given us a new birth into a living hope through the resurrection of Jesus Christ from the dead (I Peter 1:3).

> Blessed be the God and Father of our Lord Jesus Christ, who has blessed us in Christ with every spiritual blessing in the heavenly places (Ephesians 1:3).

Therefore prepare your minds for action; discipline yourselves; set all your hope on the grace that Jesus Christ will bring you when he is revealed (1 Peter 1:13).

Stand, therefore, and fasten the belt of truth around your waist (Ephesians 6:14).

He was destined before the foundation of the world, but was revealed at the end of the ages for your sake (1 Peter 1:20).

Just as he chose us in Christ, before the foundation of the world (Ephesians 1:4).

Jesus Christ, who has gone into heaven and is at the right hand of God, with angels, authorities, and powers made subject to him (1 Peter 3:21–2).

God . . . seated him at his right hand in the heavenly places, far above all rule and authority and power and dominion (Ephesians 1:20–1).

In addition, the instructions to slaves, husbands and wives in 1 Peter and Ephesians are very similar.

The argument is put forward that 1 Peter is quoting Ephesians. Although Ephesians must have been written somewhere about AD 64, Paul's letters were not collected and edited until about AD 90, If, then, Peter was also writing in AD 64, how could he know Ephesians?

This is an argument to which there is more than one reply. (a) The instructions to slaves, husbands and wives are part of the standardized ethical teaching given to all converts in all churches. Peter was not borrowing from Paul; both were using common material. (b) All the similarities quoted can well be explained from the fact that certain phrases and lines of thought were universal in the early Church. For instance, 'Blessed be the God and Father of our Lord Jesus Christ' was part of the universal devotional language of the early

Church, which both Peter and Paul would know and use without any borrowing from each other. (c) Even if there was mutual borrowing, it is by no means certain that I Peter borrowed from Ephesians; the borrowing might well have been the other way round and probably was, for I Peter is much simpler than Ephesians. (d) Last, even if I Peter borrowed from Ephesians, if Peter and Paul were in Rome at the same time, it is perfectly possible that Peter could have seen a copy of Ephesians before it was sent to Asia Minor, and he might well have discussed its ideas with Paul.

The argument that I Peter must be late because it quotes from Ephesians seems to us very uncertain and insecure, and probably mistaken.

As an Elder Myself

It is objected that Peter could not well have written the sentence: 'Now as an elder myself . . . I exhort the elders among you' (I Peter 5:1). It is maintained that Peter could not have called himself an elder. He was an apostle whose function was quite different from that of an elder. The apostle was characteristically someone whose work and authority were not confined to any one congregation, but whose remit ran throughout the whole Church; whereas the elder was the governing official of the local congregation.

That is perfectly true. But it must be remembered that among the Jews there was no office more universally honoured than that of elder. Elders had the respect of the whole community, and the community looked to them for guidance in its problems and justice in its disputes. Peter, as a Jew, would feel nothing out of place in calling himself an elder, and in so doing he would avoid the conscious claim of authority that the title of apostle might have implied, and graciously and courteously identify himself with the people to whom he spoke.

A Witness of the Sufferings of Christ

It is objected that Peter could not honestly have called himself a witness of Christ's sufferings, for after the arrest in the garden all the disciples forsook Jesus and fled (Matthew 26:56), and, apart from the beloved disciple, none was a witness of the cross (John 19:26–7). Peter could call himself a witness of the *resurrection*, and indeed to be such a witness was the function of an apostle (Acts 1:22); but a witness of the cross he was not. In a sense, that is undeniable. And yet Peter is here claiming not to be a witness of the crucifixion but to be a witness of the sufferings of Christ. He did see Christ suffer, in his continual rejection by the people, in the poignant moments of the Last Supper, in the agony in the garden and in that moment when, after he had denied him, Jesus turned and looked on him (Luke 22:61). It is an insensitive and unimaginative criticism which denies to Peter the right to say that he had been a witness of the sufferings of Christ.

Persecution for the Name

The main argument for a late date for 1 Peter is drawn from its references to persecution. It is argued that 1 Peter implies that it was already a crime to be a Christian and that Christians were brought before the courts, not for any crime but for the bare fact of their faith. First Peter speaks about being reproached for the name of Christ (4:14); it speaks of suffering as a Christian (4:16). It is argued that this stage of persecution was not reached until after AD 100, and that prior to that date their persecution was on the charge of alleged evildoing, as in the time of Nero.

There is no doubt that this was the law by AD 112. At that time, Pliny was governor of Bithynia. He was a personal friend of the Emperor Trajan, and he had a way of referring all his difficulties to Trajan for solution. He wrote to the emperor to tell how he dealt with the Christians. Pliny was well aware that they were law-abiding citizens to whose practices no crimes were attached. They told him that 'they had been accustomed to assemble on a fixed day before daylight, and sing by turns a hymn to Christ as God; that they had bound themselves with an oath, not for any crime, but to commit neither theft, nor robbery, nor adultery, nor to break their word, and not to deny a deposit when demanded'. Pliny accepted all this; but, when they were brought before him, he asked only one question. 'I have asked them whether they were Christians. Those who confessed I asked a second and a third time, threatening punishment. Those who persisted I ordered to be led away to execution.' Their sole crime was that of being Christians.

Trajan replied that this was the correct way to go about things and that anyone who denied being a Christian and proved it by sacrificing to the gods was immediately to be set free. From the letters, it is clear that there was a good deal of information being laid against the Christians, and Trajan laid it down that no anonymous letters of information were to be accepted or acted upon (Pliny, *Letters* 96 and 97).

It is argued that this stage of persecution did not emerge until the time of Trajan, and that 1 Peter therefore implies a situation which must be as late as Trajan's time.

The only way in which we can settle this is to sketch the progress of persecution and the reason for it in the Roman Empire. We may do so by setting out one basic fact and three developments from it.

(1) Under the Roman system, religions were divided into two kinds. There were those which were *religiones licitae*, permitted religions; these were recognized by the state, and

it was open to anyone to practise them. There were *religiones illicitae*; these were forbidden by the state, and it was illegal for anyone to practise them on pain of automatic prosecution as a criminal. It is to be noted that Roman toleration was very wide, and that any religion which did not affect public morality and civil order was certain to be permitted.

(2) Judaism was a *religio licita*, and in the very early days the Romans, not unnaturally, did not know the difference between Judaism and Christianity. Christianity, as far as they were concerned, was merely a sect of Judaism, and any tension and hostility between the two was a private quarrel which was no concern of the Roman government. Because of that, in the very early days Christianity was under no danger of persecution. It enjoyed the same freedom of worship as Judaism enjoyed because it was assumed to be a *religio licita*.

(3) The action of Nero changed the situation. However it came about, and most likely it was by the deliberate action of the Jews, the Roman government discovered that Judaism and Christianity were different. It is true that Nero first persecuted the Christians, not for being Christians but for burning Rome. But the fact remains that the government had discovered that Christianity was a separate religion.

(4) The consequence was immediate and inevitable. Christianity became at once a prohibited religion, and immediately every Christian by definition automatically became an outlaw. In the writings of the Roman historian Suetonius, we have direct evidence that this was precisely what happened. He gives a kind of list of the legislative reforms initiated by Nero:

> During his reign, many abuses were severely punished and put down, and not a few new laws were made; a limit was set to expenditures; the public banquets were confined to a distribution of food; the sale of any kind

of cooked viands in the taverns was forbidden, with the exception of pulse and vegetables, whereas, before, every kind of dainty was exposed for sale. Punishment was inflicted on the Christians, a class of men given to a new and mischievous superstition. He put an end to the diversions of the chariot-drivers, who from immunity of long standing claimed the right of ranging at large and amusing themselves by cheating and robbing the people. The pantomimic actors and their partisans were banished from the city.

We have quoted that passage in full because it is proof that by the time of Nero the punishment of Christians had become an ordinary police affair. It is abundantly clear that we do not need to wait until the time of Trajan for the mere fact of being a Christian to be a crime. Any time after Nero, Christians were liable to punishment and death simply for the name they bore.

This does not mean that persecution was constant and consistent, but it does mean that any Christian was liable to execution at any time, purely as a police matter. In one area, a Christian might live a whole lifetime at peace; in another, there might be outbreaks of persecution every few months. It depended very largely on two things. It depended on the governor himself, who might either leave the Christians alone or equally set the processes of the law in action against them. It depended on informers. The governor might not want to act against the Christians, but if information was laid against a Christian he had to; and there were times when the mob was out for blood, information was presented and Christians were butchered as entertainment for a Roman holiday.

To compare small things with great, the legal position of the Christians and the attitude of the Roman law can be paralleled in Britain today. There are certain actions which are illegal – to take a very small example, parking a car in a restricted area – but which for a while may be permitted. But if the authorities decide to institute a drive against such an action, or if it develops into too blatant a breaking of the law, or if someone lodges a complaint and produces evidence, the law will go into action, and due penalty and punishment will be exacted. That was the position of the Christians in the empire. Technically they were outlaws; in actual fact no action might be taken against them, but a kind of sword of Damocles was always there, suspended over them. They never knew when information would be produced against them, or when a governor would take action. They never knew when they might have to die. And that was the situation consistently after the action of Nero. Up to that time, the Roman authorities had not realized that Christianity was a new religion, but from then on Christians were automatically outlaws.

Let us, then, look at the situation as depicted in 1 Peter. Peter's people are undergoing various trials (1:6). Their faith is liable to be tried as metal is tested with fire (1:7). Clearly, they are undergoing a campaign of slander in which ignorant charges with no foundation are being maliciously directed against them (2:12, 2:15, 3:16, 4:4). At this very moment, they are in the middle of an outbreak of persecution because they are Christians (4:12, 4:14, 4:16, 5:9). Such suffering is only to be expected, and they must not be surprised at it (4:12). In any event, it gives them the happiness of suffering for what is right (3:14, 3:17), and of being sharers in the sufferings of Christ (4:13). There is no need to come down to the time of Trajan for this situation. It is one in which Christians in every part of the empire found themselves every day at any time after their true status had been disclosed by the action of Nero. The persecution situation in 1 Peter does not in any way compel us to date it after the lifetime of Peter.

Honour the King

But we must proceed with the arguments of those who cannot support the Petrine authorship. It is argued that, in the situation which existed in the time of Nero, Peter could never have written: 'For the Lord's sake accept the authority of every human institution, whether of the emperor as supreme, or of governors, as sent by him to punish those who do wrong and to praise those who do right . . . Fear God. Honour the emperor' (2:13–17). The fact is, however, that this is precisely the point of view expressed in Romans 13:1–7. The whole teaching of the New Testament, except only in the Book of Revelation in which Rome is damned, is that Christians must be loyal citizens and must demonstrate the falsity of the charges made against them by the excellence of their behaviour (1 Peter 2:15). Even in times of persecution, Christians fully acknowledged their obligation to be good citizens; and their only defence against persecution was to show by the excellence of their citizenship that they did not deserve such treatment. It is by no means impossible that Peter could have written like that.

A Sermon and a Pastoral Letter

What is the view of those who cannot believe that 1 Peter is the work of Peter himself?

First of all, it is suggested that the initial address (1:1–2) and the closing greetings and salutations (5:12–14) are later additions and no part of the original letter.

It is then suggested that 1 Peter as it stands is composed of two separate and quite different works. In 4:11, we find a doxology, a hymn of praise. The natural place for a doxology is at the end, and it is suggested that 1:3–4:11 is the first of the two works of which the letter is composed. It is further suggested that this part of 1 Peter was originally a baptismal sermon. There is indeed in it a reference to the baptism which saves us (3:21); and the advice to slaves, wives and husbands (2:18–3:7) would be entirely relevant to those who were entering the Christian Church from worship of the ancient Greek and Roman gods and setting out on the newness of the Christian life.

It is suggested that the second part of the letter, 4:12–5:11, contains the substance of a pastoral letter, written to strengthen and comfort during a time of persecution (4:12–19). At such a time, the elders were very important; the resistance power of the Church depended on them. The writer of this pastoral letter fears that greed and arrogance are creeping in (5:1–3), and he urges them faithfully to perform their important task (5:4).

On this view, 1 Peter is composed of two separate works – a baptismal sermon and a pastoral letter written in time of persecution, and neither has anything to do with Peter.

Asia Minor, not Rome

If 1 Peter is a baptismal sermon and a pastoral letter in time of persecution, where is its place of origin? If the letter is not Peter's, there is no need to connect it with Rome, and in any event it appears that the Roman church did not know or use 1 Peter. Let us put together certain facts.

(1) Pontus, Galatia, Cappadocia, Asia and Bithynia (1:1) are all in Asia Minor and all centred in Sinope.

(2) The first person to quote extensively from 1 Peter is Polycarp, Bishop of Smyrna – and Smyrna is in Asia Minor.

(3) Certain phrases in 1 Peter immediately turn our thoughts to parallel phrases in other parts of the New Testament. In 1 Peter 5:13, the church is called 'your sister church . . . chosen together with you', and in 2 John 13 the

church is described as an 'elect sister'. First Peter 1:8 speaks of Jesus Christ: 'Although you have not seen him, you love him; and even though you do not see him now, you believe in him and rejoice with an indescribable and glorious joy.' This turns our thoughts very naturally to Jesus' saying to Thomas in the Fourth Gospel: 'Blessed are those who have not seen and yet have come to believe' (John 20:29). First Peter urges the elders to tend, that is, to shepherd, the flock of God (1 Peter 5:2). That turns our thoughts to Jesus' instruction to Peter to feed his lambs and his sheep (John 21:15–17), and to Paul's farewell instruction to the elders of Ephesus to keep watch over the flock over which the Holy Spirit has made them guardians (Acts 20:28). All this is to say that the memories which 1 Peter awakens are of the Fourth Gospel, the Letters of John and of Paul at Ephesus. The Fourth Gospel and the Letters of John were most probably written at Ephesus – and Ephesus is in Asia Minor.

It seems that, in the case of 1 Peter, all roads lead to Asia Minor.

The Occasion of the Publication of 1 Peter

Assuming that 1 Peter has its origin in Asia Minor, can we suggest an occasion for its writing? It was written at a time of persecution. We know from Pliny's letters that in Bithynia about AD 112 there was a serious persecution of the Christians, and Bithynia is one of the provinces named in the address. We may well conjecture that it was to give courage to the Christians that 1 Peter was issued. It may be that at that time someone in a church in Asia Minor came upon these two documents and sent them out under the name of Peter. This would not be looked upon as forgery. Both in Jewish and in Greek practice, it was the regular custom to attach books to the name of the great writers of the past.

The Author of 1 Peter

If Peter did not write 1 Peter, is it possible to guess at the author? Let us reconstruct some of his essential qualifications. On our previous assumption, he must come from Asia Minor. On the basis of 1 Peter itself, he must be an *elder* and an *eyewitness* of the sufferings of Christ (1 Peter 5:1). Is there anyone who fits these requirements? Papias, Bishop of Hierapolis in about AD 170, who spent his life collecting all the information he could about the early days of the Church, tells of his methods and his sources: 'Nor shall I hesitate, along with my own interpretations, to set down for thee whatsoever I learned with care and remembered with care from the elders, guaranteeing its truth . . . Furthermore, if anyone chanced to arrive who had been really a follower of the elders, I would enquire as to the sayings of the elders – as to what Andrew or Peter said, or Philip, or Thomas or James, or John or Matthew, or any other of the Lord's disciples, also as to what Aristion or the Presbyter John, the Lord's disciples say. For I supposed that things out of books would not be of such use to me as the utterances of a living voice which was still with us.' Here, we have an elder called Aristion, who was a disciple of the Lord and, therefore, a witness of his sufferings. Is there anything to connect him with 1 Peter?

Aristion of Smyrna

When we turn to the *Apostolic Constitutions*, we find that one of the first bishops of Smyrna was called Ariston – which is the same name as Aristion. Now who is the one who quotes so often from 1 Peter? None other than Polycarp, a later Bishop of Smyrna. What more natural than that Polycarp should quote what might well have been the devotional classic of his own church?

Let us turn to the letters to the seven churches in the Book of Revelation and read the letter to Smyrna: 'Do not fear what you are about to suffer. Beware, the devil is about to throw some of you into prison so that you may be tested, and for ten days you will have affliction. Be faithful until death, and I will give you the crown of life' (Revelation 2:10). Can this be the very same persecution as that which originally lay behind 1 Peter? And was it for this persecution that Aristion, the Bishop of Smyrna, first wrote the pastoral letter which was afterwards to become a part of 1 Peter?

Such is the suggestion of B. H. Streeter. He thinks that 1 Peter is composed of a baptismal sermon and a pastoral letter written by Aristion, Bishop of Smyrna. Originally the pastoral letter was written to comfort and strengthen the people of Smyrna in AD 90 when the persecution mentioned in the Book of Revelation threatened the church. These writings of Aristion became the devotional classics and the cherished possessions of the church at Smyrna. Rather more than twenty years later, a much wider and more far-reaching persecution broke out in Bithynia and spread throughout northern Asia Minor. Someone remembered the letter and the sermon of Aristion, felt that they were the very thing the Church needed in its time of trial, and sent them out under the name of Peter, the great apostle.

An Apostle's Letter

We have stated in full both views of the origin, date and authorship of 1 Peter. There is no doubt about the ingenuity of the theory which B. H. Streeter has produced, nor that those who favour a later date have produced arguments which have to be considered. For our own part, however, we see no reason to doubt that the letter is the work of Peter himself, and that it was written not long after the great fire of Rome and the first persecution of the Christians with the object of encouraging the Christians of Asia Minor to stand fast when the onrushing tide of persecution sought to engulf them and take their faith away.

19

2 Peter

Against Immoral Teachers

The Neglected Book and its Contents

Second Peter is one of the neglected books of the New Testament. Very few people will claim to have read it, still less to have studied it in detail. The New Testament scholar E. F. Scott says: 'it is far inferior in every respect to 1 Peter', and goes on: 'it is the least valuable of the New Testament writings'. It was only with the greatest difficulty that 2 Peter gained entry into the New Testament, and for many years the Christian Church seemed to be unaware of its existence. But, before we approach its history, let us look at its contents.

The Threat of the Lawless Life

Second Peter was written to combat the beliefs and activities of a group of people who were a threat to the Church. It begins by insisting that Christians are people who have escaped from the corruption of the world (1:4) and must always remember that they have been purged of their past sins (1:9). There is laid upon them the duty of moral goodness, which culminates in the great Christian virtue of love (1:5–8).

Let us set out the characteristics of those whom 2 Peter rebukes. They twist Scripture to make it suit their own purpose (1:20, 3:16). They bring the Christian faith into disrepute (2:2). They are greedy and seek personal gain, and they exploit others (2:3, 2:14–15). They are doomed and will share the fate of the sinning angels (2:4), the world before the Flood (2:5), the citizens of Sodom and Gomorrah (2:6) and the false prophet Balaam (2:15). They are irrational and sensual creatures, ruled by their animal instincts (2:12) and dominated by their lusts (2:10, 2:18). Their eyes are full of adultery (2:14). They are presumptuous, self-willed and arrogant (2:10, 2:18). They spend even the daylight hours in abandoned and luxurious revelry (2:13). They speak of liberty; but what they call liberty is unrestrained licence, and they themselves are the slaves of their own lusts (2:19). Not only are they deluded, they also delude others and lead them astray (2:14, 2:18). They are worse than those who never knew the right, because they knew what goodness is and have lapsed into evil, like a dog returning to its vomit and a sow returning to the mud after it has been washed (2:20–2).

It is clear that Peter is describing antinomians, those who used God's grace as a justification for sinning. In all probability they were Gnostics, who said that only spirit was good and that matter was essentially evil and that, therefore, what we did with the body was not important and that we could follow physical appetites to excess and it made no difference. They lived the most immoral lives and encouraged others to do so, and they justified their actions by distorting grace and interpreting Scripture to suit themselves.

The Denial of the Second Coming

Further, these evil people denied the second coming (3:3–4). They argued that this was a stable world in which things remained unalterably the same, and that God was so slow to act that it was possible to assume that the second coming was never going to happen at all. The answer of 2 Peter is that this is not a stable world; that it has, in fact, been destroyed by water in the Flood and that it will be destroyed by fire in

the final conflagration (3:5–7). What they regard as unneces-
sary delay is in fact God withholding his hand in patience to
give men and women another chance to repent (3:8–9). But
the day of destruction is coming (3:10). A new heaven and a
new earth are on the way; therefore, goodness is an absolute
necessity if people are to be saved in the day of judgment
(3:11–14). With this Paul agrees, however difficult his letters
may be to understand, and however false teachers deliberately
misinterpret them (3:15–16). The duty of Christians is to stand
fast, firmly founded in the faith, and to grow in grace and in
the knowledge of Jesus Christ (3:17–18).

The Doubts of the Early Church

Such are the contents of the letter. For a long time, it was
regarded with doubt and with something very like misgiving.
There is no trace of it until after AD 200. It is not included in
the Muratorian Canon of AD 170, which was the first official
list of New Testament books. It did not exist in the Old Latin
Version of the Scriptures, nor in the New Testament of the
early Syrian church.

The famous scholars of Alexandria either did not know it
or were doubtful about it. Clement of Alexandria, who wrote
outlines of the books of Scripture, does not appear to have
included 2 Peter. The third-century biblical scholar Origen
says that Peter left behind one epistle which is generally
acknowledged; 'perhaps also a second, for it is a disputed
question'. The blind theologian Didymus, writing in the fourth
century, commented on it, but concluded his work by saying:
'It must not be forgotten that this letter is spurious; it may be
read in public; but it is not part of the canon of Scripture.'

Eusebius, the great scholar of Caesarea, who made a careful investigation of the Christian literature of his day, comes
to the conclusion: 'Of Peter, one Epistle, which is called his

former Epistle, is acknowledged by all; of this the ancient presbyters have made frequent use in their writings as indisputably genuine; but that which is circulated as his second Epistle we have received to be not canonical although, since it appeared to be useful to many, it has been diligently read with the other Scriptures.'

It was not until well into the fourth century that 2 Peter came to rest in the canon of the New Testament.

The Objections

Scholars of the past and of modern times are close to unanimity in their judgment that Peter is not the author of 2 Peter. Even the reformer John Calvin regarded it as impossible that Peter could have spoken of Paul as 2 Peter speaks of him (3:15–16), although he was willing to believe that someone else wrote the letter at Peter's request. What, then, are the arguments against Peter's authorship?

(1) There is the extreme slowness, and even reluctance, of the early Church to accept it. If it had been truly Peter's, there can be little doubt that the Church would have welcomed and honoured it from the beginning. But the reality of the situation was very different. For the first two centuries, there is no certain instance of the letter being quoted; it is regarded with doubt and suspicion for more than another century; and only late in the fourth century is it accepted.

(2) The contents make it difficult to believe that it is Peter's. There is no mention of the passion, the resurrection and the ascension of Jesus Christ; no mention of the Church as the true Israel; no mention of that faith which is a combination of undefeatable hope and trust; no mention of the Holy Spirit, of prayer, of baptism; and no passionate desire to call men and women to the supreme example of Jesus Christ. If one took away these great truths from 1 Peter, there

would be little or nothing left – and yet none of them occurs in 2 Peter.

(3) It is wholly different in character and style from 1 Peter. This was realized in the fourth century by the biblical scholar Jerome, who wrote: 'Simon Peter wrote two Epistles which are called Catholic, of which the authenticity of the second is denied by many because of the difference of the style from the first.' The Greek style of this letter is very difficult. F. B. Clogg calls it ambitious, artificial and often obscure, and remarks that it is the only book in the New Testament which is improved by translation. F. H. Chase, Bishop of Ely in the early part of the twentieth century, writes: 'The Epistle does produce the impression of being a somewhat artificial piece of rhetoric. It shows throughout signs of self-conscious effort. The author appears to be ambitious of writing in a style which is beyond his literary power.' He concludes that it is hard to reconcile the literary character of this letter with the supposition that Peter wrote it. James Moffatt says: '2 Peter is more periodic and ambitious than 1 Peter, but its linguistic and its stylistic efforts only reveal by their cumbrous obscurity a decided inferiority of conception, which marks it off from 1 Peter.'

It might be claimed, as Jerome did indeed claim, that, while Peter used Silvanus for 1 Peter, he used someone else to assist in writing down 2 Peter and that this explains the change in style. But, in his commentary on 2 Peter, J. B. Mayor compares the two letters. He quotes some of the great passages of 1 Peter and then says: 'I think that none who read these words can help feeling that, not even in Paul, not even in John, is there to be found a more beautiful or a more living description of the secret of primitive Christianity, of the force that overcame the world, than in the perfect quaternion of faith and hope and love and joy, which pervades this short epistle [i.e. 1 Peter]. No one could make the same assertion with regard to 2 Peter: thoughtful and interesting as it is, it lacks that intense sympathy, that flame of love, which marks 1 Peter . . . No change of circumstances can account for the change of tone of which we are conscious in passing from one epistle to the other.' It is the conclusion of that great and conservative scholar that no explanation, other than difference of authorship, can explain not so much the difference in style as the difference in atmosphere between 1 and 2 Peter. It is true that from the purely linguistic point of view there are 369 words which occur in 1 Peter which do not occur in 2 Peter, and there are 230 words which occur in 2 Peter and not in 1 Peter. But there is more than a difference in style. Writers can change their style and their vocabulary to suit a particular audience and occasion. But the difference between the two letters in atmosphere and attitude is so wide that it is hardly possible that the same person could have written both.

(4) Certain things within 2 Peter point strongly to a late date. So much time has passed that people have begun to abandon hope of the second coming altogether (3:4). The apostles are spoken of as figures of the past (3:2). The fathers, that is the founders of the Christian faith, are now figures of the almost dim and distant past; there have been generations between this letter and the beginnings of the Christian faith (3:4).

There are references which require the passing of the years to explain them. The reference to Peter's approaching death looks very like a reference to Jesus' prophecy in John 21:18–19; and the Fourth Gospel was not written until about AD 100. The statement that Peter is going to leave something which will continue his teaching after he has gone looks very like a reference to Mark's gospel (1:12–14).

Above all, there is the reference to the letters of Paul (3:15–16). From this, it is quite certain that Paul's letters are known and used throughout all the Church; they are public property, and furthermore they are regarded as Scripture and on a level with 'the other Scriptures' (3:16). It was not until at least AD 90 that these letters were collected and published, and it would take many years for them to acquire the position of sacred Scripture. It is practically impossible that anyone should write like this until mid-way through the second century AD.

All the evidence converges to prove that 2 Peter is a late book. It is not until the third century that it is quoted. The great scholars of the early Church did not regard it as Peter's, although they did not question its usefulness. The letter has references which require the passing of the years to explain them. The great interest of 2 Peter lies in the very fact that it was the last book in the New Testament to be written and the last to gain entry into the New Testament.

In Peter's Name

How, then, did it become attached to the name of Peter? The answer is that it was *deliberately* attached. This may seem to us a strange thing to do, but in the ancient world this was common practice. Plato's letters were written not by Plato but by a disciple in the master's name. The Jews repeatedly used this method of writing. Between the Old and the New Testament, books were written under the names of Solomon, Isaiah, Moses, Baruch, Ezra, Enoch and many others. And, in New Testament times, there is a whole literature around the name of Peter – the Gospel of Peter, the Preaching of Peter, the Apocalypse of Peter.

One significant fact makes this method of writing even more intelligible. The heretics used it. They issued misleading and damaging books under the names of the great apostles, claiming that they were the secret teaching of the great founders of the Church handed down by word of mouth to them. Faced with this, the Church retaliated in kind and issued books in which Christians set down for their own generation the things they were quite sure that the apostles would have said had they been facing this new situation. There is nothing either unusual or discreditable in a book being issued under the name of Peter although Peter did not write it. The writer, in humility, was putting the message which the Holy Spirit had given him into the mouth of Peter because he felt that his own name was unworthy to appear upon the book.

We will not find 2 Peter easy to read; but it is a book of major importance because it was written to people who were undermining the Christian ethic and the Christian doctrine and who had to be stopped before the Christian faith was wrecked by their distortion of the truth.

20

1 John

A Defence of the Faith

A Personal Letter and its Background

The First Letter of John is called a letter, but it has no opening address nor closing greetings such as the letters of Paul have. And yet no one can read it without feeling its intensely personal character. Beyond all doubt, the man who wrote it had in his mind's eye a definite situation and a definite group of people. Both the form and the personal character of 1 John will be explained if we think of it as what someone has called 'a loving and anxious sermon', written by a pastor who loved his people, and sent out to the various churches over which he had charge.

Any such letter is produced by an actual situation apart from which it cannot be fully understood. If we wish to understand 1 John, we have first of all to try to reconstruct the situation which produced it, remembering that it was written in Ephesus a little after AD 100.

The Falling Away

By AD 100, certain things had almost inevitably happened within the Church, especially in a place like Ephesus.

(1) Many were now second- or even third-generation Christians. The thrill of the first days had, to some extent at least, passed away. In 'The Prelude', Wordsworth said of one of the great moments of modern history:

Bliss was it in that dawn to be alive.

In the first days of Christianity, there was a glory and a splendour; but now Christianity had become a thing of habit, 'traditional, half-hearted, nominal'. People had grown used to it, and something of the wonder had been lost. Jesus knew human nature, and he had said: 'The love of many will grow cold' (Matthew 24:12). John was writing at a time when, for some at least, the first thrill had gone and the flame of devotion had died to a flicker.

(2) One result was that there were members of the Church who found that the standards which Christianity demanded were becoming a burden and who were tired of making the effort. They did not want to be *saints* in the New Testament sense of the term. The New Testament word for *saint* is *hagios*, which is also commonly translated as *holy*. Its basic meaning is *different*. The Temple was *hagios* because it was *different* from other buildings; the Sabbath was *hagios* because it was *different* from other days; the Jewish nation was *hagios* because it was *different* from other nations; and Christians were called to be *hagios* because they were called to be *different* from other men and women. There was always a distinct division between Christians and the world. In the Fourth Gospel, Jesus says: 'If you belonged to the world, the world would love you as its own. Because you do not belong to the world, but I have chosen you out of the world – therefore the world hates you' (John 15:19). 'I have given them your word,' said Jesus in his prayer to God, 'and the world has hated them because they do not belong to the world, just as I do not belong to the world' (John 17:14).

All of this involved an ethical demand. It demanded a new standard of moral purity, a new kindness, a new service, a new forgiveness – and it was difficult. And, once the first thrill and enthusiasm were gone, it became harder and harder to stand out against the world and to refuse to conform to the generally accepted standards and practices of the age.

(3) It is to be noted that 1 John shows no signs that the church to which it was written was being persecuted. The peril, as it has been put, was not persecution but seduction; it came from within. That, too, Jesus had foreseen. 'Many false prophets', he said, 'will arise, and lead many astray' (Matthew 24:11). This was a danger of which Paul had warned the leaders of this very church of Ephesus when he made his farewell address to them. 'I know', he said, 'that after I have gone, savage wolves will come in among you, not sparing the flock. Some even from your own group will come distorting the truth in order to entice the disciples to follow them' (Acts 20:29–30).

The trouble which 1 John seeks to combat came not from people who were out to destroy the Christian faith but from those who thought they were improving it. It came from people whose aim was to make Christianity intellectually respectable. They knew the intellectual trends and currents of the day, and felt that the time had come for Christianity to come to terms with secular philosophy and contemporary thought.

The Contemporary Philosophy

What, then, was this contemporary thought and philosophy with which the false prophets and mistaken teachers wished to align the Christian faith? Throughout the Greek world, there was a way of thinking to which the general name of Gnosticism is given. The basic belief of all Gnostic thought was that only spirit was good and that matter, the material world, was essentially evil. The Gnostics, therefore, inevitably despised the world since it was matter. In particular, they despised the body, which, being matter, was necessarily evil. Imprisoned within this body was the human spirit. That spirit was a seed of God, who was altogether good. So, the aim of life must be to release this heavenly seed imprisoned in the evil of the body. That could be done only by a secret knowledge and elaborate ritual which only true Gnostics could supply. Here was a train of thought which was written deep into Greek thinking – and which has not even now ceased to exist. Its basis is the conviction that all matter is evil and that spirit alone is good, and that the one real aim in life is to liberate the human spirit from the vile prison house of the body.

The False Teachers

With that in our minds, let us turn to 1 John and gather the evidence as to who these false teachers were and what they taught. They had been within the Church, but they had withdrawn from it. 'They went out from us, but they did not belong to us' (1 John 2:19). They were people of influence, for they claimed to be prophets. 'Many false prophets have gone out into the world' (1 John 4:1). Although they had left the Church, they still tried to disseminate their teaching within it and to deceive its members and lead them away from the true faith (1 John 2:26).

The Denial of Jesus' Messiahship

At least some of these false teachers denied that Jesus was the Messiah. 'Who is the liar', demands John, 'but the one who denies that Jesus is the Christ?' (1 John 2:22). It is most likely that these false teachers were not Gnostics in the true sense of the word, but Jews. Things had always been difficult for Jewish Christians, but the events of history made them doubly so. It was very difficult for Jews to come to believe in a crucified Messiah. But suppose they had begun to believe this, their difficulties were by no means finished. The Christians believed that Jesus would return quickly to vindicate his people. Clearly, that would be a hope that would be specially dear to the hearts of the Jews. Then, in AD 70, Jerusalem was captured by the Romans, who were so infuriated with the long intransigence and the suicidal resistance of the Jews that they tore the holy city stone from stone and drew a plough across the middle of it. In view of that, how could the Jews easily accept the hope that Jesus would come and save them? The holy city was desolate; the Jews were dispersed throughout the world. In view of that, how could it be true that the Messiah had come?

The Denial of the Incarnation

There was something even more serious than that. There was false teaching which came directly from an attempt from within the Church to bring Christianity into line with Gnosticism. We must remember the Gnostic point of view that spirit alone was good and matter utterly evil. *Given that point of view, any real incarnation is impossible.* That is exactly what, centuries later, St Augustine was to point out. Before he became a Christian, he was skilled in the philosophies of the various schools. In the *Confessions* (8:9), he tells us that somewhere in the writings of the Platonists he had read in one form or another nearly all the things that Christianity says; but there was one great Christian saying which he had never found in any of these works and which no one would ever find – and that saying was: 'The Word became flesh and lived among us' (John 1:14). Since these thinkers believed in the essential evil of matter and therefore the essential evil of the body, that was one thing they could never say.

It is clear that the false teachers against whom John was writing in this First Letter denied the reality of the incarnation and of Jesus' physical body. 'Every spirit', writes John, 'that confesses that Jesus Christ has come in the flesh is from God, and every spirit that does not confess Jesus is not from God' (1 John 4:2–3).

In the early Church, this refusal to admit the reality of the incarnation took, broadly speaking, two forms.

(1) In its more radical and wholesale form, it was called *Docetism*, which the scholar E. J. Goodspeed suggests might be translated as *Seemism*. The Greek verb *dokein* means *to seem*; and the Docetists taught that Jesus only *seemed* to have a body. They insisted that he was a purely spiritual being who had nothing but the appearance of having a body. One of the apocryphal books written from this point of view is the Acts of John, which dates from about AD 160. In it, John is made to say that sometimes when he touched Jesus he seemed to meet with a material body, but at other times 'the substance was immaterial, as if it did not exist at all', and also that, when Jesus walked, he never left any footprint upon the ground. The simplest form of Docetism is the complete denial that Jesus ever had a physical body.

(2) There was a more subtle, and perhaps more dangerous, variant of this theory connected with the name of Cerinthus. In tradition, John and Cerinthus were sworn enemies. The great early Church historian Eusebius (*Ecclesiastical History*, 4:14:6) hands down a story which tells how John went to the public bathhouse in Ephesus to bathe. He saw Cerinthus inside and refused even to enter the building. 'Let us flee,' he said, 'lest even the bathhouse fall, because Cerinthus the enemy of truth is within.' Cerinthus drew a definite distinction between the human Jesus and the divine Christ. He said that Jesus was a man, born in a perfectly natural way. He lived in special

obedience to God, and after his baptism the Christ in the shape of a dove descended upon him, from that power which is above all powers, and then he brought news of the Father who up to that point had been unknown. Cerinthus did not stop there. He said that, at the end of Jesus' life, the Christ again withdrew from him so that the Christ never suffered at all. It was the human Jesus who suffered, died and rose again.

This again comes out in the stories of the apocryphal gospels written under the influence of this point of view. In the Gospel of Peter, written in about AD 130, it is said that Jesus showed no pain upon the cross and that his cry was: 'My power! My power! Why have you forsaken me?' It was at that moment that the divine Christ left the human Jesus. The Acts of John go further. They tell how, when the human Jesus was being crucified on Calvary, John was actually talking to the divine Christ in a cave in the hillside and that the Christ said to him: 'John, to the multitude down below in Jerusalem I am being crucified, and pierced with lances and with reeds, and gall and vinegar are given me to drink. But I am speaking to you, and listen to what I say . . . Nothing, therefore, of the things they will say of me have I suffered' (Acts of John 97).

We may see from the Letters of Ignatius how widespread this way of thinking was. Ignatius was writing to a group of churches in Asia Minor which must have been much the same as the group to which 1 John was written. When Ignatius wrote, he was a prisoner and was being transported to Rome to be martyred by being flung to the wild animals in the arena. He wrote to the Trallians: 'Be deaf, therefore, when anyone speaks to you apart from Jesus Christ, who was of the family of David and Mary, who was truly born, both ate and drank, was truly persecuted under Pontius Pilate, was truly crucified and died . . . who also was truly raised from the dead . . . But if, as some affirm, who are without God – that is, who are unbelievers – his suffering was only a semblance . . . why am I a prisoner?' (Ignatius, *To the Trallians*, 9–10). To the Christians at Smyrna, he wrote: 'For he suffered all these things for us that we might attain salvation, and he truly suffered even as he also truly raised himself, not as some unbelievers say that his passion was merely in semblance' (*To the Smyrnaeans*, 2). Polycarp, writing to the Philippians, used John's very words: 'For everyone who does not confess that Jesus Christ has come in the flesh is an anti-Christ' (*To the Philippians*, 7:1).

This teaching of Cerinthus is also rebuked in 1 John. John writes of Jesus: 'This is the one who came by water and blood, Jesus Christ, *not with the water only but with the water and the blood*' (1 John 5:6). The point of that verse is that the Gnostic teachers would have agreed that the divine Christ came by *water*, that is, at the baptism of Jesus; but they would have denied that he came by *blood*, that is, by the cross, for they insisted that the divine Christ left the human Jesus before his crucifixion.

The great danger of this heresy is that it comes from what can only be called a mistaken reverence. It is afraid to ascribe to Jesus full humanity. It regards it as irreverent to think that he had a truly physical body. It is a heresy which is by no means dead but is still held today, usually quite unconsciously, by many devout Christians. But it must be remembered, as John so clearly saw, that our salvation was dependent on the full identification of Jesus Christ with us. As one of the great early Church fathers unforgettably put it, 'He became what we are to make us what he is.'

This Gnostic belief had certain practical consequences in the lives of those who held it.

1 JOHN

(1) The Gnostic attitude to matter and to all created things produced a certain attitude to the body and the things to do with the body. That attitude might take any one of three different forms.

(a) It might take the form of self-denial, with fasting and celibacy and rigid control, even deliberate ill-treatment, of the body. The view that celibacy is better than marriage and that sex is sinful goes back to Gnostic influence and belief – and this is a view which still lingers on in certain quarters. There is no trace of that view in this letter.

(b) It might take the form of an assertion that the body did not matter and that, therefore, its appetites might be satisfied without restraint. Since the body was in any event evil, it made no difference what was done with it. There are echoes of this in this letter. John condemns as liars all who say that they know God and yet do not keep God's commandments; those who say that they abide in Christ ought to walk as Christ walked (1 John 1:6, 2:4–6). There were clearly Gnostics in these communities who claimed special knowledge of God but whose conduct was a long way from the demands of the Christian ethic.

In certain quarters, this Gnostic belief went even further. Gnostics were people who had *gnōsis*, *knowledge*. Some held that real Gnostics must, therefore, know the best as well as the worst and must enter into every experience of life at its highest or at its deepest level, as the case may be. It might almost be said that such people held that it was an obligation to sin. There is a reference to this kind of belief in the letter to Thyatira in the book of Revelation, where the risen Christ refers to those who have known 'the deep things of Satan' (Revelation 2:24). And it may well be that John is referring to these people when he insists that 'God is light and in him there is no darkness at all' (1 John 1:5). These particular

Gnostics would have held that there was in God not only blazing light but also deep darkness – and that an individual must penetrate both. It is easy to see the disastrous consequences of such a belief.

(c) There was a third kind of Gnostic belief. True Gnostics regarded themselves as spiritual people in every sense, as having shed all the material things of life and released their spirits from the bondage of matter. Such Gnostics held that they were so spiritual that they were above and beyond sin and had reached spiritual perfection. It is to them that John refers when he speaks of those who deceive themselves by saying that they have no sin (1 John 1:8–10).

Whichever of these three forms Gnostic belief took, its ethical consequences were perilous in the extreme; and it is clear that the last two forms were to be found in the society to which John wrote.

(2) Further, this Gnosticism resulted in an attitude to men and women which inevitably destroyed Christian fellowship. We have seen that Gnostics aimed at the release of the spirit from the prison house of the evil body by means of an elaborate and mysterious knowledge. Clearly, such a knowledge was not for everyone. Ordinary people were too involved in the everyday life and work of the world ever to have time for the study and discipline necessary; and, even if they had had the time, many were intellectually incapable of grasping the involved speculations of Gnostic theosophy and so-called philosophy.

This produced an inevitable result. It divided people into two classes – those who were capable of a really spiritual life, and those who were not. In the ancient world, every individual was thought of as consisting of three parts. There was the *sōma*, the *body*, the physical part. There was the *psuchē*, which is often translated as *soul*; but we must be careful, because it does not mean what we mean by *soul*. To the Greeks, the *psuchē* was the principle of physical life. Everything which had physical life had *psuchē*. *Psuchē* was the life principle which human beings shared with all living creatures. Finally, there was the *pneuma*, the spirit; and it was the spirit which was possessed only by human beings and which made them kin to God.

The aim of Gnosticism was the release of the *pneuma* from the *sōma*; but that release could be won only by long and arduous study which only the intellectuals who had time on their hands could ever undertake. The Gnostics, therefore, divided people into two classes – the *psuchikoi*, who could never advance beyond the principle of physical life and never attain to anything else than what was to all intents and purposes animal living; and the *pneumatikoi*, who were truly spiritual and truly akin to God.

The result was clear. The Gnostics produced a spiritual aristocracy who looked with contempt and even hatred on lesser mortals. The *pneumatikoi* regarded the *psuchikoi* as contemptible, earthbound creatures who could never know what real religion was. The consequence was obviously the annihilation of Christian fellowship. That is why John insists throughout his letter that the true test of Christianity is love for one another. If we really are walking in the light, we have fellowship with one another (1:7). Whoever claims to be in the light and hates a fellow Christian is in fact in darkness (2:9–11). The proof that we have passed from dark to light is that we love each other (3:14–17). The marks of Christianity are belief in Christ and love for one another (3:23). God is love, and whoever does not love does not know God at all (4:7–8). Because God loved us, we ought to love each other; it is when we love each other that God dwells in us (4:10–12). The commandment is that those who love God must love their brothers and sisters also, and those who say they love God and at the same time hate their brothers and sisters are branded as liars (4:20–1). The Gnostics, to put it bluntly, would have said that the mark of true religion is contempt for ordinary men and women; John insists in every chapter that the mark of true religion is love for everyone.

Here, then, is a picture of these Gnostic heretics. They talked of being born of God, of walking in the light, of having no sin, of dwelling in God, of knowing God. These were their catchphrases. They had no intention of destroying the Church and the faith; by their way of thinking, they were going to cleanse the Church of dead wood and make Christianity an intellectually respectable philosophy, fit to stand beside the great systems of the day. But the effect of their teaching was to deny the incarnation, to eliminate the Christian ethic and to make fellowship within the Church impossible. It is little wonder that John seeks, with such fervent pastoral devotion, to defend the churches he loved from such an insidious attack from within. This was a threat far more perilous than any persecution from outside; the very existence of the Christian faith was at stake.

The Message of John

The First Letter of John is a short letter, and we cannot look within it for a systematic exposition of the Christian faith. Nonetheless, it will be of the greatest interest to examine the basic underlying beliefs with which John confronts those threatening to wreck the Christian faith.

The Object of Writing

John's object in writing is twofold; yet the two aspects are one and the same. He writes that the joy of his people may be completed (1:4), and that they may not sin (2:1). He sees clearly that, however attractive the wrong way may be, it is not in its nature to bring happiness. To bring his people joy and to preserve them from sin are one and the same thing.

The Idea of God

John has two great things to say about God. God is light, and in him there is no darkness at all (1:5). God is love, and that made him love us before we loved him, and made him send his Son as a remedy for our sins (4:7–10, 16). John's conviction is that God is self-revealing and self-giving. He is light, and not darkness; he is love, and not hate.

The Idea of Jesus

Because the main attack of the false teachers was on the person of Christ, this letter, which is concerned to answer them, is specially rich and helpful in what it has to say about him.

(1) Jesus is the one who was from the beginning (1:1, 2:14). When we are confronted with Jesus, we are confronted with the eternal.

(2) Another way of putting this is to say that Jesus is the Son of God, and for John it is essential to be convinced of that (4:15, 5:5). The relationship of Jesus to God is unique, and in him is seen God's ever-seeking and ever-forgiving heart.

(3) Jesus is the Christ, the Messiah (2:22, 5:1). That again, for him, is an essential article of belief. It may seem that here we come into a region of ideas which is much narrower and, in fact, specifically Jewish. But there is something essential here. To say that Jesus is from the beginning and that he is the Son of God is to preserve his connection with *eternity*; to say that he is the Messiah is to preserve his connection with *history*. It is to see his coming as the event towards which

God's plan, working itself out in his chosen people, was moving.

(4) Jesus was most truly and fully human. To deny that Jesus came in the flesh is to be moved by the spirit of antichrist (4:2–3). It is John's witness that Jesus was so truly human that he himself had known and touched him with his own hands (1:1–3). No writer in the New Testament holds with greater intensity the full reality of the incarnation. Not only did Jesus become a man, he also suffered for men and women. It was by water and blood that he came (5:6); and he laid down his life for us (3:16).

(5) The coming of Jesus, his incarnation, his life, his death, his resurrection and his ascension all combine to deal with human sin. Jesus was without sin (3:5); and human beings are essentially sinners, even though in our arrogance we may claim to be without sin (1:8–10); and yet the sinless one came to take away the sin of sinning humanity (3:5). In regard to our sin, Jesus is two things.

(a) He is our *advocate* with the Father (2:1). The word is *paraklētos*. A *paraklētos* is someone who is called in to help. The word could be used of a physician; it was often used of a witness called in to give evidence in favour of someone on trial, or of a defending lawyer called in to defend someone accused of an offence. Jesus pleads our case with God; he, the sinless one, is the defender of sinning men and women.

(b) But Jesus is more than that. Twice, John calls him the *expiation* for our sins (2:2, 4:10). When we sin, the relationship which should exist between us and God is broken. An expiatory sacrifice is one which restores that relationship; or, rather, it is a sacrifice through which that relationship is restored. It is an *atoning* sacrifice, a sacrifice which once again puts us *at one* with God. So, through what Jesus was and did, the relationship between God and all people, broken by sin, is restored. Jesus does not only plead the case of sinners; he sets them at one with God. The blood of Jesus Christ cleanses us from all sin (1:7).

(6) As a result of all this, through Jesus Christ, all who believe have life (4:9, 5:11–12). This is true in a double sense. Believers have life in the sense that they are saved from death; and they have life in the sense that living has ceased to be mere existence and has become life in its fullest sense.

(7) All this may be summed up by saying that Jesus is the Saviour of the world (4:14). Here, we have something which has to be set out in full. 'The Father has sent his Son as the Saviour of the world' (4:14). We have already talked of Jesus as pleading our case before God. If we were to leave that without addition, it might be argued that God wished to condemn human beings and was deflected from his dire purpose by the self-sacrifice of Jesus Christ. But that is not so, because, for John, as for every writer in the New Testament, the whole initiative lay with God. It was God who sent his Son to be the Saviour of men and women.

Within the short span of this letter, the wonder and the glory and the grace of Christ are most fully set out.

The Spirit

In this letter, John has less to say about the Spirit; for his highest teaching about the Spirit, we must turn back to the Fourth Gospel. It may be said that, in 1 John, the function of the Spirit is in some sense to be the liaison between God and his people. It is the Spirit who makes us conscious that there is within us the abiding presence of God through Jesus Christ (3:24, 4:13). We may say that it is the Spirit who enables us to grasp the precious fellowship with God which is being offered to us.

The World

The world within which Christians live is hostile; it is a world without God. It does not know Christians, because it did not know Christ (3:1). It hates Christians, just as it hated Christ (3:13). The false teachers are from the world and not from God, and it is because they speak its language that the world is ready to hear them and accept them (4:4–5). In a sweeping statement, John says that the whole world is in the power of the evil one (5:19). It is for that reason that Christians have to overcome it, and their weapon in the struggle with the world is faith (5:4).

Hostile as the world is, it is doomed. The world and all its desires are passing away (2:17). That, indeed, is why it is folly to give one's heart to the world; the world is coming to an end. Although Christians live in a hostile world which is passing away, there is no need for despair and fear. The darkness is past; the true light now shines (2:8). God in Christ has broken into time; the new age has come. It is not yet fully brought to fruition, but the consummation is sure.

Christians live in an evil and a hostile world, but they possess the means to overcome it; and, when the destined end of the world comes, they will be safe, because they already possess that which makes them members of the new community in the new age.

The Fellowship of the Church

John does more than move in the high realms of theology; he has certain most practical things to say about the Christian Church and the Christian life. No New Testament writer stresses more consistently or more strenuously the necessity of Christian fellowship. Christians, John was convinced, are not only bound to God; they are also bound to each other.

When we walk in the light, we have fellowship with each other (1:7). Those who claim to walk in the light but who hate their brothers and sisters are in reality walking in darkness; those who love their brothers and sisters are the ones who are in the light (2:9–11). The proof that people have passed from darkness to light is the fact that they love one another. To hate a fellow human being is in essence to be a murderer, as Cain was. If we are able out of our own wealth to help another's poverty and do not do so, it is ridiculous for us to claim that the love of God dwells in us. The essence of religion is to believe in the name of the Lord Jesus Christ and to love one another (3:11–17, 3:23). God is love; and, therefore, those who love are kin to God. God has loved us, and that is the best reason for loving each other (4:7–12). If we say that we love God and at the same time hate another person, we are liars. The command is that all who love God must love others too (4:20–1).

It was John's conviction that the only way in which anyone can prove love for God is by loving other people, and that that love must be not only a sentimental emotion but also a dynamic towards practical help.

Christian Righteousness

No New Testament writer makes a stronger ethical demand than John, or more strongly condemns a so-called religion which fails to produce ethical action. God is righteous, and the life of everyone who knows him must reflect his righteousness (2:29). Whoever abides in Christ, and is born of God, does not sin; whoever does not do right is not of God (3:3–10); and the characteristic of this righteousness is that it translates into love for other people (3:10–11). We show our love to God and to others by keeping God's commandments (5:2). Whoever is born of God does not sin (5:18).

For John, knowledge of God and obedience to him must always go hand in hand. It is by keeping his commandments that we prove that we really do know God. Those who say that they know him and who do not keep his commandments are liars (2:3–5).

It is, in fact, this obedience which is the basis of effective prayer. We receive what we ask from God because we keep his commandments and do what is pleasing in his sight (3:22).

The two marks which characterize genuine Christianity are love for one another and obedience to the revealed commandments of God.

The Destination of the Letter

There are certain baffling problems with regard to the letter's destination. The letter itself gives us no clue as to where it was sent. Tradition strongly connects it with Asia Minor, and especially with Ephesus, where, according to tradition, John lived for many years. But there are certain other odd facts which somehow have to be explained.

The sixth-century Roman historian Cassiodorus says that the First Letter of John was titled *Ad Parthos*, 'To the Parthians'; and St Augustine has a series of ten tractates written on the Epistle of John *ad Parthos*. One Geneva manuscript complicates the matter still further by titling the letter *Ad Sparthos*. There is no such word as *Sparthos*. There are two possible explanations of this impossible title. (1) Just possibly, what is meant is *Ad Sparsos*, which would mean 'to the Christians scattered abroad'. (2) In Greek, *Ad Parthos* would be *Pros Parthous*. Now, in the early manuscripts, there was no space between the words, and they were all written in capital letters, so that the title would run PROSPARTHOUS. A scribe writing to dictation could quite easily put that down as PROSSPARTHOUS, especially if he did not know what the title meant. *Ad Sparthos* can be eliminated as a mere mistake.

But where did 'To the Parthians' come from? There is one possible explanation. The Second Letter of John does tell us of its destination; it is written to *The elect lady and her children* (2 John 1). Let us turn to the end of 1 Peter. The Authorized Version has: 'The church that is at Babylon, elected together with you, saluteth you' (1 Peter 5:13). The phrase *the church that is* is printed in the Authorized Version in italics. This, of course, means that it has no equivalent in the Greek, which has, in fact, no actual mention of a *church* at all. This the Revised Standard Version accurately indicates: 'She who is at Babylon, who is likewise chosen [elect], sends you greetings.' As far as the Greek goes, it would be perfectly possible, and indeed natural, to take that as referring not to a *church* but to a *lady*. That is precisely what certain of the scholars in the very early Church did. Now, we find *the elect lady* again in 2 John. It was easy to identify the two elect ladies and to assume that 2 John was also written to Babylon. The natural title for the inhabitants of Babylon was Parthians, and hence we have the explanation of the title.

The process went even further. The Greek for *the elect lady* is *hē elektē*. We have already seen that the early manuscripts were written all in capital letters; and it would be just possible to take *Elektē* not as an adjective meaning *elect* but as a proper name, *Elekta*. This is, in fact, what the second-century theologian Clement of Alexandria may have done, for we have information that he said that the Johannine letters were written to a certain Babylonian lady, Elekta by name, and to her children.

So, it may well be that the title *Ad Parthos* arose from a series of misunderstandings. *The elect one* in 1 Peter is quite certainly the Church, as the Authorized Version rightly saw.

James Moffatt translates: 'Your sister church in Babylon, elect like yourselves, salutes you.' Further, it is almost certain that, in any event, *Babylon* there stands for *Rome*, which the early writers identified with Babylon, the great prostitute, drunk with the blood of the saints (cf. Revelation 17:5). The title *Ad Parthos* has a most interesting history; but clearly it arose from a simple misunderstanding.

There is one further complication. Clement of Alexandria referred to John's letters as 'written to virgins'. On the face of it, that is improbable, for it would not be a specially relevant title for them. How could that idea come about? The Greek would be *Pros Parthenous*, which closely resembles *Pros Parthous*; and, it so happens, John was regularly called *Ho Parthenos*, the Virgin, because he never married and because of the purity of his life. This further title must have come from a confusion between *Ad Parthos* and *Ho Parthenos*.

This is a case where we may take it that tradition is right and all the ingenious theories mistaken. We may take it that these letters were written in Ephesus and to the surrounding churches in Asia Minor. When John wrote, it would certainly be to the district for which he had oversight – and that was Ephesus and the surrounding territory. He is never mentioned in connection with Babylon.

In Defence of the Faith

John wrote his great letter to meet a threatening situation and in defence of the faith. The heresies which he attacked are by no means altogether echoes of what Wordsworth, in his poem 'The Solitary Reaper', called 'old unhappy far-off things and battles long ago'. They are still beneath the surface, and sometimes they even still raise their heads. To study his letter will confirm us in the true faith and enable us to have a defence against anything that would seduce us from it.

21

2 & 3 John

Love and Truth

The very shortness of these two letters is the best guarantee of their genuineness. They are so brief and so comparatively unimportant that no one would have gone to the trouble of inventing them and of attaching them to the name of John. A standard papyrus sheet measured ten by eight inches, and the length of these letters is to be explained by the fact that they would each take up almost exactly one sheet.

The Elder

Each of them is said to come from 'the elder' – 2 John begins: 'The elder to the elect lady and her children,' while 3 John begins: 'The elder to the beloved Gaius.' It is extremely unlikely that *the elder* is an official or ecclesiastical title. Elders were officials attached to one congregation whose jurisdiction did not extend outside that congregation, whereas the writer of these letters certainly assumes that he has the right to speak and that his word will carry weight in congregations where he is not actually present. He speaks as one whose authority goes out to the Church at large. The word is *presbuteros*, which originally meant *an elder*, not in the official but in the natural sense of the term. We would be better to translate it as *the ancient*, or *the aged*, for it is not from a position in the Church but from his age and personal qualities that the writer of these letters draws his authority.

In fact, we know that in Ephesus there was a very old man named John who held a very special position. In the days of the early Church, there was a churchman called Papias who lived from about AD 60 to 130. He had a passion for collecting all the information he could lay hands on about the early days of the Church. He was not a great scholar. The fourth-century Church historian Eusebius dismisses him as 'a man of very limited intelligence'; but he does transmit to us some most interesting information. He became Bishop of Hierapolis, but he had a close connection with Ephesus, and he tells us of his own methods of acquiring information. He frequently uses *elder* in the sense of *one of the fathers of the Church*, and he mentions a particularly distinguished *elder* whose name was John. 'I shall not hesitate', he writes, 'to put down for you, along with my own interpretations, whatsoever things I have at any time learned carefully from the *elders*, and carefully remembered, guaranteeing their truth. For I did not, like the multitude, take pleasure in those that speak much, but in those that teach the truth; not in those who relate strange commandments, but in those who deliver the commandments given by the Lord to faith, and springing from the truth itself. If, then, anyone came who had been a follower of the *elders*, I questioned him in regard to the words of the *elders* – what Andrew, or what Peter, had said, or what was said by Philip, or by Thomas, or by James, or by John, or by Matthew, or by any other of the disciples of the Lord; and what things Aristion, or the *Elder John* say. For I did not think that what was to be learned from books would profit me as much as what came from the living and abiding voice.' Clearly, the *Elder John*, John who had reached a great age, was a notable figure in Ephesus, although he is clearly distinguished from John the apostle.

It must be this John who wrote these two little letters. By this time, he was an old man, one of the last surviving links with Jesus and his disciples. He was a man who had the authority of a bishop in Ephesus and in the places around it; and, when he saw that a church was threatened with trouble and heresy, he wrote with gracious and loving correction to his people. Here are the letters of one of the last of the first generation of Christians, a man whom all loved and respected.

Common Authorship

That the two letters are from the one hand there is no doubt. Short as they are, they have a great deal in common. Second John begins: 'The elder to the elect lady and her children, whom I love in the truth.' Third John begins: 'The elder to the beloved Gaius, whom I love in truth.' Second John goes on: 'I was overjoyed to find some of your children walking in the truth' (verse 4); and 3 John goes on: 'I have no greater joy than this, to hear that my children are walking in the truth' (verse 4). Second John comes to an end: 'Although I have much to write to you, I would rather not use paper and ink; instead I hope to come to you and talk with you face to face, so that our joy may be complete' (verse 12). Third John comes to an end: 'I had much to write to you, but I would rather not write with pen and ink; instead I hope to see you soon, and we will talk together face to face' (verses 13–14). There is the closest possible similarity between the two letters.

There is further the closest possible connection between the situation of these letters and that in 1 John. In 1 John 4:3, we read: 'Every spirit that does not confess Jesus is not from God. And this is the spirit of the antichrist, of which you have heard that it is coming; and now it is already in the world.' In 2 John 7, we read: 'Many deceivers have gone out into the world, those who do not confess that Jesus Christ has come in the flesh; any such person is a deceiver and the antichrist.'

It is clear that 2 and 3 John are closely connected with each other, and that both are closely connected with 1 John. They are dealing with the same situation, the same dangers and the same people.

The Problem of the Second Letter

These two little letters confront us with few serious problems. The only real one is to decide whether the Second Letter was sent to an individual or to a church. It begins: 'The elder to the elect lady and her children.' The problem centres on this phrase *the elect lady*. The Greek is *eklektē kuria*, and there are three possible ways of taking it.

(1) It is just possible, though not really likely, that *Eklektē* is a proper name and that *kuria* is a quite usual affectionate address. *Kurios* (the masculine form) has many meanings. It very commonly means *sir*; it means *master* of slaves and *owner* of possessions; on a much higher level, it means *lord* and is the word so often used as a title for Jesus. In letters, *kurios* has a special use. It is practically the equivalent of the English phrase *My Dear*. So, a soldier writes home, saying: *Kurie mou patēr*, My Dear Father. In letters, *kurios* is an address combining affection and respect. It is therefore just possible that this letter is addressed to *My Dear Eklektē*. The biblical scholar Rendel Harris, indeed, went to the lengths of saying that 2 John is nothing other than a Christian love letter. This is unlikely, as we shall see, for more than one reason. But one thing is decisive against it. Second John ends: 'The children of your elect sister send you their greetings.' The Greek is again *eklektē*; and, if it is a proper name at the

beginning of the letter, it must also be a proper name at the end. This would mean that there were two sisters both called by the very unusual name of *Eklektē* – which is simply unbelievable.

(2) It is possible to take *Kuria* as a proper name, for there are examples of this usage. We would then take *eklektē* in its normal New Testament sense; and the letter would be written to the *elect Kuria*. The objections are threefold. (a) It seems unlikely that any single individual could be spoken of as loved by all those who have known the truth (verse 1). (b) Verse 4 says that John rejoiced when he found some of her children walking in the truth; the implication is that others did not walk in the truth. This would seem to imply a number greater than one woman's family could contain. (c) The decisive objection is that, throughout the letter, the *eklektē kuria* is addressed sometimes in the singular and sometimes in the plural. The singular occurs in verses 4, 5 and 13; and the plural occurs in verses 6, 8, 10 and 12. It would be almost impossible that an individual would be addressed in this way.

(3) So, we must come to the conclusion that *the elect lady* means *a church*. There is, in fact, good evidence that the expression was used with this meaning. First Peter, in the Authorized Version, ends with greetings from 'the church that is at Babylon elected together with you' (1 Peter 5:13). The words *church that is* are in italics; that, of course, means that they are not in the Greek and have been supplied in translation to fill out the sense. The Greek literally reads: 'The Elect One at Babylon'; and *The Elect One* is feminine, as is reflected in more modern translations. Few have ever doubted that the phrase means *The church which is at Babylon*; and that is how we must take it in John's letter also. No doubt, the Elect Lady goes back to the idea of the Church

as the Bride of Christ. We can be certain that 2 John is written not to an individual but to a church.

The Problem in the Early Church

Both 2 John and 3 John throw vivid light on a problem which sooner or later had to arise within the organization of the early Church. Let us see if we can reconstruct the situation which lies behind them. It is clear that John, this very old man, regards himself as having a right to act as guide and counsellor and to administer warning and rebuke in the churches whose members are his children. In 2 John, he writes of those who are doing well (verse 4), and by implication suggests that there are others who are not so satisfactory. He further makes it clear that there are travelling teachers in the district, some of whom are preaching false and dangerous doctrine, and he gives orders that such teachers are not to be accepted and not to be given hospitality (verses 7–11). Here, then, John is exercising what is to him an unquestioned right to issue orders to his churches and is seeking to guard against a situation in which travelling teachers of falsehood may arrive at any moment.

The situation behind 3 John is more complicated. The letter is written to one called Gaius, of whose character and actions John most thoroughly approves (verses 3–5). Wandering missionaries have come to the church, people who are fellow helpers of the truth, and Gaius has given them true Christian hospitality (verses 6–8). In the same church is another man called Diotrephes, who loves to put himself first (verse 9). Diotrephes is portrayed as a dictatorial character who will stand no rival to his authority. Diotrephes has refused to receive the wandering teachers of the truth and has actually tried to drive out of the church those who did receive them. He will have nothing to do with travelling teachers even when they are true preachers of the word (verse 10). Then into the picture comes a man called Demetrius, to whom John gives a personal character reference as a good man and one to be hospitably welcomed (verse 12). The simplest explanation of Demetrius is that he must be the leader of a band of wandering teachers who are on their way to the church to which John is writing. Diotrephes will certainly refuse to have anything to do with them and will try to have those who do receive them thrown out; and John is writing to urge Gaius to receive the wandering teachers and not to be intimidated by the domineering Diotrephes, whom he (John) will deal with when he visits the church in question (verse 10). The whole situation turns on the reception of the travelling teachers. Gaius has received such teachers before, and John urges him to receive them and their leader Demetrius again. Diotrephes has shut the door on them and defied the authority of the venerable John.

The Threefold Ministry

All this looks like a very unhappy situation, and indeed it was. Nonetheless, it was one which was bound to arise. In the nature of things, a problem of ministry was bound to emerge within the Church. In its earliest days, the Church had three different kinds of ministries.

(1) Unique, and above all others, stood the *apostles*, those who had been in the company of Jesus and who had been witnesses of the resurrection. They were the undisputed leaders of the Church. Their commission ran throughout the whole Church; in any country and in any congregation, their ministry was supreme.

(2) There were the *prophets*. They were not attached to any one congregation. They were wandering preachers, going where the Spirit moved them and giving to others the message

which the Spirit of God gave to them. They had given up home and occupation and the comfort and the security of a settled life to be the wandering messengers of God. They, too, had a very special place in the Church. The *Didache*, or, to give it its English name, *The Teaching of the Twelve Apostles*, is the earliest book of Church order. In it, the unique position of the prophets is made clear. The order of service for the Eucharist is laid down and the prayers are given; the service ends with the prayer of thanksgiving, which is given in full; and then comes the sentence: 'But suffer the prophets to give thanks as much as they will' (*Didache*, 10:7). The prophets were not to be brought under the rules and regulations which governed ordinary people. So, the Church had two sets of people whose authority was not confined to any one congregation and who had right of entry to every congregation.

(3) There were the *elders*. During their first missionary journey, part of the work of Paul and Barnabas was to ordain elders in all the local churches which they founded (Acts 14:23). The elders were the officials of the settled community; their work was within their congregation, and they did not move outside it. It is clear that they were the backbone of the organization of the early Church; on them the routine work and the solidity of the individual congregations depended.

The Problem of the Wandering Preachers

The position of the apostles presented no real problem; they were unique and their position could never really be disputed. But the wandering prophets did present a problem. Their position was one which was singularly liable to abuse. They had huge prestige; and it was possible for the most undesirable characters to enter into a way of life in which they moved from place to place, living in very considerable comfort at the expense of the local congregations. A clever rogue could make a very comfortable living as a wandering prophet. Even the Greek satirists saw this. The writer, Lucian, in his work called the *Peregrinus*, draws a picture of a man who had found the easiest possible way of making a living without working. He was a trickster who lived off the fat of the land by travelling round the various communities of the Christians, settling down wherever he liked and living luxuriously at their expense. The *Didache* clearly saw this danger and laid down definite regulations to meet it. The regulations are long, but they reveal so much about the life of the early Church that they are worth quoting in full (*Didache*, 11–12).

> If anyone comes and instructs you on the foregoing lines, make him welcome. But should the instructor himself then turn round and introduce teaching of a different and subversive nature, pay no attention to him. If it aims at promoting righteousness and knowledge of the Lord, though, welcome him as you would the Lord.
>
> As regards apostles and prophets, according to the gospel directions this is how you are to act. Every apostle who comes to you should be welcomed as by the Lord, but he is not to stay more than a day, or two days if it is really necessary. If he stays for three days, he is no genuine prophet. And an apostle at his departure should accept nothing but as much provisions as will last him to his next night's lodging. If he asks for money, he is not a genuine prophet.
>
> While a prophet is uttering words in a trance, you are on no account to subject him to any tests or verifications; every sin shall be forgiven, but this sin shall not be forgiven. Nonetheless, not all who speak in trances are prophets unless they also exhibit the manners

and conduct of the Lord. It is by their behaviour that you can tell the impostor from the true. Thus, if a prophet should happen to call out for something to eat while he is in a true trance, he will not actually eat of it; if he does, he is a fraud. Also, even supposing a prophet is sound enough in his teaching, yet if his deeds do not correspond with his words, he is an impostor . . . If any prophet, speaking in a trance, says, 'Give me money (or anything else)', do not listen to him. On the other hand, if he bids you to give it to someone else who is in need, nobody should criticize him.

Everyone who comes 'in the Name of the Lord' is to be made welcome, though later on you must test him and find out about him. You will be able to distinguish the true from the false. If the newcomer is only passing through, give him all the help you can – though he is not able to stay more than a couple of days with you, or three if it is unavoidable. But if he wants to settle down among you, and is a skilled worker, let him find employment and earn his bread. If he knows no trade, use your discretion to make sure that he does not live in idleness simply on the strength of being a Christian. Unless he agrees to this, he is only trying to exploit Christ. You must be on your guard against men of that sort.

The *Didache* even invents the word *Christmonger, trader in Christ, Christemporos,* to describe this kind of person.

John was entirely justified in warning his people that the wrong kind of wandering prophets might come claiming hospitality and in saying that they must on no account be received. There is no doubt that, in the early Church, these wandering prophets became a problem. Some of them were heretical teachers, even if they were sincerely convinced of their own teaching. Some were simply plausible rogues who had found an easy way to make a comfortable living. That is the picture which lies behind 2 John.

The Clash of Ministries

But the situation behind 3 John is in some ways even more serious. The problem figure is Diotrephes. He is the man who will have nothing to do with wandering teachers and who seeks to cast out anyone who dares to give them a welcome. He is the man who will not accept the authority of John and whom John brands as a domineering character. There is much more behind this than meets the eye. This was no storm in a teacup; it was a fundamental split between the local and the travelling ministry.

Obviously, the whole structure of the Church depended on a strong, settled ministry. That is to say, its very existence depended on a strong and authoritative eldership. As time went on, the settled ministry was bound to become frustrated under the remote control of even one so famous and venerable as John, and to resent the possibly upsetting invasions of wandering prophets and evangelists. It was by no means impossible that, however well-intentioned they were, these travellers could do far more harm than good.

Here is the situation behind 3 John. John represents the old apostolic control from a distance; Demetrius and his band of missionaries represent the wandering prophets and preachers; Diotrephes represents the settled ministry of the local elders, who wish to run their own congregation and who regard the wandering preachers as dangerous intruders; Gaius represents the good, well-meaning man who is torn in two and cannot make up his mind.

What happened in this case we do not know. But the end of the matter in the Church was that the wandering preachers faded from the scene, and the apostles in the nature of things passed from this earth, and the settled ministry became the ministry of the Church. In a sense, even in the Church today, the problem of the independent travelling evangelist and the settled ministry is not fully solved; but these two little letters are of the most fascinating interest because they show the organization of the Church in a transitional stage, when the clash between the travelling and the settled ministry was beginning to emerge; and – who knows? – Diotrephes may not have been as bad as he is painted nor altogether wrong.

22

Jude

Affirming the One True God

The Difficult and Neglected Letter

It may well be said that, for the great majority of modern readers, reading the little letter of Jude is a bewildering rather than a profitable undertaking. There are two verses which everyone knows – the resounding and magnificent doxology with which it ends:

> Now to him who is able to keep you from falling and to present you without blemish before the presence of his glory with rejoicing, to the only God our Saviour through Jesus Christ our Lord, be glory, majesty, dominion and authority, before all time and now and forever. Amen.

But, apart from these two great verses, Jude is largely unknown and seldom read. The reason for its difficulty is that it is written out of a background of thought, against the challenge of a situation, in pictures and with quotations, which are all quite strange to us. Without doubt, it would hit those who read it for the first time like a hammer-blow. It would be like a trumpet-call to defend the faith. James Moffatt calls Jude 'a fiery cross to rouse the churches'. But, as J. B. Mayor, one of its greatest editors and commentators, has said, 'To a modern reader it is curious rather than edifying with the exception of the beginning and the end.'

This is one of the main reasons for addressing ourselves to the study of Jude; for, when we understand Jude's thought and disentangle the situation against which he was writing, his letter becomes of great interest for the history of the earliest Church and by no means without relevance for today. There have indeed been times in the history of the Church, and especially in its revivals, when Jude was not far from being the most relevant book in the New Testament. Let us begin by simply setting down the substance of the letter without waiting for the explanations which must follow later.

Meeting the Threat

It had been Jude's intention to write a treatise on the faith which all Christians share; but that task had to be laid aside in view of the emergence of people whose conduct and thought were a threat to the Christian Church (verse 3). In view of this situation, the need was not so much to expound the faith as to rally Christians in its defence. Certain individuals who had insinuated themselves into the Church were busily engaged in turning the grace of God into an excuse for open immorality and were denying the only true God and Jesus Christ the Lord (verse 4). These people were immoral in life and heretical in belief.

The Warnings

Against these intruders, Jude marshals his warnings. Let them remember the fate of the Israelites. They had been brought in safety out of Egypt, but they had never been permitted to enter the promised land because of their lack of belief (verse 5). The reference is to Numbers 13:26–14:29. Despite receiving the grace of God, it was still possible to lose eternal salvation by drifting into disobedience and faithlessness. Some angels with the glory of heaven as their own had come to earth and corrupted mortal women with their lust (Genesis 6:2); and now they were imprisoned in deepest darkness, awaiting judgment (verse 6). Anyone who rebels against God must look for judgment. The cities of Sodom and Gomorrah had given themselves over to lust and to unnatural conduct, and their destruction in flames is a dreadful warning to everyone who similarly goes astray (verse 7).

The Evil Life

These intruders are visionaries of evil dreams; they defile their flesh, and they speak evil of the angels (verse 8). Not even Michael the archangel dared speak evil even of the evil angels. Michael had been given the task of burying the body of Moses. The devil had tried to stop him and claim the body for himself. Michael had spoken no evil against the devil, even in circumstances like that, but had simply said: 'The Lord rebuke you!' (verse 9). Angels must be respected, even when evil and hostile. These evil people condemn everything which they do not understand; and spiritual things are beyond their understanding. They do understand their physical instincts and allow themselves to be governed by them as irrational animals do (verse 10).

They are like Cain, the cynical, selfish murderer; they are like Balaam, whose one desire was for gain and who led the people into sin; they are like Korah, who rebelled against the legitimate authority of Moses and was swallowed up by the earth for his arrogant disobedience (verse 11).

They are like the hidden rocks on which a ship may come to grief; they have their own in-group in which they mix with people like themselves, and thus destroy Christian fellowship; they deceive others with their promises, like clouds which promise the longed-for rain and then pass over the sky; they are like fruitless and rootless trees, which have no harvest of good fruit; as the foaming spray of the waves casts the sea-weed and the wreckage on the beaches, they cast up shameless deeds like foam; they are like disobedient stars which refuse to keep their appointed orbit and are doomed to darkness (verse 13). Long ago, the prophet Enoch had described these people and had prophesied their divine destruction (verses 14–15). They grumble and speak against all true authority and discipline as the children of Israel murmured against Moses in the desert; they are discontented with the lot which God has appointed to them; they are dictated to by their lusts; their speech is arrogant and proud; they pander to and flatter the great for the sake of gain (verse 16).

Words to the Faithful

Having made clear his disapproval of the evil intruders in this torrent of invective, Jude turns to the faithful. They could have expected all this to happen, for the apostles of Jesus Christ had foretold the rise of evil people (verses 18–19). But the duty of all true Christians is to build their lives on the foundation of the most holy faith, to learn to pray in the power of the Holy Spirit, to remember the conditions of the covenant into which the love of God has called them, and to wait for the mercy of Jesus Christ (verses 20–1).

As for the false thinkers and those who indulge in loose living, some of them may be saved with pity while they are still hesitating on the brink of their evil ways; others have to be snatched like pieces of burning wood from the fire; and, in all this rescue work, Christians must have that godly fear which will love the sinner but hate the sin, and must avoid contamination from those they seek to save (verses 22–3).

And, all the time, there will be with them the power of that God who can keep them from falling and can bring them pure and joyful into his presence (verses 24–5).

The Heretics

Who were the heretics whom Jude blasts, what were their beliefs and what was their way of life? Jude never tells us. He was not a theologian but, as James Moffatt says, 'a plain, honest leader of the church'. 'He denounces rather than describes' the heresies he attacks. He does not seek to argue and to refute, for he writes as one 'who knows when round indignation is more telling than argument'. But, from the letter itself, we can deduce three things about these heretics.

(1) They were antinomians – people who believed that the moral law did not apply to them. Antinomians have existed in every age of the Church. They are people who pervert grace. Their position is that the law is dead and they are under grace. The prescriptions of the law may apply to other people, but they no longer apply to them. They can do absolutely what they like. Grace is supreme; it can forgive any sin; the greater the sin, the more the opportunities for grace to abound (Romans 6). The body is of no importance; what matters is the inward heart. All things belong to Christ, and, therefore, all things are theirs. And so, for them, there is nothing forbidden.

So, Jude's heretics turn the grace of God into an excuse for flagrant immorality (verse 4); they even indulge in shameless unnatural conduct, as the people of Sodom did (verse 7). They defile the flesh and do not consider it to be a sin (verse 8). They allow their animal instincts to rule their lives (verse 10). With their sensual ways, they are likely to wreck the Love Feasts of the Church (verse 12). It is by their own lusts that they direct their lives (verse 16).

Modern Examples of the Ancient Heresy

It is a curious and tragic fact of history that the Church has never been entirely free of this antinomianism; and it is natural that it has flourished most in the ages when the wonder of grace was being rediscovered.

It appeared in the Ranters of the seventeenth century. The Ranters were pantheists and antinomians. A pantheist believes that God is everything; literally *all things* are Christ's, and Christ is the end of the law. They talked of 'Christ within them', took no notice of the Church or its ministry, and belittled Scripture. One of them, Jacob Bottomley, in a book entitled *The Light and Dark Sides of God*, wrote: 'It is not safe to go to the Bible to see what others have spoken and written of the mind of God as to see what God speaks within me, and to follow the doctrine and leading of it in me.' When the Quaker George Fox rebuked them for their lewd practices, they answered: 'We are God.' This may sound very fine; but, as John Wesley, the founder of Methodism, was to say, it most often resulted in 'a gospel of the flesh'. It was their argument that 'swearing, adultery, drunkenness and theft are not sinful unless the person guilty of them apprehends them to be so'. When Fox was a prisoner at Charing Cross, they came to see him and greatly offended him by calling for drink and tobacco. They swore terribly and, when Fox rebuked them, justified themselves by saying that Scripture tells us that Abraham, Jacob, Joseph, Moses, the priests and the angel all swore. To this, Fox replied that the one who was before Abraham commanded: 'Swear not at all.' The seventeenth-century Puritan, Richard Baxter, said of them: 'They conjoined a cursed doctrine of libertinism, which brought them to all abominable filthiness of life; they taught . . . that God regardeth not the actions of the outward man, but of the heart; and that to the pure all things are pure (even things forbidden) and so, as allowed by God, they spoke most hideous words of blasphemy, and many of them committed whoredoms commonly . . . The horrid villainies of this sect did speedily extinguish it.' Doubtless, many of the Ranters were insane; doubtless, some of them were pernicious and deliberate pleasure-seekers; but doubtless, too, some of them were earnest but misguided people who had misunderstood the meaning of grace and freedom from the law.

Later, John Wesley was to have trouble with the antinomians. He talks of them preaching a gospel of flesh and blood. At Jenninghall, he says that 'the antinomians had laboured hard in the Devil's service'. At Birmingham, he says that 'the fierce, unclean, brutish, blasphemous antinomians' had utterly destroyed the spiritual life of the congregation. He tells of a certain Roger Ball who worked his way into the life of the congregation at Dublin. At first, he seemed to be so spiritually minded that the congregation welcomed him as being well suited for the service and ministry of the Church. He showed himself in time to be 'full of guile and of the most abominable errors, one of which was that a believer had a right to all women'. He would not take communion, for under grace a man must 'touch not, taste not, handle not'. He would not preach, and abandoned the church services because, he said, 'The dear Lamb is the only preacher.'

Wesley, deliberately to show the position of these antinomians, related in his *Journal* a conversation which he had with one of them at Birmingham. It ran as follows. 'Do you believe that you have nothing to do with the law of God?' 'I have not; I am not under the law; I live by faith.' 'Have you, as living by faith, a right to everything in the world?' 'I have. All is mine, since Christ is mine.' 'May you then take anything you will anywhere? Suppose out of a shop without the consent or knowledge of the owner?' 'I may, if I want, for it is mine. Only I will not give offence.' 'Have you a right to all the women in the world?' 'Yes, if they consent.' 'And is not that a sin?' 'Yes, to him who thinks it is a sin; but not to those whose hearts are free.'

Repeatedly, Wesley had to meet these people, as George Fox had to meet them. John Bunyan, too, came up against the Ranters, who claimed complete freedom from the moral law and looked with contempt on the ethics of stricter Christians. 'These would condemn me as legal and dark, pretending that they only had attained perfection that could do what they would and not sin.' One of them, whom Bunyan knew, 'gave himself up to all manner of filthiness, especially uncleanness . . . and would laugh at all exhortations to sobriety. When I laboured to rebuke his wickedness, he would laugh the more.'

Jude's heretics have existed in every Christian generation; and, even if they do not go all the way, there are still many who in their heart of hearts trade upon God's forgiveness and make his grace an excuse to sin.

The Denial of God and of Jesus Christ

(2) Of the antinomianism and blatant immorality of the heretics whom Jude condemns, there is no doubt. The other two faults with which he charges them are not so obvious in their meaning. He charges them with, as the Revised Standard Version has it, 'denying our only Master and Lord, Jesus Christ' (verse 4). The closing doxology is to 'the only God', a phrase which occurs again in Romans 16:27 and 1 Timothy 1:17 (cf. 1 Timothy 6:15). The reiteration of the word *only* is significant. If Jude talks about our *only* Master and Lord and about the *only* God, it is natural to assume that there must have been those who questioned the uniqueness of Jesus Christ and of God. Can we trace any such line of thought in the early Church; and, if so, does it fit in with any other evidence which may be supplied by hints within the letter itself?

As so often in the New Testament, we are again in contact with that type of thought which came to be known as Gnosticism. Its basic idea was that this was a dualistic universe, a universe with two eternal principles in it. From the beginning of time, there had always been spirit and matter. Spirit was essentially good; matter was essentially evil. Out of this flawed matter, the world was created. Now, God is pure spirit and, therefore, could not possibly have contact with matter because it was essentially evil. How then was creation brought about? God put out a series of aeons or divine powers; each of these aeons was further away from him. At the end of this long chain, remote from God, there was an aeon who was able to touch matter; and it was this aeon, this distant and secondary god, who actually created the world.

Nor was this all that was in Gnostic thought. As the aeons in the series grew more distant from God, they grew more ignorant of him – and also grew more hostile to him. The creating aeon, at the end of the series, was both totally ignorant of and totally hostile to God.

Having gone that far, the Gnostics took another step. They identified the true God with the God of the New Testament, and they identified the secondary, ignorant and hostile god with the God of the Old Testament. As they saw it, the God of creation was a different being from the God of revelation and redemption. Christianity, on the other hand, believes in the *only* God, the one God of creation, providence and redemption.

This was the Gnostic explanation of sin. It was because creation was carried out, in the first place, from evil matter and, in the second place, by an ignorant god, that sin and suffering and all imperfection existed.

This Gnostic line of thought had one curious but perfectly logical result. If the God of the Old Testament was ignorant of and hostile to the true God, it must follow that the people whom that ignorant God hurt were in fact *good* people. Clearly, the hostile God would be hostile to the people who were the true servants of the true God. The Gnostics, therefore, so to speak, turned the Old Testament upside down and regarded its heroes as villains and its villains as heroes. So, there was a sect of these Gnostics called Ophites, because they worshipped the serpent of Eden (the Greek word for snake is *ophis*); and there were those who regarded Cain and Korah and Balaam as great heroes. It is these very people whom Jude uses as tragic and terrible examples of sin.

So, we may take it that the heretics whom Jude attacks are Gnostics who denied the oneness of God, who regarded the God of creation as different from the God of redemption, who saw in the Old Testament God an ignorant enemy of the true God and who, therefore, turned the Old Testament upside down to regard its sinners as servants of the true God and its saints as servants of the hostile God.

Not only did these heretics deny the oneness of God, they also denied 'our only Master and Lord Jesus Christ'. That is to say, they denied the uniqueness of Jesus Christ. How does that fit in with the Gnostic ideas as far as they are known to us? We have seen that, according to Gnostic belief, God put out a series of aeons between himself and the world. The Gnostics regarded Jesus Christ as one of these aeons. They did not regard him as our *only* Master and Lord; he was only one among the many who were links between God and human beings, although he might be the highest and the closest of all.

There is still one other hint about these heretics in Jude, a hint which also fits in with what we know about the Gnostics. In verse 19, Jude describes them as 'these who set up divisions'. The heretics introduce some kind of class distinctions within the fellowship of the Church. What were these distinctions?

We have seen that, between human beings and God, there stretched an infinite series of aeons. The aim of men and women must be to achieve contact with God. To obtain this, their souls must cross this infinite series of links between themselves and God. The Gnostics held that, to achieve this, a very special and secret knowledge was required. So deep was this knowledge that only very few could attain to it.

The Gnostics, therefore, divided people into two classes – the *pneumatikoi* and the *psuchikoi*. The *pneuma* was the human spirit, that which made human beings kin to God; and the *pneumatikoi* were the *spiritual* people, the people whose spirits were so highly developed and intellectual that they were able to climb the long ladder and reach God. These *pneumatikoi*, the Gnostics claimed, were so spiritually and intellectually equipped that they could become as good as Jesus. Irenaeus, the second-century Bishop of Lyons, says that some of them believed that the *pneumatikoi* could become *better* than Jesus and attain direct union with God.

On the other hand, the *psuchē* was simply the principle of physical life. All things which lived had *psuchē*; it was something which human beings shared with the animal creation and even with growing plants. The *psuchikoi* were ordinary people; they had physical life, but their *pneuma* was undeveloped, and they were incapable of ever gaining the intellectual wisdom which would enable them to climb the long road to God. The *pneumatikoi* were a very small and select minority; the *psuchikoi* were the vast majority of ordinary people.

It is clear that this kind of belief inevitably produced spiritual snobbery and pride. It introduced into the Church the worst kind of class distinction.

So, the heretics whom Jude attacks were people who denied the oneness of God and split him into an ignorant creating God and a truly spiritual God. They denied the uniqueness of Jesus Christ and saw him as only one of the links between God and human beings, and they created class distinctions within the Church and limited fellowship with God to the intellectual few.

The Denial of the Angels

(3) It is further implied that these heretics denied and insulted the angels. It is said they 'reject authority, and revile the glorious ones' (verse 8). The words 'authority' and 'glorious ones' describe ranks in the Jewish hierarchy of angels. Verse 9 is a reference to a story in *The Assumption of Moses* (see above, page 181). If Michael, the archangel, on such an occasion said nothing against the prince of evil angels, clearly no one can speak evil of the angels.

The Jewish belief in angels was very elaborate. Every nation had a protecting angel. Every person, even every child, had an angel. All the forces of nature, the wind and the sea and the fire and all the others, were under the control of angels. It could even be said: 'Every blade of grass has its angel.' Clearly, the heretics attacked the angels. It is likely that they said that the angels were the servants of the ignorant and hostile creator God and that Christians must have nothing to do with them. We cannot quite be sure what lies behind this; but, to all their other errors, the heretics added the despising of the angels, and to Jude this seemed an evil thing.

Jude and the New Testament

We must now examine the questions regarding the date and the authorship of Jude.

Jude had some difficulty in getting into the New Testament at all; it is one of the books whose position was always insecure and which were late in gaining full acceptance as part of the New Testament. Let us briefly set out the opinions of the great fathers and scholars of the early Church about it.

Jude is included in the Muratorian Canon, which dates to about AD 170 and may be regarded as the first semi-official list of the books accepted by the Church. The inclusion of Jude is strange when we remember that the Muratorian Canon does not include in its list Hebrews and 1 Peter. But, for a long time thereafter, Jude is spoken of with some doubt. In the middle of the third century, the biblical scholar Origen knew and used it, but he was well aware that there were many who questioned its right to be Scripture. Eusebius, the great scholar of the middle of the fourth century, made a deliberate examination of the position of the various books which were in use, and he classed Jude among the books which were disputed.

Jerome, who completed the Latin version of the Bible, the Vulgate, in the early years of the fifth century, had his doubts about Jude; and it is in him that we find one of the reasons for the hesitation which was felt towards it. The strange thing about Jude is the way in which it quotes as authorities books which are *outside* the Old Testament. It uses as Scripture certain books which were written between the Old and the New Testaments and were never generally regarded as Scripture. Here are two definite instances. The reference in verse 9 to Michael arguing with the devil about the body of Moses is taken from an apocryphal book called *The Assumption of Moses*. In verses 14–15, Jude confirms his argument with a quotation from prophecy, as, indeed, is the habit of all the New Testament writers; but Jude's quotation is, in fact, taken from the Book of Enoch, which he appears to regard as Scripture. Jerome tells us that it was Jude's habit of using non-Scriptural books as Scripture which made some people regard him with suspicion; and, towards the end of the third century in Alexandria, it was from the very same charge that the blind theologian Didymus defended him. It is perhaps the strangest thing in Jude that he uses these non-Scriptural books as other New Testament writers use the prophets; and in verses 17–18 he makes use of a saying of the apostles which is not identifiable at all.

Jude, then, was one of the books which took a long time to gain an assured place in the New Testament; but, by the fourth century, its place was secure.

The Date

There are definite indications that Jude is not an early book. It speaks of the faith that was once delivered to the saints (verse 3). That way of speaking seems to look back a long way and to come from the time when there was a body of belief that was orthodoxy. In verses 17–18, he urges his people to remember the words of the apostles of the Lord Jesus Christ. That seems to come from a time when the apostles were no longer there and the Church was looking back on their teaching. The atmosphere of Jude is of a book which looks back.

Beside that, we have to set the fact that, as it seems to us, 2 Peter makes use of Jude to a very large extent. Anyone can see that its second chapter has the closest possible connection with Jude. It is quite certain that one of these writers was borrowing from the other. On general grounds, it is much more likely that the author of 2 Peter would incorporate the whole of Jude into his work than that Jude would, for no apparent reason, take over only one section of 2 Peter. Now, if we believe that 2 Peter uses it, Jude cannot be very late, even if it is not early.

It is true that Jude looks back on the apostles; but it is also true that, with the exception of John, all the apostles were dead by AD 70. Taking together the fact that Jude looks back on the apostles and the fact that 2 Peter uses it, a date about AD 80–90 would suit the writing of Jude.

The Authorship of Jude

Who was the Jude, or Judas, who wrote this letter? He calls himself the servant of Jesus Christ and the brother of James. In the New Testament, there are five people called Judas.

(1) There is the Judas of Damascus in whose house Paul was praying after his conversion on the Damascus road (Acts 9:11).

(2) There is Judas Barsabas, a leading figure in the councils of the Church, who, along with Silas, was the bearer to Antioch of the decision of the Council of Jerusalem when the door of the Church was opened to the Gentiles (Acts 15:22, 27, 32). This Judas was also a prophet (Acts 15:32).

(3) There is Judas Iscariot.

None of these three has ever been considered seriously as the author of this letter.

(4) There is the second Judas in the apostolic band. John calls him Judas, not Iscariot (John 14:22). In Luke's list of the Twelve, there is an apostle whom the Authorized Version calls Judas *the brother* of James (Luke 6:16; Acts 1:13). If we were to depend solely on the Authorized Version, we might well think that here we have a serious candidate for the authorship of this letter; and, indeed, the Church father Tertullian calls the writer the Apostle Judas. But, in the Greek, this man is simply called *Judas of James*. This is a very common idiom in Greek, and almost always it means not

brother of but *son of* – so that *Judas of James* in the list of the Twelve is not Judas the *brother* of James but Judas the *son* of James, as all the more modern translations show.

(5) There is the Judas who was the brother of Jesus (Matthew 13:55; Mark 6:3). If any of the New Testament Judases is the writer of this letter, it must be this one, for only he could truly be called *the brother of James*.

Is this little letter to be taken as a letter of the Judas who was the brother of our Lord? If so, it would give it a special interest. But there are objections.

(1) If Jude – to use the form of his name with which we are familiar – was the brother of Jesus, why does he not say so? Why does he identify himself as Jude the brother of James rather than as Jude the brother of Jesus? It would surely be explanation enough to say that he shrank from taking so great a title of honour to himself. Even if it was true that he was the brother of Jesus, he might well prefer in humility to call himself his servant, for Jesus was not only his brother but also his Lord. Further, Jude the brother of James would in all probability never have gone outside Palestine in all his life. The church he would know would be the one in Jerusalem, and of that church James was the undoubted head. If he was writing to churches in Palestine, his relationship to James was the natural thing to stress. When we come to think of it, it would be more surprising that Jude should call himself the brother of Jesus than that he should call himself the servant of Jesus Christ.

(2) The objection is raised that Jude calls himself the servant of Jesus Christ and thereby calls himself an apostle. 'Servants of God' was the Old Testament title for the prophets. God would not do anything without revealing it first to his servants the prophets (Amos 3:7). What had been a prophetic title in the Old Testament became an apostolic title in the

New Testament. Paul speaks of himself as the servant of Jesus Christ (Romans 1:1; Philippians 1:1). In the Pastoral Epistles, he is spoken of as the servant of God (Titus 1:1), and that is also the title which James takes for himself (James 1:1). The conclusion is reached, therefore, that by calling himself 'the servant of Jesus Christ' Jude is claiming to be an apostle.

There are two answers to that. First, the title of servant of Jesus Christ is not confined to the Twelve, for it is given by Paul to Timothy (Philippians 1:1). Second, even if it is regarded as a title confined to the apostles in the wider sense of the word, we find the brothers of the Lord associated with the eleven after the ascension (Acts 1:14), and Jude, like James, may well have been among them; and we learn that the brothers of Jesus were prominent in the missionary work of the Church (1 Corinthians 9:5). Such evidence as we have would tend to prove that Jude, the brother of our Lord, was one of the apostolic circle and that the title of servant of Jesus Christ is perfectly applicable to him.

(3) It is argued that the Jude of Palestine, who was the brother of Jesus, could not have written the Greek of this letter, as he would have been an Aramaic-speaker. That is not a safe argument. Jude would certainly know Greek, for it was the common language of the ancient world, which people spoke in addition to their own language. The Greek of Jude is unrefined and forceful. It might well have been within Jude's competence to write it for himself; and, even if he could not do so, he may well have had a helper and translator such as Peter had in Silvanus.

(4) It might be argued that the heresy which Jude is attacking is Gnosticism, and that Gnosticism is much more a Greek than a Jewish way of thought – and what would Jude of Palestine be doing writing to Greeks? But an odd fact about this heresy is that it is the very opposite of orthodox Judaism.

All Jewish action was controlled by sacred law; the first basic belief of Judaism was that there was one God, and the Jewish belief in angels was highly developed. It is by no means difficult to suppose that, when certain Jews entered the Christian faith, they swung to the other extreme. It is easy to imagine Jews, who all their lives had been slaves to the law, suddenly discovering grace and plunging into antinomianism as a reaction against their former legalism, and reacting similarly against the traditional Jewish belief in one God and in angels. In the heretics whom Jude attacks, it is in fact easy to see Jews who had come into the Christian Church more as deserters from Judaism than as truly convinced Christians.

(5) Last, it might be argued that, if this letter had been known to have been the work of Jude the brother of Jesus, it would not have been so long in gaining an entry into the New Testament. But, before the end of the first century, the Church was largely Gentile, and the Jews were regarded as the enemies and the slanderers of the Church. During his lifetime, Jesus' brothers had in fact been his enemies; and it could well have happened that a letter as Jewish as Jude might have had a struggle against prejudice to get into the New Testament, even if its author was the brother of Jesus.

Jude the Brother of Jesus

If this letter is not the work of Jude the brother of Jesus, what are the alternative suggestions? There are two.

(1) The letter is the work of a man called Jude of whom nothing is otherwise known. This theory has to meet a double difficulty. First, there is the coincidence that this Jude is also the brother of James. Second, it is hard to explain how so small a letter ever came to have any authority at all, if it is the work of someone quite unknown.

(2) The letter is pseudonymous. That is to say, it was written by someone else and then attached to the name of Jude. That was a common practice in the ancient world. Between the Old and the New Testament, scores of books were written and attached to the names of Moses, Enoch, Baruch, Isaiah, Solomon and many others. No one saw anything wrong in that. But two things are to be noted about Jude.

(a) In all such publications, the name to which the book was attached was a famous name; but Jude, the brother of our Lord, was a person who was completely obscure; he is not numbered among the great names of the early Church. There is a story that, in the days of the Emperor Domitian, there was a deliberate attempt to see to it that Christianity did not spread. News came to the Roman authorities that certain descendants from the family of Jesus were still alive, among them the grandsons of Jude. The Romans felt that it was possible that rebellion might gather around these men, and they were ordered to appear before the Roman courts. When they did so, they were seen to be labourers and land workers and were dismissed as being unimportant and quite harmless. Obviously, Jude was Jude the obscure, and there could have been no possible reason for attaching a book to the name of a man whom nobody knew.

(b) When a book was written under a pseudonym, the reader was never left in any doubt as to the person whose name it was being attached to. If this letter had been issued as the work of Judas the brother of our Lord, he would certainly have been given that title in such a way that no one could mistake it; and yet, in fact, it is quite unclear who the author is.

Jude is obviously Jewish; its references and allusions are such that only a Jew could understand them. It is simple and unrefined; it is vivid and pictorial. It is clearly not the work of a theologian. It fits Jude the brother of our Lord. It is attached to his name, and there could be no reason for doing that unless he did in fact write it.

It is our opinion that this little letter is actually the work of Judas, the brother of Jesus.

23

Revelation

Visions of God's Power

The Strange Book

When we embark upon the study of Revelation, we feel ourselves projected into a different world. Here is something quite unlike the rest of the New Testament. Not only is Revelation different; it is also notoriously difficult to understand. The result is that it has sometimes been abandoned as quite unintelligible and it has sometimes become the playground of religious eccentrics, who use it to map out celestial timetables of what is to come or who find in it evidence for their own eccentricities. One despairing commentator said that there are as many riddles in Revelation as there are words, and another that the study of Revelation either finds or leaves the reader mad.

The founder of the Protestant Reformation, Martin Luther, would have denied Revelation a place in the New Testament. Along with James, Jude, 2 Peter and Hebrews, he relegated it to a separate list at the end of his New Testament. He declared that in it there are only images and visions such as are found nowhere else in the Bible. He complained that, notwithstanding the obscurity of his writing, the writer had the boldness to add threats and promises for those who disobeyed or kept his words, unintelligible though they were. In it, said Luther, Christ is neither taught nor acknowledged; and the inspiration of the Holy Spirit is not perceptible in it. Another Reformation scholar, Huldreich Zwingli, is equally hostile to Revelation. 'With the Apocalypse,' he writes, 'we have no concern, for it is not a biblical book ... The Apocalypse has no savour of the mouth or the mind of John. I can, if I so will, reject its testimonies.' Most voices have stressed the unintelligibility of Revelation, and not a few have questioned its right to a place in the New Testament.

On the other hand, there are those in every generation who have loved this book. In his commentary, T. S. Kepler quotes the verdict of the early Church historian and Archbishop of Quebec, Philip Carrington, and makes it his own: 'In the case of Revelation, we are dealing with an artist greater than Stevenson or Coleridge or Bach. St John has a better sense of the right word than Stevenson; he has a greater command of unearthly supernatural loveliness than Coleridge; he has a richer sense of melody and rhythm and composition than Bach ... It is the only masterpiece of pure art in the New Testament ... Its fulness and richness and harmonic variety place it far above Greek tragedy.'

We shall no doubt find this book difficult and bewildering; but doubtless, too, we shall find it infinitely worth while to wrestle with it until it gives us its blessing and opens its riches to us.

Apocalyptic Literature

In any study of Revelation, we must begin by remembering the basic fact that, although unique in the New Testament, it is nonetheless representative of a kind of literature which was the most common of all in the period between the Old and the New Testaments. Revelation is commonly called the Apocalypse – in Greek *apokalupsis*. Between the Old and the New Testaments, there grew up a great mass of what is called apocalyptic literature, the product of an indestructible Jewish hope.

The Jews could not forget that they were the chosen people of God. To them, that involved the certainty that some day they would arrive at world supremacy. In their early history, they looked forward to the coming of a king of David's line who would unite the nation and lead them to greatness. A shoot was to come forth from the stump of Jesse (Isaiah 11:1, 11:10). God would raise up a righteous branch for David (Jeremiah 23:5). Some day, the people would serve David, their king (Jeremiah 30:9). David would be their shepherd and their king (Ezekiel 34:23, 37:24). The booth of David would be repaired (Amos 9:11); out of Bethlehem there would come a ruler who would be great to the ends of the earth (Micah 5:2–4).

But the whole history of Israel contradicted these hopes. After the death of Solomon, the kingdom – small enough to begin with – split into two under Rehoboam and Jeroboam, and so lost its unity. The northern kingdom, with its capital at Samaria, vanished in the last quarter of the eighth century BC before the assault of the Assyrians, never again reappeared in history and is now referred to as the lost ten tribes. The southern kingdom, with its capital at Jerusalem, was reduced to slavery and exile by the Babylonians in the early part of the sixth century BC. It later came under the rule of the Persians, the Greeks and finally the Romans. History for the Jews was a catalogue of disasters from which it became clear that no human deliverer could rescue them.

The Two Ages

Jewish thought stubbornly held to the conviction of the chosenness of the Jews but had to adjust itself to the facts of history. It did so by working out a scheme of history. The Jews divided all time into two ages. There was *this present age*, which is wholly bad and beyond redemption. For it, there can be nothing but total destruction. The Jews, therefore, waited for the end of things as they are. There was *the age which is to come*, which was to be wholly good, the golden age of God, in which would be peace, prosperity and righteousness, and the place of God's chosen people would at last be upheld as theirs by right.

How was this present age to become the age which is to come? The Jews believed that the change could never be brought about by human agency and, therefore, looked for the direct intervention of God. He would come striding on to the stage of history to blast this present world out of existence and bring in his golden time. The day of the coming of God was called the day of the Lord and was to be a terrible time of fear and destruction and judgment, which would be the signs of the coming new age.

All apocalyptic literature deals with these events – the sin of the present age, the terrors of the time between, and the blessings of the time to come. It is entirely composed of dreams and visions of the end. That means that all apocalyptic literature is inevitably cryptic. It is continually attempting to describe the indescribable, to say the unsayable and to paint the unpaintable.

This is further complicated by another fact. It was only natural that these apocalyptic visions should flame the more brightly in the minds of people living under tyranny and oppression. The more some alien power held them down, the more they dreamed of the destruction of that power and of their own recognition and restoration. But it would only have worsened the situation if the oppressing power could have understood these dreams. Such writings would have seemed the works of rebellious revolutionaries. These books, there-fore, were frequently written in code, deliberately couched in language which was unintelligible to the outsider; and inevitably there are many cases in which they remain unintelligible because the key to the code no longer exists. But the more we know about the historical background of such books, the better we can interpret them.

The Book of Revelation

All this is the precise picture of our Revelation. There are any number of Jewish apocalypses – Enoch, the Sibylline Oracles, the Testaments of the Twelve Patriarchs, the Ascension of Isaiah, the Assumption of Moses, the Apocalypse of Baruch, 4 Ezra. Our Revelation is a Christian apocalypse. It is the only one in the New Testament, although there were many other similar writings which did not gain admission. It is written exactly on the Jewish pattern and follows the basic idea of the two ages. The only difference is that, for the day of the Lord, it substitutes the coming in power of Jesus Christ. Not only the pattern but also the details are the same. The Jewish apocalypses had a standard sequence of events which were to happen at the last time; these events all have their place in Revelation.

Before we go on to outline that pattern of events, another question arises. Both *apocalyptic* and *prophecy* deal with the events which are to come. What, then, is the difference between them?

Apocalyptic and Prophecy

The difference between the prophets and the writers of apocalyptic was very real. There were two main differences – one of message and one of method.

(1) The prophets thought in terms of this present world. Their message was often a cry for social, economic and political justice, and was always a summons to obey and

serve God within this present world. To the prophets, it was this world which was to be reformed and in which God's kingdom would come. This has been expressed by saying that the prophets believed in history. They believed that, in the events of history, God's purpose was being worked out. In one sense, the prophets were optimists – for, however sternly they condemned the present state of affairs, they nonetheless believed that things could be put right if men and women would accept the will of God. To the apocalyptists, the world was beyond help in the present. They believed not in the reformation but in the destruction of this present world. They looked forward to the creation of a new world when this one had been shattered by the avenging wrath of God. In one sense, therefore, the apocalyptists were pessimists, for they did not believe that things as they were could ever be cured. True, they were quite certain that the golden age would come – but only after this world had been destroyed.

(2) The message of the prophets was spoken; the message of the apocalyptists was always written. Apocalyptic is a literary production. Had it been delivered by word of mouth, people would never have understood it. It is difficult, involved, often unintelligible; it has to be pored over before it can be understood. Further, the prophets always spoke under their own names; but all apocalyptic writings – except our New Testament one – are pseudonymous. They are put into the mouths of great ones of the past, like Noah, Enoch, Isaiah, Moses, the Twelve Patriarchs, Ezra and Baruch. There is something rather sad about this. Those who wrote the apocalyptic literature had the feeling that greatness had gone from the earth; they did not have the confidence in their own position and authority to put their names to their works, and attributed them to the great figures of the past, thereby seeking

to give them an authority greater than their own names could have given. As the New Testament scholar Adolf Jülicher put it: 'Apocalyptic is prophecy turned senile.'

The Pattern of Apocalyptic

Apocalyptic literature has a pattern: it seeks to describe the things which will happen at the last times and the blessedness which will follow; and the same pictures occur over and over again. It always, so to speak, worked with the same materials; and these materials find their place in our Book of Revelation.

(1) In apocalyptic literature, the Messiah was a divine, pre-existent, other-worldly figure of power and glory, waiting to descend into the world to begin his all-conquering career. He existed in heaven before the creation of the world, before the sun and the stars were made; and he is preserved in the presence of the Almighty (1 Enoch 48:3, 48:6, 62:7; 4 Ezra 13:25–6). He will come to put down the mighty from their seats, to dethrone the kings of the earth and to break the teeth of sinners (1 Enoch 42:2–6, 48:2–9, 62:5–9, 69:26–9). In apocalyptic, there was nothing human or gentle about the Messiah; he was a divine figure of avenging power and glory before whom the earth trembled in terror.

(2) The coming of the Messiah was to be preceded by the return of Elijah, who would prepare the way for him (Malachi 4:5–6). Elijah was to stand upon the hills of Israel, so the Rabbis said, and announce the coming of the Messiah with a voice so great that it would sound from one end of the earth to the other.

(3) The last terrible times were known as 'the travail of the Messiah'. The coming of the messianic age would be like the agony of birth. In the gospels, Jesus is depicted as

foretelling the signs of the end and is reported as saying: 'All this is but the beginning of the birth pangs' (Matthew 24:8; Mark 13:8).

(4) The last days will be a time of terror. Even the mighty will cry bitterly (Zephaniah 1:14); the inhabitants of the land shall tremble (Joel 2:1); people will be terrified and will seek some place to hide and will find none (1 Enoch 102:1, 102:3).

(5) The last days will be a time when the world will be shattered, a time of cosmic upheaval when the universe, as we know it, will disintegrate. The stars will be extinguished; the sun will be turned into darkness and the moon into blood (Isaiah 13:10; Joel 2:30–1, 3:15). The firmament will crash in ruins; there will be a torrent of raging fire, and creation will become a molten mass (Sibylline Oracles 3:83–9). The seasons will lose their order, and there will be neither night nor dawn (Sibylline Oracles 3:796–806).

(6) The last days will be a time when human relationships will be destroyed. Hatred and enmity will reign upon the earth. People will turn against their neighbours (Zechariah 14:13). Brothers will kill each other; parents will murder their own children; from dawn to sunset they shall slay one another (1 Enoch 100:1–2). Honour will be turned into shame, strength into humiliation, and beauty into ugliness. Jealousy will arise in those who did not think much of themselves, and passion will take hold of those who were peaceful (2 Baruch 48:31–7).

(7) The last days will be a time of judgment. God will come like a refiner's fire – and who can endure the day of his coming (Malachi 3:1–3)? It is by the fire and the sword that God will plead with people (Isaiah 66:15–16). The Son of Man will destroy sinners from the earth (1 Enoch 69:27), and the smell of brimstone will pervade all things (Sibylline Oracles

3:58–61). The sinners will be burned up as Sodom was long ago (Jubilees 36:10–11).

(8) In all these visions, the Gentiles have their place – but it is not always the same place.

(a) Sometimes the vision is that the Gentiles will be totally destroyed. Babylon will become such a desolation that there will be no place for the wandering Arabs to plant their tents among the ruins, no place for the shepherds to graze their sheep; it will be nothing more than a desert inhabited by the beasts (Isaiah 13:19–22). God will trample down the Gentiles in his anger (Isaiah 63:6). The Gentiles will come over in chains to Israel (Isaiah 45:14).

(b) Sometimes one last gathering of the Gentiles against Jerusalem is depicted, and one last battle in which they are destroyed (Ezekiel 38:14–39:16; Zechariah 14:1–11). The kings of the nations will throw themselves against Jerusalem; they will seek to ravage the shrine of the Holy One; they will place their thrones in a ring round the city, with their faithless people with them; but it will be only for their final destruction (Sibylline Oracles 3:663–72).

(c) Sometimes there is the picture of the conversion of the Gentiles through Israel. God has given Israel as a light to the Gentiles, that God's salvation may reach to the ends of the earth (Isaiah 49:6). The coastlands wait upon God (Isaiah 51:5); the ends of the earth are invited to look to God and be saved (Isaiah 45:20–2). The Son of Man will be a light to the Gentiles (1 Enoch 48:4–5). Nations shall come from the ends of the earth to Jerusalem to see the glory of God (Psalms of Solomon 17:31).

Of all the pictures in connection with the Gentiles, the most common is that of the destruction of the Gentiles and the exaltation of Israel.

(9) In the last days, the Jews who have been scattered throughout the earth will be gathered into the holy city again. They will come back from Assyria and from Egypt and will worship the Lord in his holy mountain (Isaiah 27:12–13). The hills will be removed and the valleys will be filled in, and even the trees will gather to give them shade as they come back (Baruch 5:5–9). Even those who died as exiles in far countries will be brought back.

(10) In the last days, the New Jerusalem, which is already prepared in heaven with God (4 Ezra 10:44–59; 2 Baruch 4:2–6), will come down among men and women. It will be more beautiful than anything else, with foundations of sapphires, pinnacles of agate, and jewelled gates on walls of precious stones (Isaiah 54:11–12; Tobit 13:16). The glory of the latter house will be greater than the glory of the former (Haggai 2:9).

(11) An essential part of the apocalyptic picture of the last days was the resurrection of the dead. 'Many of those who sleep in the dust of the earth shall awake, some to everlasting life, and some to shame and everlasting contempt' (Daniel 12:2–3). Sheol and the grave will give back that which has been entrusted to them (1 Enoch 51:1). The scope of the resurrection of the dead varied. Sometimes it was to apply only to the righteous in Israel; sometimes to all Israel; and sometimes to all people everywhere. Whatever form it took, it is true to say that now for the first time we see emerging a strong hope of a life beyond the grave.

(12) There were differences as to how long the messianic kingdom was to last. The most natural – and the most usual – view was to think of it as lasting forever. The kingdom of the saints is an everlasting kingdom (Daniel 7:27). Some believed that the reign of the Messiah would last for 400 years. They arrived at this figure from a comparison of

Genesis 15:13 and Psalm 90:15. In Genesis, Abraham is told that the period of affliction of the children of Israel will be 400 years; the psalmist's prayer is that God will make the nation glad for as many days as he has afflicted them and as many years as they have seen evil. In Revelation, the view is that there is to be a reign of the saints for 1,000 years; then the final battle with the assembled powers of evil; then the golden age of God.

Such were the events which the apocalyptic writers pictured in the last days; and practically all of them find their place in the pictures of Revelation. To complete the picture, we may briefly summarize the blessings of the coming age.

The Blessings of the Age to Come

(1) The divided kingdom will be united again. The house of Judah will walk again with the house of Israel (Jeremiah 3:18; Isaiah 11:13; Hosea 1:11). The old divisions will be healed, and the people of God will be one.

(2) There will be in the world an amazing fertility. The wilderness will become a field (Isaiah 32:15); it will become like the garden of Eden (Isaiah 51:3); the desert will rejoice and blossom like the crocus (Isaiah 35:1). The earth will yield its fruit ten thousandfold; on each vine will be 1,000 branches, on each branch 1,000 clusters, in each cluster 1,000 grapes, and each grape will give a cor (120 gallons) of wine (2 Baruch 29:5-8). There will be a situation of plenty, such as the world has never known, and the hungry will rejoice.

(3) A consistent part of the dream of the new age was that in it all wars would cease. The swords will be beaten into ploughshares and the spears into pruning-hooks (Isaiah 2:4). There will be no sword or noise of battle. There will be a common law for everyone and a great peace throughout the

earth, and king will be friendly with king (Sibylline Oracles 3:751–60).

(4) One of the loveliest ideas concerning the new age was that in it there would be no more conflict between wild animals or between human beings and the animal world. The leopard and the kid, the cow and the bear, the lion and the calf will play and lie down together (Isaiah 11:6–9, 65:25). There will be a new covenant between human beings and all living creatures (Hosea 2:18). Even a child will be able to play where the poisonous reptiles have their holes and their dens (Isaiah 11:6–9; 2 Baruch 73:6). In all nature, there will be a universal reign of friendship in which none will wish to do another any harm.

(5) The coming age will bring the end of weariness, of sorrow and of pain. The people will not faint or pine any more (Jeremiah 31:12); everlasting joy will be upon their heads (Isaiah 35:10). There will be no such thing as an untimely death (Isaiah 65:20–2); no one will say: 'I am sick' (Isaiah 33:24); death will be swallowed up, and God will wipe tears from all faces (Isaiah 25:8). Disease will withdraw; anxiety, anguish and lamentation will pass away; childbirth will have no pain; the reaper will not grow weary and the builder will not be toilworn (2 Baruch 73:2–74:4). The age to come will be one when what the Roman poet Virgil called 'the tears of things' will be no more.

(6) The age to come will be an age of righteousness. There will be perfect holiness among human beings. This generation will be a good generation, living in the fear of the Lord in the days of mercy (Psalms of Solomon 17:28–49, 18:9–10).

The Book of Revelation is the New Testament representative of all these apocalyptic works which tell of the terrors before the end of time and of the blessings of the age to come; and it uses all the familiar imagery. It may often be difficult and even unintelligible to us; but, for the most part, it was using pictures and ideas which those who read it would have known and understood.

The Author of Revelation

(1) Revelation was written by a man called John. He begins by saying that God sent the visions he is going to relate to his servant John (1:1). The main body of the book begins with the statement that it is from John to the seven churches in Asia (1:4). 'I, John,' he says, 'am the one who heard and saw these things' (22:8).

(2) This John was a Christian who lived in Asia in the same sphere as the Christians of the seven churches. He calls himself the brother of those to whom he writes; and he says that he too shares in the tribulations through which they are passing (1:9).

(3) He was most probably a Jew of Palestine who had come to Asia Minor late in life. We can deduce this from the kind of Greek that he writes. It is vivid, powerful and pictorial, but from the point of view of grammar it is easily the worst Greek in the New Testament. He makes mistakes which even those with only a basic knowledge of Greek would never make. Greek is certainly not his native language; and it is often clear that he is writing in Greek and thinking in Hebrew. He has a detailed knowledge of the Old Testament. He quotes it or alludes to it 245 times. These quotations come from about twenty Old Testament books; his favourites are Isaiah, Daniel, Ezekiel, Psalms, Exodus, Jeremiah and Zechariah. Not only does he know the Old Testament intimately; he is also familiar with the apocalyptic books written between the Testaments.

(4) His claim for himself is that he is a prophet, and it is on that fact that he bases his right to speak. The command of the risen Christ to him is that he must prophesy (10:11). It is

through the spirit of prophecy that Jesus gives his witness to the Church (19:10). God is the God of the holy prophets and sends his angel to show his servants what is going to happen in the world (22:6). The angel speaks to him of his brothers the prophets (22:9). His book is characteristically prophecy or the words of prophecy (22:7, 22:10, 22:18–19).

It is here that John's authority lies. He does not call himself an apostle, as Paul does when he wants to underline his right to speak. He has no 'official' or administrative position in the Church; he is a prophet. He writes what he sees; and, since what he sees comes from God, his word is faithful and true (1:11, 1:19).

When John was writing, the prophets had a very special place in the Church. He was writing, as we shall see, in about AD 90. By that time, the Church had two kinds of ministry. There was the local ministry; those engaged in it were settled permanently in one congregation as the elders, the deacons and the teachers. There was also the travelling ministry of those whose sphere of work was not confined to any one congregation. In it were the apostles, whose authority ran throughout the whole Church; and there were the prophets, who were wandering preachers. The prophets were greatly respected; the *Didache* says (11:7) that to question the words of a true prophet was to sin against the Holy Spirit. The accepted order of service for the celebration of the Eucharist is laid down in the *Didache*, but at the end comes the sentence: 'But allow the prophets to hold the Eucharist as they will' (10:7). The prophets were regarded as uniquely coming from God; and John was a prophet.

(5) It is unlikely that he was an apostle. Otherwise, he would hardly have put such emphasis on the fact that he was a prophet. Further, he speaks of the apostles as if he was looking back on them as the great foundations of the Church. He speaks of the twelve foundations of the wall of the holy city, and then says:

'and on them were the twelve names of the twelve apostles of the Lamb' (21:14). He would scarcely have spoken of the apostles like that if he himself had been one of them.

This conclusion is made even more likely by the title of the book. In the Authorized and Revised Versions, it is called *the Revelation of St John the Divine*. In the Revised Standard Version and in James Moffatt's and in J. B. Phillips' translations, *the Divine* is omitted, because it is absent from the majority of the oldest Greek manuscripts; but it does go a long way back. The Greek is *theologos*, and the word is used here in the sense in which scholars speak of 'the Puritan divines'. It means not John the saintly but John the theologian; and the very addition of that title seems to distinguish this John from the John who was the apostle.

As long ago as AD 250, Dionysius, the great scholar who was head of the Christian school at Alexandria, saw that it was well nigh impossible that the same man could have written both Revelation and the Fourth Gospel, if for no other reason than that the Greek is so different. The Greek of the Fourth Gospel is simple but correct; the Greek of Revelation is rugged and vivid, but notoriously incorrect. Further, the writer of the Fourth Gospel studiously avoids any mention of his own name; the John of Revelation repeatedly mentions his. Still further, the ideas of the two books are different. The great ideas of the Fourth Gospel – light, life, truth and grace – do not dominate Revelation. At the same time, there are enough resemblances in thought and language to make it clear that both books come from the same centre and from the same world of thought.

The Date of Revelation

We have two sources which enable us to fix the date.

(1) There is the account which tradition gives to us. The consistent tradition is that John was banished to Patmos in

the time of the Roman emperor Domitian, and that he saw his visions there; at the death of Domitian, John was liberated and came back to Ephesus, and there set down the visions he had seen. Victorinus, who wrote towards the end of the third century AD, says in his commentary on Revelation: 'John, when he saw these things, was in the island of Patmos, condemned to the mines by Domitian the emperor. There, therefore, he saw the revelation ... When he was afterwards set free from the mines, he handed down this revelation which he had received from God.' The biblical scholar Jerome, who wrote at the end of the fourth century and the beginning of the fifth, is even more detailed: 'In the fourteenth year after the persecution of Nero, John was banished to the island of Patmos, and there wrote the Revelation ... Upon the death of Domitian, and upon the repeal of his acts by the senate, because of their excessive cruelty, he returned to Ephesus, when Nerva was emperor.' The early Church historian Eusebius says: 'The apostle and evangelist John related these things to the churches, when he had returned from exile in the island after the death of Domitian.' Tradition makes it certain that John saw his visions in exile in Patmos; the only thing that is doubtful – and it is not important – is whether he wrote them down during the time of his banishment or when he returned to Ephesus. On this evidence, we will not be wrong if we date Revelation about AD 95.

(2) The second line of evidence is the material in the book. There is a completely new attitude to Rome and to the Roman Empire.

In Acts, the tribunal of the Roman magistrate was often the safest refuge of the Christian missionaries against the hatred of the Jews and the fury of the mob. Paul was proud that he was a Roman citizen, and he repeatedly claimed the rights to which every Roman citizen was entitled. In Philippi, he put the local magistrates in their place by revealing his citizenship (Acts 16:36–40). In Corinth, Gallio dismissed the complaints against Paul with impartial Roman justice (Acts 18:1–17). In Ephesus, the Roman authorities protected him from the rioting mob (Acts 19:23–41). In Jerusalem, the Roman tribune rescued him from what might have become a lynching (Acts 21:30–40). When the Roman tribune in Jerusalem heard that there was to be an attempt on Paul's life on the way to Caesarea, he took every possible step to ensure Paul's safety (Acts 23:12–31). When Paul despaired of justice in Palestine, he exercised his right as a citizen and appealed direct to Caesar (Acts 25:10–11). When he wrote to the Romans, he urged upon them obedience to the powers that be, because they were ordained by God and were a terror only to the evil and not to the good (Romans 13:1–7). Peter's advice is exactly the same. Governors and kings are to be obeyed, for their task is given to them by God. It is a Christian's duty to fear God and honour the emperor (1 Peter 2:12–17). In writing to the Thessalonians, it is likely that Paul points to the power of Rome as the one thing which is controlling the threatening chaos of the world (2 Thessalonians 2:7).

In Revelation, there is nothing but blazing hatred for Rome. Rome is a Babylon, the mother of prostitutes, drunk with the blood of the saints and the martyrs (Revelation 17:5–6). John hopes for nothing but Rome's total destruction.

The explanation of this change in attitude lies in the wide development of Caesar-worship, which, with its accompanying persecution, is the background of Revelation.

By the time of Revelation, Caesar-worship was the one religion which covered the whole Roman Empire; and it was because of their refusal to conform to its demands that Christians were persecuted and killed. Its essence was that the reigning Roman emperor, who was seen to embody the spirit of Rome, was divine. Once a year, everyone in the Empire had to appear before the magistrates to burn a pinch of incense to the godhead of Caesar and to say: 'Caesar is Lord.' After they had done that, people were able to go away and worship any god or goddess they liked, as long as that worship did not infringe decency and good order; but they had to go through this ceremony in which they acknowledged the emperor's divinity.

The reason was very simple. Rome had a vast and diverse empire, stretching from one end of the known world to the other. It had in it many languages, races and traditions. The problem was how to weld this varied mass into a unity. There was no unifying force such as a common religion, and none of the national religions could conceivably have become universal. Caesar-worship could. It was the one common act and belief which turned the Empire into a unity. To refuse to burn the pinch of incense and to say: 'Caesar is Lord' was not an act against religion; it was an act of political disloyalty. That is why the Romans dealt with the utmost severity with anyone who would not say: 'Caesar is Lord.' And Christians could never give the title Lord to anyone other than Jesus Christ. This was the centre of their creed.

We must see how this Caesar-worship developed and how it was at its peak when Revelation was written.

One basic fact must be noted. Caesar-worship was not imposed on the people from above. It arose from the people; it might even be said that it arose in spite of efforts by the early emperors to stop it, or at least to curb it. And it is to be noted that, of all the people in the Empire, only the Jews were exempt from it.

Caesar-worship began as a spontaneous outburst of gratitude to Rome. The people of the provinces knew very well what they owed to Rome. Impartial Roman justice had taken the place of inconsistent and tyrannical oppression. Security had taken the place of insecurity. The great Roman roads spanned the world, and were safe from robbers; and the seas were clear of pirates. The *pax Romana*, the Roman peace, was the greatest thing which ever happened to the ancient world. As Virgil had it, Rome felt its destiny to be 'to spare the fallen and to cast down the proud'. Life had a new order about it. The American biblical scholar E. J. Goodspeed writes: 'This was the *pax Romana*. The provincial under Roman sway found himself in a position to conduct his business, provide for his family, send his letters, and make his journeys in security, thanks to the strong hand of Rome.'

Caesar-worship did not begin with the deification of the emperor. It began with the deification of Rome. The spirit of the Empire was deified under the name of the goddess Roma. Roma stood for all the strong and benevolent power of the Empire. The first temple to Roma was erected in Smyrna as far back as 195 BC. It was no great step to think of the spirit of Rome as being incarnated in one man, the emperor. The worship of the emperor began with the worship of Julius Caesar after his death. In 29 BC, the Emperor Augustus granted to the provinces of Asia and Bithynia permission to erect temples in Ephesus and Nicaea for the joint worship of the goddess Roma and the deified Julius Caesar. At these shrines, Roman citizens were encouraged and even exhorted to worship. Then another step was taken. To provincials who were *not* Roman citizens, Augustus gave permission to erect temples in Pergamum in Asia and in Nicomedia in Bithynia, for the worship of Roma and *himself*. At first, the worship of the reigning emperor was considered to be something permissible for provincial non-citizens, but not for those who had the dignity of the citizenship.

There was an inevitable development. It is human to worship a god who can be seen rather than a spirit. Gradually, people began more and more to worship the emperor himself instead of the goddess Roma. It still required special permission from the senate to build a temple to the living emperor; but, by the middle of the first century, that permission was more and more freely given. Caesar-worship was becoming the universal religion of the Roman Empire. A priesthood developed, and the worship was organized into groups of ministers and elders called presbyteries, whose officials were held in the highest honour.

This worship was never intended to wipe out other religions. Rome was essentially tolerant. People might worship Caesar *and* their own god. But, more and more, Caesar-worship became a test of political loyalty; it became, as has been said, the recognition of the dominion of Caesar over an individual's life and soul. Let us, then, trace the development of this worship up to, and immediately beyond, the writing of Revelation.

(1) Augustus, who died in AD 14, allowed the worship of Julius Caesar, his great predecessor. He allowed non-citizens in the provinces to worship himself, but he did not permit citizens to do so; and he made no attempt to enforce this worship.

(2) Tiberius (AD 14–37) could not halt Caesar-worship. He forbade temples to be built and priests to be appointed for his own worship; and, in a letter to Gython, a Laconian city, he definitely refused divine honours for himself. So, far from enforcing Caesar-worship, he actively discouraged it.

(3) Caligula (AD 37–41), the next emperor, was an epileptic, a madman and a megalomaniac. He insisted on divine honours. He attempted to enforce Caesar-worship even on the Jews, who had always been and who always were to remain exempt from it. He planned to place his own image in the Holy of Holies in the Temple in Jerusalem, a step which would certainly have provoked unyielding rebellion.

Mercifully, he died before he could carry out his plans. But, in his reign, we have an episode when Caesar-worship became an imperial demand.

(4) Caligula was succeeded by Claudius (AD 41–54), who completely reversed his insane policy. He wrote to the governor of Egypt – there were 1,000,000 Jews in Alexandria – fully approving the Jewish refusal to call the emperor a god and granting them full liberty to enjoy their own worship. On his accession to the throne, he wrote to Alexandria saying: 'I deprecate the appointment of a high priest to me and the erection of temples, for I do not wish to be offensive to my contemporaries, and I hold that sacred fanes [temples] and the like have been by all ages attributed to the immortal gods as peculiar honours.'

(5) Nero (AD 54–68) did not take his own divinity seriously and did nothing to insist on Caesar-worship. It is true that he persecuted the Christians; but this was not because they would not worship him, but because he had to find scapegoats for the great fire of Rome.

(6) On the death of Nero, there were three emperors in eighteen months – Galba, Otho and Vitellius – and in such a time of chaos the question of Caesar-worship did not arise.

(7) The next two emperors, Vespasian (AD 69–79) and Titus (AD 79–81), were wise rulers, who made no insistence on Caesar-worship.

(8) The coming of Domitian (AD 81–96) brought a complete change. He was a devil. He was the worst of all things – a cold-blooded persecutor. With the exception of Caligula, he was the first emperor to take his divinity seriously and to *demand* Caesar-worship. The difference was that Caligula was an insane devil; Domitian was a sane devil, which is much more terrifying. He erected a monument to 'the deified Titus, son of the deified Vespasian'. He began a campaign

of bitter persecution against all who would not worship the ancient gods – 'the atheists', as he called them. In particular, he launched his hatred against the Jews and the Christians. When he arrived in the theatre with his empress, the crowd were urged to rise and shout: 'All hail to our Lord and his Lady!' He behaved as if he himself were a god. He informed all provincial governors that government announcements and proclamations must begin: 'Our Lord and God Domitian commands ...' Everyone who addressed him in speech or in writing must begin: 'Lord and God.'

Here is the background of Revelation. All over the Empire, men and women had to call Domitian god – or die. Caesar-worship was the deliberate policy; all must say: 'Caesar is Lord.' There was no escape.

What were the Christians to do? What hope did they have? Not many of them were wise, and not many of them were powerful. They had no influence or status. Against them had risen the might of Rome, which no nation had ever resisted. They were confronted with the choice – Caesar or Christ. It was to encourage men and women in such times that Revelation was written. John did not shut his eyes to the terrors; he saw dreadful things, and he saw still more dreadful things on the way; but beyond them he saw glory for those who defied Caesar for the love of Christ. Revelation comes from one of the most heroic ages in all the history of the Christian Church. It is true that Domitian's successor Nerva (AD 96–8) repealed the savage laws; but the damage was done, the Christians were outlaws, and Revelation is a clarion call to be faithful to death in order to win the crown of life.

The Book Worth Studying

We cannot shut our eyes to the difficulty of Revelation. It is the most difficult book in the Bible; but its study brings infinite rewards, for it contains the blazing faith of the Christian Church in the days when life was an agony and people expected the end of the heavens and the earth as they knew them but still believed that beyond the terror was the glory and above human raging was the power of God.

Scripture Index

OLD TESTAMENT

Genesis
1:3	37
6:2	279
15:13	307
32:30	161
49	201–2
49:3	202
49:5–7	202
49:14–15	202
49:18	202
49:19	202
49:20	202
49:21	202
49:22–26	202
49:27	202

Exodus 309
24:3–8	161
33:20	161

Numbers
13:26–14:29	278

Judges
13:23	161

Psalms 309
90:15	307

Isaiah 309
2:4	307
11:1	299
11:6–9	308
11:10	299

11:13	307
13:10	304
13:19–22	305
25:8	308
27:12–13	306
32:15	307
33:24	308
35:1	307
35:10	308
40:3–5	27
45:14	305
45:20–22	305
49:6	305
51:3	307
51:5	305
54:11–12	306
63:6	305
65:20–22	308
65:25	308
66:15–16	304

Jeremiah 309
3:18	307
23:5	299
30:9	299
31:12	308

Ezekiel 309
34:23	299
37:24	299
38:14–39:16	305

Daniel 309
7:27	306

12:2–3	306

Hosea
1:11	307
2:18	308

Joel
2:1	304
2:30–31	304
3:15	304

Amos
3:7	292
9:11	299

Micah
5:2–4	299

Zephaniah
1:14	304

Haggai
2:9	306

Zechariah 309
14:1–11	305
14:13	304

Malachi
3:1–3	304
4:5–6	303

NEW TESTAMENT

Matthew 1–14, 36
1:1–17	10
1:2	25

SCRIPTURE INDEX

Matthew (*continued*)		12:15	3	25:14–30	9	
1:21–23	7	12:24	8	25:31–46	9	
1:24–25	189	12:46–50	177	26:56	226	
2:2	11	13	9, 10	27:9	7	
2:14–15	7	13:55	18, 176,	27:11	11	
2:16–18	7		183, 188,	27:35	7	
2:23	7		292	27:37	11	
3:3	27	13:58	3	27:56	46, 175, 184	
3:7–10	5	14:12–21	1, 13	28:18	11	
3:7–12	8	15:13	8	28:19	7	
3:34–35	7	15:22	10			
4:1	18	15:24	7	**Mark**	1–5, 12–21,	
4:12	30	16:3	8		242	
4:21	176	16:12	8	1:1	18	
5–7	9	16:13–23	9	1:3	27	
5:3	27	17:1	176	1:12	18	
5:17–20	8	18	9	1:14	30	
5:22	11	18:2	19	1:19	176	
5:28	11	18:17	9	1:19–20	46	
5:34	11	19:13–15	19	1:20	46	
5:34–37	191	19:24	58	1:22	18	
5:39	11	20:17	19	1:27	18	
5:44	11	20:20	4, 47	1:29	176	
6:14–15	191	21:1–11	11	1:34	3	
7:3	5	21:3–5	7	1:41	39	
7:16–20	191	21:9	11	2:1–12	1, 13	
8:11	7	21:12–13	33	2:14	175	
8:16	3	21:15	11	2:17	20	
9:1–8	1, 13	21:41	8	2:23	33	
9:9	6, 175	23	8, 10	3:5	4, 18	
9:11	8	23:2	8	3:10	3	
10	9	23:37	31	3:17	46, 176	
10:2	176	24	9	3:18	175	
10:3	175	24–25	9	3:21	4, 177, 187	
10:4	25	24:8	304	3:31–35	177, 187	
10:5	27	24:11	247	4:38	19	
10:5–6	7	24:12	246	4:41	18	
11:25–27	5	24:14	7	5:22	39	
12:14	8	25:1–13	9	5:37	46, 176	

5:41	21	16:1	46	7:36–50	27
6:3	18, 176, 183,	16:8	17	8:51	176
	184, 188, 292	16:9–20	17	9:10–17	1, 13
6:5–6	3			9:18	25
6:6	18	**Luke**	1–5, 12–14,	9:18–22	9
6:30–44	1, 13		22–28	9:28	176
6:31	19	1:1–4	24	9:29	25
6:34	18	1:3	59	9:38	58
6:39	33	1:46–55	26	9:49	46
6:40	19	1:68–70	26	9:51–56	26
6:51	18	2:7	189	9:54	47, 176
7:11	21	2:24	27	10:21–22	5
7:34	18, 21	2:29–32	26	10:30–37	26
8:12	18	3:1–2	24	11:5–13	25
8:27–33	9	3:4	27	13:29	27
8:33	18	3:6	27	13:34	31
9:2	46, 176	3:7–9	5	15:11–32	27
9:5	33	3:18	30	16:19–31	27
9:14	39	3:21	25	17:11–19	26
9:36	19	3:23	188	18:1–8	25
9:38	46	3:38	25	18:15–17	19
10:13–16	19	4:1	18	18:25	58
10:14	4, 19	4:25–27	26	18:31	19
10:21	19, 50	4:35	58	19:1–10	27
10:25	58	4:40	3	19:45–46	33
10:26	18	5:7–10	46	22:31–32	146
10:32	19	5:10	176	22:32	25
10:35	4, 47, 176	5:16	25	22:61	226
10:41	176	5:17–26	1, 13	23:43	27
11:1–2	20	6:12	25	23:46	25
11:12	19	6:14	176		
11:15–17	33	6:15	25, 175	**John**	29–56
13:3	176	6:16	175, 291	1	159
13:8	304	6:19	3	1:3	43
14:33	46, 176	6:20	27	1:8	42
14:36	21	6:41–42	5	1:9	38
14:43	20	7:9	26	1:14	43, 249
15:34	21	7:15	39	1:20ff.	42
15:40	175, 184	7:22	27	1:23	27

John (*continued*)		6:8–9	34	14–17	34
1:28	35	6:9	34	14:5	34
1:40–41	34	6:19	34	14:8–9	34
1:44	35	6:20	44	14:22	291
2:1	35, 188	6:32	38	15:1	38
2:1–11	34	6:33–38	45	15:19	246
2:1–13	31	6:61–64	45	16:12–13	56
2:4	45	7:1–5	187	17:5	45
2:6	34	7:2	31	17:14	246
2:11	39	7:3–9	177	18:1	35
2:13	31, 32	7:5	177	19:11	45
2:13–22	33	7:10	31, 45	19:13	35
2:15	44	7:21–23	35	19:17	35
2:20	35	8:16	38	19:23	34
3:1–15	34	8:58	45	19:25	175, 184,
3:16	43	9	39		186
3:22–30	30	9:3	39	19:25–27	50
3:28	42	9:7	35	19:26–27	187, 226
4	34	9:14	35	19:28	44
4:1	42	10:18	31, 45	19:35	50
4:1–2	30	10:22	31	19:39	34
4:5	35	10:23	35	20:2	50
4:6	44	10:41	42	20:24–29	34
4:9	26, 35	11	34, 39	20:29	233
4:16–17	45	11:3	50	21:2	35
4:31	44	11:4	39	21:15–17	233
4:35–5:1	31	11:5	50	21:18–19	242
4:46	35	11:14	45	21:20	50
5:1	31	11:16	34	21:24	50
5:2	35	11:33	44		
5:6	45	11:35	44	**Acts**	57–63
5:10	35	11:38	44	1:1	59
5:36	42	12:1	35	1:1–6:7	61
6	39	12:3	34	1:8	61
6:1–7:14	31	12:4–5	34	1:13	47, 175,
6:4	32	12:21	35		176, 291
6:5	44	12:22	34	1:14	177, 183,
6:5–7	34	13:1–17	34		293
6:6	45	13:23–25	50	1:21–22	91–92

1:22	226	13:50	219	19:21	70
1–5	63	14:14	185	19:21–28:31	62
1–15	62	14:23	272	19:23–41	313
2:14–16	209	15	61, 177	19:31	60
2:19–20	218	15–16	63	19:37	60
2:20–31	209	15:14	215	20:5–16	63
2:22–26	210	15:17	192	20:17–35	98
2:38–39	210	15:22	186, 213, 291	20:28	233
3:1ff.	47	15:23	192	20:29–30	247
3:12–26	209	15:27	213, 291	20:31	98
3:13	210	15:32	213, 291	21:1–18	63
3:13–14	209	15:37–40	15, 213	21:18–25	177, 182
3:19	210	16	110–11	21:30–40	313
3:19–23	210	16–28	63	23:11	71
4:1–13	47	16:6–10	110, 128	23:12–31	313
4:8–12	209	16:6–19:20	62	23:26–30	192
4:11	210	16:10–17	63	23:29	60
4:36	167	16:19	213	25:10–11	313
5:30–31	210	16:20–21	110	25:25	60
5:31	210	16:25	213	27:1–28:16	63
6:8–9:31	61	16:29	213	28:30–31	144
8:14	47	16:35ff.	60		
8:26–40	63	16:36–40	313	**Romans**	69–80
9:11	291	16:37	213	1–8	74
9:31–10:48	63	17:1–10	130	1:1	66, 185, 293
9:32–12:24	61	17:2	130	1:7	66, 79
10:34–43	209	17:10–12	130	1:8	67
10:39–42	210	18:1–17	85, 88,	1:11	71
10:42	210		313	1:15	71, 79
10:43	209, 210	18:2	77	4:15	174
11:19–30	63	18:5	213	6	281
12:2	57, 183	18:12–17	216	6:4	140
12:12	14	18:12ff.	60	7:10–11	174
12:17	177	18:14	60	9–11	74
12:25	14	18:18	77	12	76, 192
12:25–14:28	63	18:24ff.	167	12–15	74
12:25–16:5	62	18:26	167	13:1–7	231, 313
13:12	60	19:1–7	41	14–15	76
13:13	14	19:10	118	14–16	79

Romans (*continued*)
14:15–23	79
15	79, 146
15:23–24	72
15:24	145
15:25	71
15:28	72, 145
15:30–31	72
16	67, 74, 76–80
16:5	167
16:7	186
16:17	77
16:22	68
16:25–27	79
16:27	284

1 Corinthians 81–90
1–4	90
1:1	66, 185
1:3	66
1:4	67
1:11	87
1:12	167, 215
1:26–27	197
3:4	167
3:22	215
4:17	87
5:9	86
6:9–10	85
7:1	87
8:6	126
9:5	215, 293
9:6	185
12:13	152
15	178
15:5	215
15:7	178
16:1ff.	71
16:17	87

16:19	67, 77
16:21	68

2 Corinthians 81–90
1–9	88, 89
1:1	66, 185
1:2	66
1:3	67
1:19	213
2:4	88
2:13	88, 89
6:13–7:2	87
6:14–7:1	87, 89
7:5	89
7:8	88
7:13	88, 89
9:1ff.	71
10–13	88, 89
11:9	111
12:14	87
13:1–2	87
13:13	67

Galatians 91–95
1–2	92
1:1	66, 92, 185
1:3	66
1:18	215
1:19	177, 183
2:6–10	92
2:9	47, 177, 191, 215
2:11	215
2:14	215
3:23–24	174
3:28	152

Ephesians 96–107, 208
1–3	101

1:1	66, 99
1:3	67, 223
1:3–14	100
1:4	224
1:9–10	101
1:15	98
1:15–23	100
1:20–21	224
2:1–9	100
2:11–12	98
3:1	97
3:1–7	100
3:2	99
4:1	97
4:17	98
6:5–9	153
6:14	224
6:20	97
6:21	97

Philippians 108–14
1:1	66, 293
1:1–3:1	113
1:3	67
1:7	111
1:28–30	111, 112
2:1–11	112
2:24	144–45
2:29–30	112
3:1	113
3:2	112, 113
3:2–4:3	113
3:20	110
4:1	111–12
4:2	112
4:4–23	113
4:10–11	112
4:16	111
4:21–22	67

SCRIPTURE INDEX

Colossians	115–27
1:1–2	66
1:2	67
1:4	119
1:6	119
1:7	118
1:8	119
1:14	101
1:15	120
1:16	120, 121
1:17	120
1:19	101, 120
1:21	119
1:22	120
1:27	119
1:28	122
2:1	118
2:2	120
2:3	101
2:5	119
2:8	120, 121
2:9	101, 120
2:10	121
2:15	121
2:16	121, 122
2:18	122
2:20	120
2:21	122
3:5–7	119
3:5–8	122
3:11	129, 152
3:22–4:1	153
4:7	97
4:9	155
4:10	15
4:11	58
4:12	58
4:12–13	118
4:12–15	67

4:13	154
4:14	22, 58
4:15	154
4:16	105, 106–7, 154
4:17	154
4:18	68

1 Thessalonians	128–33
1:1	66, 67, 213
2:5	132
2:6–7	132
2:9	132
2:11	132
2:14	131
2:17	131
2:20	131
3:1–2	131
3:4–6	131
3:5	131
4:3–8	132
4:9	132
4:9–10	131
4:11	131
4:13–18	131
5:2	132
5:6	132
5:12–14	132
5:13	132
5:26	67

2 Thessalonians	128–33
1:1	66, 213
1:3	67
2:3–12	132
2:7	313
3:17	68

1 Timothy	134–48
1:4	138, 140
1:7	140
1:15	147
1:17	284
2:4	139
3:1–7	136
3:8–13	136
3:15	134
3:16	138
4:1	137
4:4–5	139
4:6	137
5:3–16	136–37
5:17–18	136
5:17–19	136
5:23	147
6:4	138, 139
6:5	139
6:15	284
6:20	140

2 Timothy	134–48
1:14	137
2:8	138
2:18	140
2:23	138
3:6	139
3:8	137
4	147
4:11	15
4:19	77
4:20	146

Titus	134–48
1:1	293
1:5	144
1:5–6	136
1:7–16	136
1:10	140

Titus (*continued*)

1:11	139
1:13	137
1:14	140
1:15	139
1:16	139
2:4	139
2:11	139
3:9	138, 140
3:12	144

Philemon 149–57

2	153
10	149
11	151
12	154–55
13	150
13–14	155
14	150
15	151
16	151
18–19	149
19	155
20	155
21	155
22	145
24	15

Hebrews 158–68, 289, 297

2:3	163, 164
5:12	163, 164, 165
6:10	164
10:19–22	159
10:32	163
10:32–34	164
12:4	163
13:7	163, 164
13:22	165, 167
13:24	164

James 169–204, 297

1:1	175, 190, 192, 193, 194, 201, 202, 205, 293
1:2	199
1:7	190
1:9–11	202
1:10	199
1:11	199
1:12	202
1:15	198
1:17	195, 199
1:18	190, 202
1:19–20	202
1:25	174, 190
1:26–27	202
2:1	194, 201
2:1–3	196
2:2	191, 196
2:4–5	198
2:7	192
2:8	190
2:12	174
2:12–13	191
2:13	198, 199
2:14	198
2:14–16	198
2:14–19	199
2:14–26	192
2:18–19	198
2:20	199
2:21–23	199
2:24	192
2:25	199
2:26	199

3:1	196
3:3–6	199
3:6	195
3:11–12	198
3:11–13	191
3:18	202
4:1	198
4:1–2	202
4:4	198, 199
4:6	199
4:10	190
4:12	199
4:13	198
4:15	190
5:1–6	196, 199
5:3	198
5:6	191, 198
5:7	190, 191, 199, 202
5:7–9	195
5:8	190
5:9	191
5:10	190
5:11	190, 199
5:12	191
5:13–14	198
5:13–18	202
5:14	190, 196
5:15	190
5:17	199
5:20	199, 202

1 Peter 205–36, 237, 241–42, 289

1:1	205, 232
1:1–2	231
1:3	209, 223
1:3–4:11	231

1:4	224	4:12–5:11	232	2:15	238
1:5	207, 210	4:13	207, 210,	2:18	238
1:6	215, 230		230	2:19	238
1:7	207, 210, 230	4:14	226, 230	2:20–22	238
1:8	210, 233	4:16	226, 230	3:2	242
1:10–12	209	4:17	208	3:3–4	238
1:13	207, 210,	4:17–18	210	3:4	242
	211, 224	4:19	215	3:5–7	239
1:13–25	210	5:1	208, 210,	3:8–9	239
1:14	215		225, 234	3:10	239
1:19	210	5:1–13	232	3:11–14	239
1:20	224	5:2	233	3:15–16	239, 240,
1:20–21	209, 224	5:4	208, 210,		243
1:21	210, 211		232	3:16	237, 243
2:1–3	210	5:9	215, 230	3:17–18	239
2:7	210	5:12	212		
2:9–10	215	5:12–14	231	**1 John**	205, 245–64
2:12	207, 211,	5:13	16, 232,	1:1	257
	230		263, 269	1:1–3	258
2:12–17	313	5:14	218	1:4	256
2:13–17	231			1:5	253, 257
2:15	230, 231	**2 Peter**	237–44,	1:6	253
2:16	210		290–91, 297	1:7	255, 259, 261
2:18–3:7	232	1:1	215	1:8–10	254, 258
2:22	211	1:4	237	2:1	256, 258
2:24	210, 211	1:5–8	237	2:2	258
3:14	215, 230	1:9	237	2:3–5	262
3:16	215, 230	1:12–14	242	2:4–6	253
3:17	230	1:20	237	2:8	260
3:21	232	2:2	237	2:9–11	255, 259,
3:22	210	2:3	237		261
4:1–5	210	2:4	238	2:14	257
4:3–4	215	2:5	238	2:17	260
4:4	230	2:6	238	2:19	248
4:5	210	2:10	238	2:22	248, 257
4:7	207, 209	2:12	238	2:26	248
4:11	231	2:13	238	2:29	261
4:12	215, 230	2:14	238	3:1	260
4:12–19	232	2:14–15	237	3:3–10	261

SCRIPTURE INDEX

1 John (*continued*)

3:5	258
3:10–11	261
3:11–17	261
3:13	260
3:14–17	255
3:16	258
3:22	262
3:23	255, 261
3:24	259
4:1	248
4:2–3	250, 258
4:3	43, 267–68
4:4–5	260
4:7–8	255
4:7–10	257
4:7–12	261
4:9	259
4:10	258
4:10–12	255
4:13	259
4:14	259
4:15	257
4:16	257
4:20–21	256, 261
5:1	257
5:2	261
5:4	260
5:5	257
5:6	252, 258
5:11–12	259
5:18	261
5:19	260

2 John 205, 265–76

1	55, 263, 265, 267, 268, 269
4	267, 269, 270
5	269
6	269
7	268
7–11	270
8	269
10	269
12	267, 269
13	232–33, 269

3 John 205, 265–76

1	55, 265, 267
3–5	270
4	267
6–8	270
9	270
10	271
12	271
13–14	267

Jude 277–96, 297

3	278, 290
4	278, 281, 284
5	278
6	279
7	279, 281
8	279, 281, 288
9	279, 288, 289
10	279, 281
11	279
12	281
13	279–80
14–15	280, 289–90
16	280, 281
17–18	290
18–19	280
19	286
20–21	280
22–23	280
24–25	277, 280

Revelation 231, 297–319

1:1	309
1:4	309
1:9	309
1:11	310
1:19	310
2:10	235
2:24	253
3:14–22	106
3:16	106
3:17	115
4:7	29
10:11	309
17:5	264
17:5–6	313
19:10	310
21:14	311
22:6	310
22:7	310
22:8	309
22:9	310
22:10	310
22:18–19	310

Subject Index

Abraham, 75, 94, 174, 282

Achaicus, 87, 89

Acts
 aim of, 57, 59–62
 apostles in, 57
 authorship of, 58
 definition of apostle in, 91–92
 ending of, 144, 145–46
 as history, 57
 Peter in, 57
 sources of, 62–63
 on spread of Christianity, 61–62
 theology of early Church and, 209–10
 Theophilus and, 59, 146

Acts of John, 250

Aeschylus, 212

Agape (Love Feast), 218

Agrippa, 60

Albinus, 179–80

Alexander the Great, 108, 128–29

Aliturus, 219

Alphaeus, 175, 183, 184

Ananus, 179–80

Andrew, 34, 53

Andronicus, 186

angels, 122, 278–79, 288, 289, 294, 310

animals, 308

Anna, 26, 186–87

antichrist, 43, 267–68

antinomianism, 122, 238, 281–84, 294

Antioch, 63, 213, 219, 291

Antiochus the Great, 117

Anton, Paul, 135

Apion, 65–66

apocalyptic literature
 and blessings of age to come, 307–9
 Elijah in, 303
 Gentiles in, 305
 Jews and, 298–99, 302–9
 judgment day in, 304–5
 on last days, 303–4
 Matthew's gospel and, 9
 Messiah in, 303–4
 pattern of, 303–7
 prophets versus, 301–2
 resurrection of the dead and, 306
 Revelation as, 298, 301, 308–9
 and two ages in Jewish thought, 299–301, 307–9
 as written message, 302–3

Apocrypha, 201, 251

Apollos, 167

apostles
 definition of, in Acts, 91–92
 after first Twelve Apostles, 185–86
 Jerome on, 183, 185
 as leaders of Church, 271
 Revelation on, 310–11
 as servants of God, 292, 293
 See also specific apostles

SUBJECT INDEX

Apostolic Constitutions, 234
Aquila, 77, 78, 86, 167
Aquinas, Thomas. *See* Thomas
  Aquinas
Aramaic language, 204
Archippus, 153–55
Aristion of Smyrna, 234–35,
  266
Aristotle, 129, 151–52
Armytage, A. H. N. Green, 54
asceticism. *See* self-denial
Asia, 214–15, 214–16, 232–35.
  See also specific locations
Assumption of Moses, The, 288,
  289, 301
Athanasius, Bishop of Alexandria,
  163, 171–72
Attalus III, 214
Augustine, St., 43, 166, 170, 171
  Confessions, 249
Augustus, Emperor, 315, 316

Balaam, 279, 286
baptism of Jesus Christ, 251, 252
Barnabas, 14–15, 166, 167, 185,
  202, 206, 272
Bartholomew, 203
Baruch, 201, 243, 295, 301, 302,
  304, 306, 307, 308
Basilides, 142
Beare, F. W., 207, 212
beatitudes. *See* Sermon on the
  Mount
Benedictus, 26
Bigg, Charles, 212, 221–22
bishops, 136, 208
Bithynia, 214–15, 216, 232, 233,
  235

body, Gnostic view of, 122,
  123–24, 139–40, 141, 247,
  253
Bottomley, Jacob
  *The Light and Dark Sides of
  God*, 282
Boxter, Richard, 282–83
Bruce, A. B., on Mark's gospel, 17
Bunyan, John, 284

Caesar, Julius, 84, 315, 316
Caesarea, 24, 63, 313
Caesar-worship, 313–18
Cain, 261, 279, 286
Caligula, Emperor, 316–17
Calvin, John, 96, 166, 240
Cappadocia, 214–15, 232
Carrington, Philip, 298
Cassander, 129
Cassiodorus, 262
Catholic or General Epistles,
  205–6
Cerinthus, 42, 49, 250–51, 252
Chase, F. H., 241
Chloe, 87, 89
Christ. *See* Jesus Christ
Christianity
  Acts on spread of, 61–62
  creeds and, 137–38, 144
  Gentiles and, 60–61, 93, 177,
  191, 195–96, 291, 294
  Jewish Christians, 60, 92–93,
  190–92, 194
  Lord's Supper and, 218
  love and, 218, 255–56, 261
  persecution of Christians, 60,
  111, 163–64, 207, 215–21,
  226–31, 313, 317–18

332

SUBJECT INDEX

righteousness and, 74–75,
  261–62
second coming of Christ and, 9,
  131, 132–33, 195, 207–8, 218
slavery and, 151–53
as universal, 60–61
See also Church
Church
  in Antioch, 63, 213
  apostles as leaders of, 271
  bishops of, 136
  as body of Christ, 103–4, 152–53
  as Bride of Christ, 269–70
  in Colosse, 118–19
  in Corinth, 86–90
  creeds and, 137–38, 144
  deacons of, 136
  elders of, 136, 190–91, 208,
    272, 310
  in Ephesus, 245–47, 270–71,
    275–76
  fellowship of, 260–61
  function of, 103–4
  in Galatia, 62
  gospel of Matthew on, 8–9
  in Jerusalem, 61, 62–63, 71,
    177–78, 191, 192–93, 196
  Jews as enemy of, 294
  organization of, 136–37, 144,
    208
  in Philippi, 111–12
  Syrian Church, 170–71, 223,
    239
  theology of early Church,
    208–10
  in Thessalonica, 131–32
  traveling ministry in, 270–76,
    310

types of ministry in, 271–76,
  310
See also Christianity
Cicero, 160
circumcision, 93, 140
Claudius, Emperor, 77, 317
Claudius Lysias, 60, 192
Clement of Alexandria
  on Epistle to the Hebrews, 163,
    165–66
  on James as bishop of
    Jerusalem, 177–78
  on John's gospel, 40, 52
  on John's letters, 263–64
  on John the apostle, 47
  on Second Letter of Peter, 239
Clement of Rome, 145, 206, 210
Codex Corbeiensis, 169, 176
Codex Toletanus, 52
Coleridge, Samuel Taylor, 96, 97,
  298
Colosse
  Church at, 118–19, 155
  geographic location of, 115
  heresy at, 107, 117, 119–22,
    125–26
  history of, 116, 117
Colossians, Letter to
  on all-sufficiency of Jesus
    Christ, 101, 102–3, 107, 120,
    126
  Archippus and, 153, 154
  authorship of, 125–26
  on Christ's role in creation, 120
  compared with First Corinthi-
    ans, 126
  compared with Letter to the
    Ephesians, 97, 101, 107

333

SUBJECT INDEX

Colossians, Letter to (*continued*)
  heresy at Colosse and, 119–26
  humanity of Christ in, 120
  on Mark, 15
  Onesimus and, 155
  as prison letter from Paul, 15
  significance of, 126–27
  on slaves and masters, 153
Columella, 72
Confessions (Augustine), 249
Corinth
  greatness of, 81–83
  history of, 84–85
  Paul in, 62, 71, 73, 85–89, 111,
    213, 313
  problems with Church in, 86–90
  wickedness of, 83, 85
  See also Corinthians, First and
    Second Letters to
Corinthians, First and Second Let-
    ters to
  compared with Colossians, 126
  correct order of, 86, 88
  Letter of Reconciliation in,
    88, 89
  letter previous to, 86–89
  as response to problems in
    Corinth, 87–90
  Severe Letter in, 88–89
Cornelius, 61
Council of Jerusalem, 177,
    192–93, 196, 213, 291
Council of Trent, 172, 173, 176
covenant, 161
creation, 120, 123, 140, 285
Crispus, 86
crucifixion
  of Jesus, 31, 32, 33, 44, 50,
    184–85, 226, 251–52

  of slaves, 150, 151
Cyprian, 163
Cyrus, 117

darkness and light, 253–54, 257,
    261, 280
David, 299
deacons, 136, 208, 310
Deissmann, Adolf, 67
deity of Jesus Christ, 18, 45–46,
    250–52
Demetrius, 64, 271, 275
demonic spirits, 121
Denney, James, 23
deutero-canonical books of Bible,
    172
devil, 279, 289
Dibelius, Martin, 69
Didache
  *Teaching of the Twelve Apostles,
    The*, 272, 273–74, 310
Didymus, 239, 290
Dionysius the Great, 55, 311
Diotrephes, 270–71, 275–76
disobedience. *See* obedience and
    disobedience
Docetism, 43, 250
Dodd, C. H., 209
Domitian, Emperor, 47, 164, 295,
    312, 317–18

eagle symbol of John, 23, 29
earthquakes, 115
Easton, B. S., 201
Egypt, 15
elders
  Aristion as, 234–35
  of Church, 136, 190–91, 208,
    272, 310

of Ephesus, 233
Jewish elders, 190–91
John the elder, 55, 56, 265–67,
    270–71
in Letter of James, 190–91
Paul's ordination of, 272
Peter as, 208, 225, 234
Elijah, 303
Elizabeth, 26
Enoch, 201, 243, 290, 295, 301–6
Epaenetus, 77, 119
Epaphras, 118, 150
Epaphroditus, 112
Ephesians, Letter to
    absence of second coming from,
        208
    authorship of, 99–101, 104–5
    on Church as body of Christ,
        103–4
    as circular letter, 106–7
    circumstances behind writing
        of, 96–97
    compared with First Letter of
        Peter, 223–25
    compared with Letter to the
        Colossians, 97, 101, 107
    Gentiles and, 98–99
    origin of Paul's thought in,
        102–3
    prayer in, 101
    problems of, 97–101
    recipients of, 97–99, 105–7
    significance of, 96, 107
    on slaves and masters, 153,
        224
    style of, 100–101
    on unity of all things in Jesus
        Christ, 101–4
    vocabulary of, 99–100

Ephesus
    Church in, 245–47, 270–71,
        275–76
    collection of Paul's letters at,
        86, 104, 156
    elders of, 233
    false prophets and teachers in,
        245–56, 260, 270–71
    John (author of Revelation) in,
        312
    John the apostle in, 47–49, 55,
        264
    John the Elder in, 55, 265–67,
        270–71
    Letter to the Romans and,
        77–78
    Onesimus as Bishop of, 156
    Paul in, 62, 77, 86, 98, 233, 313
    Roman magistrates on Chris-
        tians in, 60, 312
    traveling Christian teachers in,
        270–71
Epimachus, 65–66
Epiphanian Theory, 186–88
Epiphanius, 186
epistles. See letters of Paul; spe-
    cific letters
ethics. See righteousness
Eucharist, 218, 310
Euripides, 212
Eusebius
    on death of James, 180–82
    on First Letter of Peter, 222
    on John the apostle, 31, 32, 40,
        47–49, 312
    on John the elder, 266
    on Letter of James, 171
    on Matthew, 31
    on Paul, 145–46

SUBJECT INDEX

Eusebius (*continued*)
 on Second Letter of Peter, 239–40
 on tombs of John the apostle and John the elder in Ephesus, 55
evil
 of body, 122, 123–24, 139–40, 141, 248
 disobedience against God and, 278–79
 John on evil of world, 260
 Letter to Ephesians on, 102
 of material world, 42, 122–23, 125–26, 140, 238, 247–48, 249, 285
 warnings on, in Letter of Jude, 278–80
 See also immorality; sins
Ezekiel, Book of, 309
Ezra, 243, 301, 302, 303, 306

Faber, F. W., 28
faith, 137–38, 171, 174, 192, 194–96, 207
false prophets and teachers, 245–56, 260, 270–71. *See also* heresies
Farrar, Dean, 82
Farrar, F. W., 217
Festus, 60, 179–80
Flaccus, 118
Fortunatus, 87, 89
Fox, George, 282, 284

Gaius, 270, 275
Galatia, 62, 128, 214–15, 232. *See also* Galatians, Letter to
Galatians, Letter to, 91–92, 94–95

Galba, Emperor, 317
Gallio, 60, 86, 313
genealogies
 Gnosticism and, 140, 141
 of Jesus, 10, 36, 40
General or Catholic Epistles, 205–6
Gentiles
 in apocalyptic literature, 305
 Christianity and, 60–61, 93, 177, 195–96, 291, 294
 in Colossian Church, 119
 First Letter of Peter and, 215
 John's gospel and, 36–40
 Letter to the Ephesians and, 98–99
 Luke's gospel and, 24–27
 Paul and, 191
 sins of, 119
Gibbon, Edward, 216
Gnosticism
 aim of, 255, 256
 antinomianism and, 122, 238, 281–84, 294
 on the body, 122, 123–24, 139–40, 141, 247, 253
 class distinctions within, 255–56, 286–88
 denial of incarnation and, 249–56
 and dualistic universe, 285
 on evil of matter, 42, 122–23, 125–26, 140, 238, 247–48, 249, 285
 genealogies and, 140, 141
 on God, 42–43, 123, 140–41, 285–86
 immorality and, 122, 124, 132, 139, 253–54

on Jesus Christ, 43–44, 123,
249–53, 286
Jews and, 124–25, 141–42,
293–94
and knowledge, 254
Ophites and, 286
self-denial and, 122, 123–24,
139–40, 141, 253
on sin, 285–86
and spiritual perfection,
254–56, 287
God
access to, 159
conceptions of religion on,
158–59
disobedience against, 278–79
Gnostic beliefs on, 42–43, 123,
140–41, 285–86
grace of, 95, 281
inward fellowship with, 158
Jesus as Son of, 257
Jews' relationship with,
160–62
as light, 253–54, 257
love and mercy of, 28, 255–56,
257
obedience to, 261–62
Philo on, 160
Ranters on, 282–83
right relationship with, 74–75
and unity of all things in Christ,
101
See also kingdom of God
Good Samaritan parable, 26
Goodspeed, E. J., 36, 104, 149,
155–56, 200, 206, 250, 315
gospels
symbols of gospel writers,
23, 29

synoptic gospels, 1–2, 12
See also specific gospels
grace, 95, 207, 281
Greek Church, 171–72
Greek edition of Scriptures. See
Septuagint
Greek ideas
in John's gospel, 37–38, 40
in Letter of James, 195
in Letter to the Hebrews,
159–60, 162
Greek language
of First Letter of Peter, 211–13
of John's gospel, 311
of Letter of James, 203–4
of Letter of Jude, 293
of Luke's gospel, 24, 25
of Revelation, 309, 311
of Second Letter of Peter, 241
Greek preachers, 197–200

hagios, 246
Harnack, Adolf von, 106, 167
Harris, Rendel, 268
heaven. See kingdom of God
Hebrews, gospel to, 178–79
Hebrews, Letter to
on access to God, 159
authorship of, 162, 165–68
on Christ as priest and sacrifice,
162
dating of, 163–64
Greek ideas in, 159–60, 162
history of, 162–63
Jewish ideas in, 160–62
Luther and, 163, 166, 167, 173
recipients of, 164–65
Hegesippus, 177, 180–82
Helvidian Theory, 188–90

SUBJECT INDEX

heresies
  antinomianism as, 122, 238,
    281–84, 294
  at Colosse, 107, 117, 119–22,
    125–26
  Gnosticism, 42–44, 122–26,
    140–42, 238, 247–56
  John's gospel and, 41–44
  Letter to the Colossians and,
    119–26
  Marcion and, 136
  Pastoral Epistles and, 138–42
  and wandering prophets,
    274–75
  writings by heretics, 243–44
Herod, 57
Herod Agrippa I, 176
Herodotus, 117, 129
Hierapolis, 115, 116–17, 118, 155
Hieronymian Theory, 183–86
Hilary of Poitiers, 170
Holy Spirit, 34, 54, 56, 210, 259,
    298, 310
humanity of Jesus Christ, 4,
    18–19, 39, 44, 120,
    250–52, 258

Ignatius, 156, 206, 208, 251–52
immorality, 122, 124, 132, 139,
    253–54, 278, 281. See also
    evil; sins
incarnation, denial of, 249–56
Irenaeus, 49, 51–52, 210
Isaiah, 201, 243, 295, 301, 302,
    309
Israelites, 278, 299

Jacob, 161, 201–2
James (apostle)

as author of Letter of James,
    169, 176, 190–95
  conception of religion by, 158
  death of, as martyr, 57, 176, 183
  family of, 46, 47
  kingdom of God and, 4, 47
  personality of, 46–47
  as servant of God, 293
James (brother of Jesus)
  Aramaic language and, 204
  as author of Letter of James,
    170, 176, 190–95, 203–4
  as bishop of Jerusalem Church,
    177–78, 182, 191, 196
  death of, as martyr, 179–82, 192
  Epiphanian Theory of, 186–88
  Helvidian Theory of, 188–90
  Hieronymian Theory of, 183–86
  Jesus' ministry and, 176–77,
    187–88
  Jewish law and, 182
  meaning of word brother,
    183, 185
  mother of, 184–85
  resurrection appearances of
    Jesus and, 178–79
James (father of Judas, not Iscar-
    iot), 175, 291–92
James (son of Alphaeus), 175,
    183, 184
James (teacher), 203
James, Book of, 186–87
James, gospel of, 202
James, Letter of
  authorship of, 169, 175–78,
    190–95, 201–4
  compared with Paul's teachings,
    192, 194–95
  dating of, 195–97

SUBJECT INDEX

early Christian fathers and, 169–70
Epiphanian Theory of, 186–88
Greek Church and, 171–72
Greek ideas in, 195
Helvidian Theory of, 188–90
Hieronymian Theory of, 183–86
identity of James and, 175–78
James as martyr and, 179–83
Jesus' relationship with James and, 178–79, 183
Jews and, 190–92, 201–2
justification by works in, 174, 192, 194–95
Luther on, 169, 172–75, 193
preachers of ancient world and, 197–200
recipients of, 205
on rich people, 196–97, 199
scarcity of references to Jesus Christ in, 174, 193–94, 196, 201, 203, 204
Sermon on the Mount and, 191–92, 194
Syrian Church and, 170–71
James of Compostella, 176
James the younger, 175, 184
Jeroboam, 299
Jerome
on apostles, 183, 185
on brothers of Jesus, 183–86, 189
on First Letter of Peter, 241
on John's last words, 49
on Letter of James, 203
on Letter of Jude, 289, 290
on Letter to Hebrews, 166
on Paul, 146, 166
on Revelation, 312

Vulgate by, 170, 289
Jerusalem
capture of, by Romans, 249
Church in, 61, 62–63, 71, 177–78, 191, 192–93, 196
James as leader of Church in, 177–78, 191, 196
Jesus in, 30–31, 35, 45
Paul in, 92, 177, 313
Paul's collections for Church in, 71, 182
See also Council of Jerusalem
Jesus Christ
as advocate, 258
all-sufficiency of, 101, 102–3, 107, 120, 126
baptism of, 251, 252
beloved disciple of, 49–51
children and, 19
Church as body of, 103–4, 153
Church as Bride of, 269–70
cleansing of Temple by, 32, 33, 44
creation and, 120
crucifixion of, 31, 32, 33, 44, 50, 184–85, 226, 251–52
deity of, 18, 45–46, 250–52
denial of Incarnation of, 249–56
denial of Messiahship of, 248–49
expiation for sins by, 258–59
feeding of 5,000 by, 1, 3, 13, 19, 32, 39
as friend of outcasts and sinners, 27
genealogy of, 10, 36, 40
Gnostic beliefs on, 43–44, 123, 249–53, 286
healings by, 1, 3, 13

SUBJECT INDEX

Jesus Christ (*continued*)
  on Holy Spirit, 34
  humanity of, 4, 18–19, 39, 44,
      120, 250–52, 258
  incarnation of, 249–56
  James as brother of, 170,
      176–78, 183–90
  Jude as brother of, 291–94, 295,
      296
  as King, 10–11, 36
  Last Supper and, 226
  Logos and, 37
  as Messiah, 7, 23, 194, 209–10,
      248–49, 257–58
  ministry of, 30–32
  miracles of, 1, 3, 13, 34,
      38–40, 45
  in Nazareth as carpenter, 188,
      189
  omniscience of, 45
  parables of, 7, 9, 25, 26, 27
  poor and, 27
  prayer by, 25
  pre-existence of, 45
  as priest and sacrifice, 162,
      258–59
  Ranters on, 282–83
  resurrection of, 178–79, 209–10
  as Savior, 23, 29, 258–59
  second coming of, 9, 131,
      132–33, 195, 207–8, 210,
      218, 238–39, 242
  self-determination of, 45
  Sermon on the Mount by, 9, 11,
      27, 76, 191–92, 194
  as Son of God, 257
  sufferings of, 226, 251–52
  supremacy of, 120
  temptations of, 18

  transfiguration of, 33
  unity of all things in, 101–4
Jews
  in Alexandria, 317
  angels and, 288, 294
  apocalyptic literature and,
      298–99, 302–9
  banishment of, from Rome, 77
  as chosen people, 60, 74, 75,
      92–93, 299
  Christianity and, 60, 92–94,
      190–92, 194
  circumcision and, 93
  covenant and, 161
  Day of Atonement and, 161
  denial of Jesus' Messiahship by,
      248–49
  as enemies of Church, 294
  Gnosticism and, 124–25,
      141–42, 293–94
  God's relationship with, 160–62
  history of, 299
  law of, 93–94, 124, 140,
      161–62, 177, 182, 190, 294
  Letter of James and, 190–92,
      201–2
  Matthew's gospel and, 6–8, 23
  names associated with writings
      by, 243
  Paul on, 75
  Paul's stay in Thessalonica and,
      130–31
  in Phrygia, 117–18
  preaching and, 200
  in Roman Empire, 216, 228
  and two ages of history,
      299–301, 307–9
  women and Judaism, 218–19
Joachim, 186–87

SUBJECT INDEX

John (apostle)
  as author of gospel, 46, 50–56
  as beloved disciple, 49–51
  conception of religion by, 159
  death of, 49
  eagle symbol of, 23, 29
  family of, 46, 47
  kingdom of heaven and, 4
  on Laodicaea, 115
  life of, 46–49
  personality of, 46–49
  Peter's relationship with, 47
  Polycarp as student of, 51
  purity of, 264
  stories on, 47–49, 250–51
John (author of Revelation),
    309–11, 311–12
John, First Letter of
  Christian fellowship in, 255–56
  Christian righteousness in,
    261–62
  connection between Second and
    Third Letters of John and,
    268–69
  fellowship of the Church in,
    260–61
  God in, 257
  Holy Spirit in, 259
  Jesus Christ in, 250–52, 257–59
  object of writing, 256–57
  personal character of, 245
  recipients of, 205, 262–64,
    268–70
  as response to Gnosticism and
    false teachers, 245–56, 260
  world as hostile and evil in, 260
John, gospel of
  aims of, 35–46
  authorship of, 46, 50–56

  beloved disciple in, 49–51
  compared with other gospels,
    30–35, 54
  compared with Revelation, 311
  dating of, 35, 51, 242
  deity of Jesus in, 45–46
  eagle symbol of, 23, 29
  eyewitness details of, 34
  Gentiles and, 36–40
  geographic knowledge of Pales-
    tine and Jerusalem in, 35
  Greek ideas in, 37–38, 40
  Greek language of, 311
  heresies and, 41–44
  Holy Spirit in, 34, 259
  John the Baptist in, 41–42
  Logos in, 37
  ministry of Jesus in, 30–33
  miracles in, 32, 34, 38–40, 45
  specialized knowledge of writer
    of, 33–35
  speeches of Jesus in, 51
  as theological gospel, 23, 29,
    40, 54
  witness in, 50, 55
John, Second and Third Letters of
  authorship of, 55, 267–68
  connection between First Letter
    of John and, 268–69
  length of, 265
  problem of Second Letter of
    John, 268–70
  recipients of, 205, 263, 267,
    270–71
  as responses to problems in
    early Church, 267–68,
    270–71, 274–76
  wandering prophets and,
    270–71, 274–76

341

SUBJECT INDEX

John Cassian, 49

John Chrysostom, 15, 146

John of Damascus, 171

John the Baptist, 8, 24, 27, 30, 32, 41–42

John the elder, 55, 56, 265–67, 270–71

Joseph
  death of, 188, 189
  Mary and, 187, 188, 189
  sons of, as half-brothers of Jesus, 186

Josephus, 179–80

Jubilees, Book of, 305

Judaism. *See* Jews

Judas Barsabas, 291

Judas Iscariot, 34, 45, 91, 291

Judas of Damascus, 291

Judas of James, 175, 291–92

Jude (brother of Jesus), 291–94, 295, 296

Jude, Letter of
  acceptance of, into New Testament, 289–90, 294
  authorship of, 291–96
  dating of, 290–91
  on denial of angels, 288
  on denial of God and Jesus Christ, 284–88
  as difficult and neglected, 277–78
  doxology in, 277, 284
  Gnosticism and, 284–88, 293–94
  Greek language of, 293
  heresies and, 281, 284–88
  Jewishness of, 293–96
  Luther and, 173
  references to non-Scriptural books in, 289–90

and Second Letter of Peter, 290–91
  warnings on evil life in, 278–80
  words to faithful in, 280

judgment day, 304–5

Jülicher, Adolf, 303

Junia, 186

justification by faith, 192, 194–96

justification by works, 174, 192, 194–95

Juvenal, 150

Kepler, T. S., 298

kingdom of God
  apocalyptic literature on, 306–7
  James and John on, 4, 47
  Matthew's gospel on, 9

Knox, John, 96

Korah, 279, 286

Kurios, 268–69

Laodicea, 105–7, 115, 116, 118, 154, 155

law
  First Letter to Peter and, 231
  in gospel of Matthew, 8
  grace and, 95
  Greeks and, 132
  Jewish law, 93–94, 124, 140, 161–62, 177, 182, 190, 294
  Letter of James and, 174

Lazarus, 34, 39, 45, 50

letters, ancient, 65–66, 97–98, 243

letters of Paul
  dating of collection of, 86, 104, 156, 224, 243
  dictation of, 68
  difficulty of, 64–65
  epistles versus, 65

knowledge about Paul and, 64
language of, 99–100, 142–43
Pastoral Epistles, 77, 135–38,
    142–44, 147–48, 208, 293
as responses to immediate situa-
    tions, 67–68, 100
sections of, 66–67, 193
style of, 100–101
translation of, 213, 293
See also specific letters
light and darkness, 253–54, 257,
    261, 280
Light and Dark Sides of God, The
    (Bottomley), 282
Lightfoot, J. B., 115, 117, 151
lion symbol of Matthew, 23, 29
Logos, 37
Lord's Supper, 218, 310
love, 237, 255–56, 257, 261
Lucan, 72
Lucian, 273
Lucius Mummius, 84
Luke
    as author of Acts, 58, 59–63
    as author of gospel, 22
    as doctor, 22, 28, 58, 59
    as Gentile, 22, 24, 58
    imprisonment of, with Paul, 24,
        58, 63
    Letter to the Hebrews and,
        165–66
    ox symbol of, 23, 29
    Paul's relationship with, 24, 58
    See also Acts; Luke, gospel of
Luke, gospel of
    accuracy of, 24
    authorship of, 22
    birth narrative of, 189
    characteristics of, 24–28

compared with gospels of
    Matthew and Mark, 1–5,
    12–14, 18
compared with John's gospel,
    30–33
for Gentiles, 24–27
Greek language of, 24, 25
healings by Jesus in, 1, 3, 13
Jesus as friend of outcasts and
    sinners in, 27, 54
Jesus as Savior in, 23, 29
John the Baptist in, 24
kingdom of God in, 26–27
medical words in, 58
ministry of Jesus in, 30–33
number of verses in, 2,
    4–5, 13
ox symbol of, 23, 29
parables in, 25, 26, 27
poor in, 27
praising God in, 26
prayer in, 25
Sermon on the Mount in, 27
as synoptic gospel, 1–2, 12
teaching of Jesus in, 5
Theophilus and, 23, 24, 59
as universal gospel, 26–27
women in, 25–26
lusts. *See* immorality
Luther, Martin
    on Letter of James, 169,
        172–75, 193
    on Letter of Jude, 173
    on Letter to Hebrews, 163, 166,
        167, 173
    on Revelation, 173, 297–98
Lycus Valley, 115–16
Lydia, 110–11
Lyrical Ballads (Wordsworth), 54

SUBJECT INDEX

Macedonia, 128–29
Macgregor, W. M., 54
Magnificat, 26
Manoah, 161
man symbol of Mark, 23, 29
Marcion, 136
Mark
  Church of Alexandria and, 15
  death of, 17
  family of, 14
  imprisonment of, 15
  man symbol of, 23, 29
  Paul's missionary journey and, 14–15
  Paul's relationship with, 15
  Peter's relationship with, 16, 40
  sources of information for, 15–16
Mark, gospel of
  Aramaic words in, 20–21
  authorship of, 14–15
  characteristics of, 17–21, 23
  compared with gospels of Matthew and Luke, 1–5, 12–14, 18, 19
  compared with John's gospel, 30–33, 54
  divinity of Jesus in, 18
  as earliest gospel, 2, 12–14, 16, 21
  ending of, 17
  events of Jesus' life in, 5, 6, 17, 19–20, 54
  eyewitness details of, 19–20
  healings by Jesus in, 1, 3, 13
  humanity of Jesus in, 4, 18–19, 39, 44
  man symbol of, 23, 29
  ministry of Jesus in, 30, 32, 33

  number of verses in, 2, 5, 13
  realistic and simple style of, 20–21, 23
  sources of information for, 15–16, 20, 21
  as synoptic gospel, 1–2, 12
Martha and Mary, 26
Martial, 72
martyrdom, 57, 176, 179–82, 183
Mary (mother of Jesus), 26, 50, 184–89
Mary (wife of Clopas), 184–85, 186
Mary and Martha, 26
Mary Magdalene, 26, 184–85
Matthew (apostle), 5–6, 9
Matthew, gospel of
  apocalyptic interest in, 9
  authorship of, 5–6
  birth narrative of, 189
  characteristics of, 6–11
  Church in, 8–9
  compared with gospels of Mark and Luke, 1–5, 12–14, 18, 19
  compared with John's gospel, 30–33
  genealogy of Jesus in, 10, 36, 40
  healings by Jesus in, 1, 3, 13
  Jesus as King in, 10–11, 36
  Jewishness of, 6–8, 23
  kingdom of God in, 9
  law in, 8
  lion symbol of, 23, 29
  ministry of Jesus in, 30–31, 33
  number of verses in, 2, 4–5, 13
  numbers three and seven in, 10
  parables in, 7, 9
  Sermon on the Mount in, 9, 11
  as synoptic gospel, 1–2, 12
  as teaching gospel, 9–10, 54

teaching of Jesus in, 5–6, 54
Mayor, J. B., 203–4, 212, 241–42, 277
McNeile, A. H., 100, 190
Messiah
  in apocalyptic literature, 303–4
  denial of Jesus' Messiahship, 248–49
  Elijah and, 303
  Jesus as, 7, 23, 194, 209–10, 248–49, 257–58
  prophesies of, in Old Testament, 7, 23, 24, 209, 299
  reign of, 306–7
Methodism, 282
Meyer, Heinrich, 201–2
Michael (archangel), 279, 288, 289
Milligan, G., 65–66
miracles
  feeding of 5,000, 1, 13, 19, 32, 39
  healings by Jesus, 1, 3, 13
  in John's gospel, 32, 34, 38–40, 45
  marriage feast at Cana, 34, 39, 45, 188
  raising of Lazarus, 34, 39
Mithradates, 214
Moffatt, James, 100, 206, 212, 220–21, 241, 264, 277, 281, 311
Moses, 161, 201, 203, 243, 279, 289, 295, 302
Muratorian Canon, 52–53, 134, 146, 163, 169, 222–23, 239, 289

Nero, Emperor
  fire of Rome and, 216–19, 317

James as bishop of Jerusalem during time of, 178
  Paul and, 146
  persecution of Christians by, 164, 207, 216–20, 226, 228–29, 317
  and Peter on obedience to civil authorities, 231
  Seneca as tutor of, 72
Nerva, Emperor, 312, 318
New Jerusalem, 306
Newman, John Henry, 160
Nicodemus, 34, 202
Noah, 302
Nunc Dimittis, 26

obedience and disobedience, 231, 261–62, 278–79, 313
Old Testament
  apocalyptic literature in, 303–9
  prophecies of, on Messiah, 7, 23, 24, 209, 299
  prophets in, 292–93, 301–2
  quotations from, in Revelation, 309
  See also Jews; *specific people*
Onesimus, 145, 149–51, 153–56
Ophites, 286
Origen, 163, 166, 167, 171, 176, 239, 289
orthodoxy, 137–38, 144
Otho, Emperor, 317
ox symbol of Luke, 23, 29

pantheism, 282
Papias, 5, 16, 55
papyrus, papyri, 65–66, 97–98, 265
parables, 7, 9, 25, 26, 27

SUBJECT INDEX

Pastoral Epistles, 77, 135–38,
142–44, 147–48, 208, 293
Paul
apostleship of, 91–92, 185, 193,
310
attack on apostleship of, 91–92
authority of, 92
as author of Letter to the Ephesians, 99–101, 104–5
as author of Pastoral Epistles,
136, 142–43, 147–48, 293
Church in Corinth and, 86–90
collections for Jerusalem
Church by, 71, 182
conception of religion by, 158
conversion of, 61, 92, 291
in Corinth, 62, 71, 73, 85–89,
111, 213, 313
death of, 105, 144, 146, 147
at end of life, 15
in Ephesus, 62, 77, 86, 98,
233, 313
friendship between Philippi
Church and, 111–12
Gentiles and, 191
imprisonment of, 15, 24, 58, 60,
62, 63, 97, 101, 111, 112,
119, 144–46, 153
interest of, in Rome, 70–71
on James (brother of Jesus), 183
in Jerusalem, 92, 177, 313
justification by faith and, 192,
194–95
letters of generally, 64–68
Letter to the Hebrews and,
165–66
Luke's relationship with, 24
in Macedonia, 128–29

Mark's relationship with, 15
missionary journeys of, 14–15,
61, 62, 85, 110, 144–47
Onesimus and, 149–50, 153–56
opponents of, 71–72, 86, 91–92,
130–31, 132, 219
in Philippi, 110–12, 129, 213,
312–13
as Roman citizen, 103,
312–13
Roman magistrates and, 60,
216, 312–13
on second coming, 239
as servant of Jesus, 293
Silvanus and, 213, 293
Spain and, 72–73, 145–46
in Thessalonica, 111, 129–31
See also letters of Paul; specific
letters
Paul of Nisibis, 171
peace, 307–8
Peregrinus (Lucian), 273
persecution of Christians, 60, 111,
163–64, 207, 215–21,
226–31, 313, 317–18
Peshitto, 170–71
Peter
in Acts, 57
as author of First Letter of
Peter, 207, 221, 235–36
conception of religion by, 158
confession of, at Caesarea
Philippi, 9
death of, 16, 242
denial of Jesus by, 226
as elder, 225
as fisherman, 46
James and, 177, 178

SUBJECT INDEX

Jesus' prayer for, 25
John's relationship with, 47
literature using name of,
  202, 243
Mark's relationship with, 16, 40
name of, 215
on obedience to civil authority,
  231, 313
preaching material of, 16
preaching of, in Jerusalem,
  61, 191
transfiguration of Jesus and, 33
as witness of sufferings of
  Christ, 226
Peter, First Letter of
Aristion of Smyrna and, 234–35
authorship of, 207, 211–13,
  221–23, 225–31, 234, 235–36
as Catholic or General Epistle,
  205–6
circumstances behind, 215–21
compared with other books of
  New Testament, 223–25,
  232–33
compared with Second Letter of
  Peter, 240–42
dating of, 207, 226, 235–36
elect one in, 263–64
Gentiles and, 215
Greek language of, 211–13
occasion of publication of, 233
organization of Church and, 208
persecution of Christians and,
  215–21, 226–30
Peter as elder and, 225
Peter as witness of sufferings of
  Christ and, 226
place of origin of, 232–33

quotations from, by early Christian fathers and preachers,
  210–11
recipients of, 214–15
second coming in, 207–8
as sermon and pastoral letter,
  231–32, 235
significance of, 206
Syrian Church and, 223
theology of early Church and,
  208–10
Peter, Gospel of, 202, 243, 251
Peter, Second Letter of
authorship of, 240–44
compared with First Letter of
  Peter, 240–42
dating of, 242–43
denial of second coming and,
  238–39, 242
doubts of early Church on,
  239–40
Greek style of, 241
and Letter of Jude, 290–91
neglect of, 237
significance of, 243, 244
on threat of lawless life, 237–38
Pharisees and scribes, 8
Philemon, Letter to
Archippus and, 153–55
on Mark, 15
Onesimus and, 145, 149–51,
  153–56
Paul's release from prison and,
  145
as prison letter from Paul, 15
as private letter, 149, 156
slavery and, 149–56
Philip (disciple), 34, 47, 61

SUBJECT INDEX

Philip of Macedon, 108–9, 129–30
Philippi
    friendship between Paul and
        Philippi Church, 111–12
    history of, 108–10
    Paul in, 110–12, 129, 213,
        312–13
    persecution against Christians
        in, 111
    as Roman colony, 109–10
    See also Philippians, Letter to
Philippians, Letter to, 112–14
Phillips, J. B., 311
Philo, 160
Phoebe, 74, 76
Phrygia, 117–18, 128, 214
Pilate, 11
Pilate, Pontius, 251
Plato, 38, 40, 158, 159–60, 243
Platonism, 249
Pliny, 226–27, 233
pneuma, 255, 287
pneumatikoi, 255–56, 286–88
Polycarp, 51, 206, 210–11, 232,
    234, 252
Pomponius Mela, 72
Pontus, 214–15, 232
Popaea, 219
prayer, 25, 101
"Prelude, The" (Wordsworth),
    245–46
pride, 139
priest and sacrifice, 162, 258–59
Prisca, 77, 78, 167
Priscilla, 86
prodigal son parable, 27
prophets, 271–75, 292, 301–2,
    309–10. See also false
    prophets and teachers

Protevangelium, 186–87
proto-canonical books of Bible,
    172
Psalms of Solomon, 305, 308
pseudonymous books of Bible,
    203, 295
psuchikoi, 255–56, 286–88
Puritans, 282–83

Q, 5–6
Quakers, 282
Quintilian, 72

Rabbula, Bishop of Edessa,
    170–71
Ranters, 282–83
Rehoboam, 299
religion
    Caesar-worship, 313–18
    conceptions of, 158–59
    in Roman Empire, 216, 227–28,
        313–18
    See also Christianity; Jews
Renan, Joseph Ernest, 207
resurrection
    apocalyptic literature and, 306
    of body, 140
    of dead, 306
    of Jesus Christ, 178–79, 209–10
Revelation, Book of
    as apocalyptic literature, 298,
        301, 308–9
    on apostles, 310–11
    authorship of, 309–11
    Caesar-worship and, 318
    compared with John's gospel,
        311
    dating of, 311–18
    Greek language of, 309

kingdom of the saints in, 307
Luther on, 173, 297–98
quotations from Old Testament
in, 309
significance of, 318–19
strange nature and difficulty of,
297–98, 318–19
title of, 311
righteousness, 74–75, 261–62, 308
"Rock of Ages," 94
Roman Catholic Bible, 172,
173, 176
Roman magistrates, 60, 216,
312–13
Romans, Letter to
aim of, 71–73
compared with other letters by
Paul, 69
dating of, 71
on ethical character of Christian
faith, 74, 76
on Jews as chosen people, 74, 75
layout of, 73–76
Paul's interest in Rome and,
70–71
problems of Chapter 16 in,
76–80
as prophylactic, 70
recommendation on behalf of
Phoebe in, 74, 76
on righteousness, 74–75
as testamentary, 70
Rome
as Babylon, 263–64, 313
banishment of Jews from, 77
Caesar-worship in, 313–18
fire of, 216–19
Jews and Roman Empire, 216,
228

Letter to the Hebrews and,
164–65
obedience to, 313
Paul's imprisonment in, 15, 58,
62, 112, 119, 144–46, 153
Paul's interest in, 70–71
pax Romana and, 315
persecution of Christians in,
215–21, 226–30, 313, 317–18
Peter and Paul in, 225
religion in Roman Empire, 216,
227–28
slavery in Roman Empire,
150–51
unity of Roman Empire, 103,
314–15
See also Romans, Letter to; *specific emperors*
Ropes, J. H., 203
Russell, George, 158

sacrifice, 162, 258–59
saints, 246–47
Salome, 184
Samaritans, 7, 26, 27, 35, 47, 61
Sanday, William, 70
Scott, E. F., 102, 104, 162, 237
scribes and Pharisees, 8
second coming of Jesus Christ, 9,
131, 132–33, 195, 207–8,
210, 218, 238–39, 242
self-denial, 122, 123–24, 139–40,
141, 253
Selwyn, E. G., 208–9, 212
Seneca, 72
Septuagint, 190–91
Sergius Paulus, 60
Sermon on the Mount, 9, 11, 27,
76, 191–92, 194

sermons
  of Greek preachers, 197–200
  Jewish sermons, 200
  Letter of James and, 204
Shakespeare, William, 100
Sibylline Oracles, 301, 304–5, 308
Silas, 86, 130–31, 186, 212, 291
Silvanus, 212–13, 215, 241, 293
Simon the Pharisee, 26, 27
sins
  expiation of, by Jesus, 258–59
  of Gentiles, 119
  and Gnosticism, 253–54, 256,
    285–86
  grace and forgiveness of, 281
  Jesus as friend of sinners, 27, 54
  law and definition of, 95
  Letter of James on, 196–97
  Letter of Jude on, 278–80
  Letter to Ephesians on, 102
  Letter to Hebrews on, 162
  Second Letter of Peter on,
    237–38
  See also evil; immorality
slavery, 110–11, 149–56, 224
Smyrna, 234–35, 252, 315
Sodom and Gomorrah, 279, 305
"Solitary Reaper, The,"
    (Wordsworth), 264
Solomon, 201, 243, 295, 299,
    305, 308
soul, 254–55
Spain, 72–73, 145–46, 176
Stalker, James, 89
Stephanas, 87, 89
Stephen, 61
Strabo, 115
Streeter, B. H., 221, 235
Sulpicius, 220

symbols of gospel writers, 23, 29
synoptic gospels, 1–2, 12
Syrian Church, 170–71,
    223, 239

Tacitus, 217, 219–20
Tatian, 223
The Teaching of the Twelve
    Apostles (Didache), 272,
    273–74, 310
Tennyson, Alfred Lord, 102, 158
Tertius, 68
Tertullian, 135, 163, 166, 167,
    169, 189, 222, 291
Testaments of the Twelve Patri-
    archs, 201, 301, 302
Theophilus, 23, 24, 59, 146
Thessalonians, Letters to, 131–33,
    313
Thessalonica
  Church in, 131–32
  history of, 129–30
  opponents of Paul in, 132
  Paul in, 111, 129–31
  See also Thessalonians,
    Letters to
Thomas, 34
Thomas, gospel of, 202
Thomas Aquinas, 135
Thucydides, 84, 212
Tiberius, Emperor, 316
Timothy, 86, 130–31, 144, 147,
    293
Timothy, Letters to
  aim of, 134–35
  authorship of, 136, 142–44,
    147–48
  creeds and, 137–38, 144
  as ecclesiastical letters, 134–37

heresy and, 138–42
language of, 142–43
as pastoral letters, 135–38,
    142–44, 147–48
Paul's activities in, 143–44
as personal letters, 134, 147
Titus (disciple), 88–89
Titus, Emperor, 317
Titus, Letter to
aim of, 135
authorship of, 136, 142–44,
    147–48
creeds and, 137–38, 144
as ecclesiastical letter, 134–37
heresy and, 138–42
as pastoral letter, 135–38,
    142–44, 147–48
Paul's activities in, 143–44
as personal letter, 134
Tobit, 306
Toplady, A. M., 94
Trajan, Emperor, 227
transfiguration of Jesus, 33
Turner, C. H., 61
Twelve Patriarchs, 201, 301, 302
Tychicus, 97

Valentinus, 142
Vespasian, Emperor, 317
Victorinus, 312
Virgil, 315
Vitellius, Emperor, 317
Vulgate, 170, 289

Walton, Izaak, 206
Wesley, John, 282, 283–84
Westcott, B. F., 17, 222
widows, 136
Wisdom of Solomon, 201
women
    Judaism and, 25–26
    in Luke's gospel, 25–26
Wordsworth, William
    Lyrical Ballads, 54
    "Prelude, The," 245–56
    "Solitary Reaper, The," 264
works, justification by, 174, 192,
    194–95

Xerxes, 117, 129

Zachaeus, 27
Zwingli, Huldreich, 298

CPSIA information can be obtained at www.ICGtesting.com
Printed in the USA
BVOW04s0054050514

352422BV00019B/353/P